The First Oregonians

Second Edition

The First Oregonians

Edited by Laura Berg

with the Oregon Council for the Humanities

OREGON COUNCIL FOR THE HUMANITIES
Portland, Oregon

Printed in the United States of America

Library of Congress Cataloging-in-Publication Data

The first Oregonians / edited by Laura Berg ; with the Oregon Council for the Humanities.—
2nd ed.
    p. cm.
Includes bibliographical references and index.
  ISBN-13: 978-1-880377-02-4 (alk. paper)
  1. Indians of North America—Oregon. I. Berg, Laura. II. Oregon Council for the Humanities.
E78.O6F57 2007
979.5004'97--dc22
                    2007016618

812 SW Washington Street, Suite 225, Portland, OR 97205
(503) 241-0543
www.oregonhum.org

For the native peoples of Oregon

Table of Contents

Part 2 *Cultural Continuum*

Preface to the Second Edition (2007)

With virtually no publicity or marketing, the first edition of *The First Oregonians*, which was for sale beginning in June 1992, went through two printings and by 1996 every last saleable copy was gone. Since then, the Oregon Council for the Humanities (OCH) has continued to receive purchase requests and inquires about republication.

Impatient to have the book available again, the Tribal Education Cluster of the Government-to-Government Task Force sent a resolution to Governor John Kitzhaber in 2001, calling both for *The First Oregonians* to be used as a resource by state educational institutions and school districts and for the book to be updated and republished. The governor signed the resolution and—the state not being in the book publishing business—forwarded the resolution to the Oregon Council for the Humanities.

Thus began the odyssey of a second, revised edition. OCH approached this editor and, after an advisory committee meeting of tribal representatives and other knowledgeable individuals, we began our work in 2002 under the guidance of then OCH executive director Christopher Zinn. Later the leadership of OCH associate director Katherine Deumling and OCH's exceptional editor Kathleen Holt were critical. The unwavering assistance of OCH office manager Sarah Van Winkle, the amazing talent of graphic designer Jennifer Viviano, and especially the cooperation and contributions of the tribes and the authors were indispensable in bringing this project to fruition.

With the help of the advisory committee, we defined our main tasks as bringing the stories about Oregon's nine federally recognized tribes and the book as a whole into the twenty-first century. The rapid and largely positive changes that occurred in Indian Country during the some fifteen years between the first and second editions required both a new look at the tribes today and a stronger focus on the cultural and historical continuity of the first Oregonians.

The genesis of the first edition as a report on conference results and OCH-sponsored heritage recovery work (see Preface to the First Edition on page xi), meant that most of the tribal chapters were about work undertaken under the OCH grants. A second, revised edition compelled us to tell the tribes' stories in more detail; as a result, the tribal chapters, along with the opening chapter by Elizabeth Woody, became the heart of this new edition of *The First Oregonians*. We think you'll find the book a valuable contribution to understanding the indigenous communities of Oregon.

—*Laura Berg*

Preface to the First Edition (1992)

This book is the culmination of a three-year program focus on the native peoples of Oregon. Based mainly on a special grant from the National Endowment for the Humanities, that focus had three principal parts.

The first was a series of grants from the Oregon Council for the Humanities to the nine federally recognized tribal communities, allowing them to undertake heritage-recovery work within their tribes. Archival research, oral histories, and videotaping were the principal recovery activities, which in many instances have led to further heritage work. Second was a statewide public conference of native people, teachers, and the general public. This two-day event was called "The First Oregonians" and featured workshop presentations by Indians describing their own history, language, and culture. The conference drew more than four hundred people, including representatives of all the tribal groups.

The third element in our focus on Oregon's native peoples is the publication you are about to read. It looks outward from the tribes to the general public, with essays drawn from eighteen writers and scholars. The publication is aimed at teachers and students, at those who work with Oregon's native people, and at the general public. Its purpose is to offer as full and varied a set of perspectives on Oregon Indian experience as that experience deserves. We hope that it will be read widely and carefully and will enrich the state's understanding of these remarkable people.

When the idea of a publication was first proposed, we envisioned a tabloid-style reader that could be issued in great numbers. As the project went forward, the sheer scale and importance of the subject changed our minds and moved us to undertake this fuller treatment in a more durable format. We hope that both native and nonnative people will agree that this was the right decision.

Introduction

by Laura Berg

The chronicle of native peoples in Oregon is a story of continuity. Since the 1980s, Indian tribes in the state have realized economic and social gains from tribal gaming and, even more so, from the cumulative efforts of successive generations who worked to better the lives of their people. This second, revised edition of *The First Oregonians* tells the stories of how tribes withstood the worst of times, held on to their cultural, legal, and moral bearings, and, by century's close, emerged with new vigor.

These are stories rich with different voices, told largely from the native perspective. True to the complexity of the history, culture, and geography of the tribes in Oregon, the book's various authors employ different styles in writing their chapter essays. Several recount their tribes' stories thorough personal accounts, while others rely more on relating their tribes' collective past. Some weave a web to make their central points. Others move their narrative from present to past. While one finds history and culture to be the compelling way to narrate its story, another finds landscape and myth more convincing.

The first section, "Tribal Heritage," covers the present, past, and future prospects of the nine federally recognized tribes in Oregon: the Burns Paiute Tribe; the Confederated Tribes of Coos, Lower Umpqua, and Siuslaw Indians; the Coquille Indian Tribe; the Cow Creek Band of Umpqua Indians; the Confederated Tribes of Grand Ronde; the Klamath Tribes; the Confederated Tribes of Siletz Indians; the Confederated Tribes of Umatilla Indian Reservation; and the Confederated Tribes of Warm Springs.

The tribes' leaders and cultural experts chose the authors who would write these nine tribal chapters. Authors of other chapters were also known to the tribes and, in some instances, tribal representatives made suggestions about appropriate writers.

Burns Paiute elder Minerva Soucie expressed a sentiment shared by the tribes, their authors, and other tribal members and employees who provided research, photographs, and other assistance: "Contributing to *The First Oregonians* was worthwhile. I want to educate our children and our communities about the real lives of Indian people, about the struggles and the joys of growing up as an Indian child in Oregon. With this revision of *The First Oregonians*, we have a new start in telling Oregon's history. Now we as tribal members are recounting, in our own words, the stories of our own peoples, our histories and our cultures."

Some of the tribal chapters offer more history than current facts, because, as tribal elders remind me, the Indian present and future cannot be understood without trying to comprehend the Indian past. These authors show us that the past, its traditions and values, have been brought forward to the present, or, as George Wasson puts it in his chapter about the Coquille tribe, "the past colors the future."

Elizabeth Woody's chapter, "The Tribe Next Door: Tradition, Innovation, and Multiculturalism," begins the story of *The First Oregonians*, with an examination of the contemporary life of Oregon tribes and their members. Her chapter gives voice to the diverse range of cultural expressions and experiences among Oregon tribes and to the diversity within Oregon as a whole. While describing examples of the discrimination and injustice suffered by people of color in the state, she celebrates the prospects that such diversity holds for Oregon and, particularly, for the nine federally recognized tribes.

While acknowledging similar experiences with other racial and ethnic minorities in the state, Woody describes what is fundamentally different about Indian tribes and their members: the tribes' inherent sovereignty and occupation of this land prior to European contact meant that European and then United States governments dealt with Indian peoples by means of treaties. While native peoples may in many ways be culturally distinct from other Americans, it is this political status of federally recognized tribes as semi-sovereign nations within a nation that makes them unique.

Woody's explanation about treaties and sovereignty—along with Stephen Dow Beckham's chapter "Federal-Indian Relations" in part two—will help readers understand how the nine tribes became "federally recognized." These tribes have an historical and ongoing political relationship with the federal government, based on treaties, the U.S. Constitution, statutes, and court decisions. Their sovereignty and exercise of governmental powers are part of the country's political and legal fabric and are a large part of the reason for the persistence of Native America generally.

Several other Indian communities and Indian people from many of the nation's other approximately 560 tribes and Alaska native villages also reside in Oregon, but this book focuses on the state's nine federally recognized tribes and their members. For example, the Nez Perce Tribe once occupied lands in northeastern Oregon and still has an interest in ceded lands and other Oregon places. Also, the Fort McDermitt Paiute-Shoshone Tribe is partially located in southeastern Oregon, but its reservation population centers are in Nevada, making the tribe's primary relationship with that state.

Oregon tribes have made significant strides in government-to-government relations, whether between tribal and federal or tribal and state governments. The concept is not a new one. Indian peoples and Europeans, then Americans, as representatives of separate sovereigns or nations, made treaties to sue for peace, for trading privileges, and particularly, to acquire or relinquish title to Indian lands. This relationship—now preserved in Constitutional law—has taken on new life in recent times as tribal officials pressed their federal and state counterparts to work with the tribes as cogovernments.

In a 1994 executive order to all federal departments and agencies, President Bill Clinton clarified agency responsibility to consult with the tribes, government to government, before making decisions or taking actions that affect them. In 2001, the Oregon Legislature passed and Governor John Kitzhaber signed legislation formally directing that interactions between the state and Oregon Indian tribes also be conducted on a government-to-government basis. Today's elected tribal officials are meeting with someone of comparable government status or authority to share information, make comanagement decisions, and address common problems.

As the result of economic clout, positive legislation, and better relations, Oregon tribes can boast of new achievements and promising future improvements. For example, the Burns Paiute and the Malheur National Wildlife Refuge agreed in 2000 to a set of guidelines regarding the finding and dispossession of human remains on the refuge. The Umatilla tribe spearheaded the restoration of salmon beginning in the 1980s in the Umatilla River decades after their decimation around 1914. In 1996, the Siletz Dance House was built, the first traditional ceremonial house at Siletz since the local Indian agent ordered all of them burned in the 1870s. The Coquille tribe is now the sponsor of Changing Landscapes, a broadly attended and respected native cultural preservation conference. The Grand Ronde now has a language immersion class in Chinuk Wawa (formerly called Chinook Jargon), and, for the first time, tribal members were allowed to fulfill college foreign language credits by learning Chinuk Wawa.

All Oregon tribes now have their own tribal court systems, allowing tribes jurisdiction over civil and sometime criminal matters on their reservations, depending on individual tribal codes. This potentially far-reaching cultural and political breakthrough permits tribal judges to take into consideration tribal customs and traditions as well as tribal law.

Despite changes for the better, the tribes would like to do much more, particularly in regards to land. The reacquisition of tribal lands lost because of termination, allotment, and misdealing remains a long-standing goal. Individual tribal chapters, such as Robert Kentta's on the Siletz tribe, explain the machinations leading to the diaspora of peoples and the dispossession of homelands. Most tribes have made steady, if slow progress in recovering small parcels of their former lands. For example, in 2005, after over twenty years of tribal effort, the Coos tribe regained ownership of the former military facility and culturally significant lands at Coos Head. Anticipating the eventual return of some areas that were once reservation lands, the Klamath tribe has developed a sustainable forest plan to manage and protect the Winema National Forest, part of the tribes' historic homelands.

Over the years, I have heard the misconception that Indian reservations are comparable to apartheid. Reservations are tribal property, and tribes have no intention of giving up more land or resources. Ted Strong, a Yakama Indian leader from across the river in Washington, described treaties as "what we have left." In that phrase, he is referring to reservations, that is, what remained of the lands ceded to the United States (and other rights and assets not taken or limited by treaties). In fact, Oregon tribes still feel a sense of responsibility for the ceded lands they no longer own. For example, the Grand Ronde tribe has stewardship agreements with the Siuslaw National Forest and the Bureau of Land Management, which allow tribal access to and tribal assessment of the health of their ceded areas.

Reading *The First Oregonians*, I hope will help dispel other commonly held misconceptions. One is that Indians pay no taxes. Tribal members do pay taxes. In general, they are only exempt from state income tax if they both live and work on the reservation or on off-reservation Indian trust land. What Elizabeth Woody underlines in her chapter is the substantial amount of tax revenue generated by the tribes, either because of their governmental status or because of tribal enterprises, for Oregon's non-Indian community.

Another misunderstanding is about Indians receiving payments from the federal government just for being Indian. On rare occasions, there may be payments to right a past wrong. Tribes frequently share profits from tribal business activities, often called "per capitas," directly with tribal members much like shareholders receive dividends. Tribes commonly both give per capitas and reinvest profits in reservation infrastructure and programs. In general, Indians must rely on their own resources whether they live on or off reservation. This is why some tribes have programs to help members develop their own small businesses and other tribes, such as the Warm Springs, have a long history of financial assistance to tribal members who attend college. Tribal membership is another fuzzy area for some non-Indians, although the answer is simple: Each tribe determines who is a member and what the criteria are for membership. For addition information to clarify specific questions you may have about Indian tribes, I recommend the web pages of the Oregon Commission on Indian Services.

The book's second section, "Cultural Continuum," looks largely to the past to see continuity with the present. Bill Mercer's chapter, "From Petroglyphs to Powwows," incorporates a back and forth examination of both the past and present of Oregon Indian art. Although conceived for the first edition, an introduction to native art traditions and contemporary artists in Oregon did not come to fruition until this edition. With difficulty, author Mercer chose only six artists—among many fine native artists in the state—to represent artwork from different Oregon tribes and artists using different media and styles.

Other chapters in the "Cultural Continuum" section contain more traditional ethnographic works. Dell Hymes describes the linguistic heritage of Oregon, while other scholars cover the geo-cultural areas where they have special expertise. As mentioned, Stephen Dow Beckham contributes a key chapter on federal-Indian relations and that relationship's effect on the history and lives of Oregon tribes. These chapters provide a bridge between the knowledge base built over the years by these and other dedicated academics, researchers, and native peoples. This edition's new direction—tribal peoples telling their own stories—makes it a unique contribution to Native American scholarship and sets it apart from many other volumes, however useful, by non-Indian historians, ethnographers, and anthropologists.

As in the first edition, authors were given the opportunity to provide photographs to accompany their stories in order to chronicle information pictorially as well as through words. While retaining many images from the earlier edition, the authors and I found and used many new contemporary photographs to remind readers, in yet another way, that Indians are not just peoples of the past. Among the older photographs are ones by Edward S. Curtis and Major Lee Moorhouse that some consider controversial. They are criticized for romanticizing Indians, using props, and in other ways, staging the settings for their work. On the other hand, native people, knowing these shortcomings, also appreciate the record made by these priceless images. Both men photographed dignified images of Indian people, giving pause to those whose ideas about Indians were shaped by the prevailing negative representations of Indians predominant during much of the twentieth century. Curtis is appreciated for documenting many natural settings that are much altered today. Moorhouse is almost unique is his identification of his subjects by name. His photographs contain the only images, in many cases, of Umatilla tribal ancestors.

Before you start reading, you want to be prepared for variations in the spelling of Indian cultural or tribal names, languages, and other words. This phenomenon is part of the historical record: Indian languages were not written and individuals who took down information about various bands and languages did not know how to convey the sounds of the unfamiliar words in English. This fact, combined with the vagaries of nineteenth-century spelling, resulted in multiple spellings for the same words. Historians and scholars, whether Indian or non-Indian, have different preferences. Additionally, most of the tribal names were not names Indians gave themselves but what others called them, and these often changed over time.

As you will read, individual tribes have their own histories, languages, and cultures. While cultural differences are very real and consequential within the nine federally recognized tribes of Oregon, a few generalizations can be made about some of the shared cultural values and traditions. Many of these are more implicit than explicit in the book. Summarizing them may help the reader trace the continuity between the native past and present. Some of the major, shared elements of Oregon Indian cultures include the importance of consensus, tradition, and self-government; the special significance of children and elders in the community; the influence of the past on the present and the present's influence on the future; thinking and communicating in ways that are often different than non-Indian ways; a reverence for ancestors and a concern for future generations; and a spiritual and practical connection to the earth and natural resources.

Indian people sometimes use a communication style based on oral speech-making traditions. It is holistic, often incorporating ideas, stories, and retellings of historical events; this way of communicating allows for complexity and nuance. Another feature is expressing the same idea in several ways to accommodate and respect the diversity of words and understandings used by members of the community. In the Walla Walla dialect of the Sahaptin language, examining and describing things in different ways is part of *supaneeqx*. Donald Sampson, a direct descendant of Chief PeoPeoMoxMox and a former chair of the Umatilla tribe, explains, "There's no good English translation, but *supaneeqx* allows us to expand our vision by analyzing a situation from a variety of perspectives." I hope that the different perspectives in this book do just that—expand awareness and knowledge of our tribal neighbors.

Oregon Tribes' Official Websites

Burns Paiute Tribe
www.burnspaiute-nsn.gov

Confederated Tribes of Coos, Lower Umpqua, and Siuslaw Indians
www.ctclusi.org

Coquille Indian Tribe
www.coquilletribe.org

Cow Creek Band of Umpqua Indians
www.cowcreek.com

Confederated Tribes of Grand Ronde
www.grandronde.org

The Klamath Tribes
www.klamathtribes.org

Confederated Tribes of Siletz Indians
http://ctsi.nsn.us/

Confederated Tribes of Umatilla Indian Reservation
www.umatilla.nsn.us/main.html

Confederated Tribes of Warm Springs
www.warmsprings.com

Chapter 1

The Tribe Next Door
Tradition, Innovation, and Multiculturalism

BY ELIZABETH WOODY

Most people in Oregon have given little thought to the likelihood that the places where they live or the fields that they till were once native villages or homelands. For some, that is simply the past; they assume that the good in our lives is solely American in origin. They do not know that the good—whether it is rights, knowledge, or property—may have resulted from previous struggles or long-standing agreements with the native tribes, our ancestors, who originally lived here.

For millennia, Oregon's diverse landscape, with its natural prosperity, nurtured many distinctive tribes. This land was bountiful and pleasant even before it gained its glossy reputation for livability and natural beauty. A few namesakes of the older nations and their native languages have been retained in Oregon place-names and geographic locations. "The Northwest Territory" (which included the "Old Northwest," an area north of the Ohio River and east of the Mississippi), then "Oregon Territory," and finally, "Oregon," are the English names of our ancestral homelands. Rumored to be full of wonders, the Northwest drew inevitable exploration by the fledgling United States. The Corps of Discovery, led by Meriwether Lewis and William Clark, described our region's exceptional qualities and ensured its future settlement.

Presently, Oregon has nine federally recognized tribes located within its borders. They are the Burns Paiute Tribe; the Confederated Tribes of Coos, Lower Umpqua, and Siuslaw Indians; the Confederated Tribes of Grand Ronde; the Confederated Tribes of Siletz Indians; the Confederated Tribes of Warm Springs; the Confederated Tribes of Umatilla Indian Reservation; the Coquille Indian Tribe; the Cow Creek Band of Umpqua Indians; and the Klamath Tribes.

The relationships between the language families in this region reveal patterns of human history that show the longevity of our affiliation with this place. The cultural groups of the Columbia River Plateau, the Great Basin, the Sierra Nevada, and the Northwest Coast have historical, cultural, familial, and sometimes linguistic connections because of the interface of trading caravans that frequented our region's commercial hubs. (See Chapter 12, "Languages and Their Uses," for more about the state's past and present native languages.)

In other words, many peoples have been living here for thousands of years, not only creating diverse cultures, languages, and traditions, but also making connections through commerce, trading stories and knowledge, and sometimes making the closer ties of alliance and marriage.

Cultural forms reflect a long history of interrelationship. Collections of traditional native literature show how stories and protagonists relate to one another by tribe and geographical area. One story may share a common element with another, but the specifics fit the landscape of the teller at the time of the collection. Individuals have rights to regulate their story collections. Communal stories, on the other hand, belong to all. Items you see in museums—for example, imbricated Klickitat baskets and those from Thompson

River—are exceedingly beautiful, but may also function as cooking pots or water carriers. Cross-cultural trade meant that these and many other items traveled up and down the Pacific coast. South American feathers arrived here in the Northwest, just as Northwest shells went south. Medicines of great value crossed many landscapes, expanding the native tribes' knowledge of natural pharmacopoeias.

Despite a history of dynamic cultural exchange, the state of Oregon has not always fostered a pluralistic society. In 1844, Oregon passed acts that prohibited slavery, not out of moral outrage against possessing human chattel, but to exclude blacks and mulattos from the state. In 1923, Idaho, Montana, and Oregon passed alien land laws, which prohibited those not eligible for citizenship from owning land, and the following year the federal Immigration Act denied entry to all Asians. Later laws forbade African Americans from living within the city limits of Portland and Chinese women from entering the country even if they were married to Chinese miners and railroad workers who were already here. Such historical legislation is not only symptomatic of past attitudes; it is also reflected in the cur-

The Institute for Tribal Government

Oregon is home to a unique organization that demonstrates the level of political sophistication and national leadership achieved by the tribes and their supporters in the state. Since its inception in 1998, the Institute for Tribal Government (www.tribalgov.pdx.edu) in the Mark O. Hatfield School of Government at Portland State University serves elected tribal governments from Oregon and across the nation.

Until now, no national institution has provided training specifically designed for elected tribal leaders, despite the existence of more than 560 tribal governments in the United States. Newly elected officials are often unfamiliar with the responsibilities of office and must assume multiple leadership duties with little or no systematic training. At the internal level, this can contribute to instability in the tribal community. At the external level, tribal government officials are increasingly required to address complex intergovernmental issues with local, state, and federal jurisdictions. A primary goal of the Institute, therefore, is to assist tribes who want to cultivate the necessary expertise and governance skills from within their own tribe.

The director and founder of the Institute for Tribal Government is Elizabeth Furse, a former three-term U.S. Congresswoman (1992–1998), who was instrumental in helping many Oregon tribes regain federal recognition during the 1980s as director of the tribal restoration project for the Native American Program at Oregon Legal Services. At the heart of the Institute is a national board of accomplished Indian leaders, intellectuals, and instructors. The Institute also has an important oral history project, Great Tribal Leaders of Modern Times, which has recorded many of Oregon's seminal Indian leaders of recent past decades.

rent demographics of rural Oregon: Outside of current or former Indian reservations, European Americans are an even larger majority in the state's rural areas than in its urban centers.

It is also important to understand the significance of treaties and sovereignty and the way these fundamental concepts operate in the daily lives of the Oregon tribes, and, whether acknowledged or not, they are the foundational agreements that allow other Oregonians to live here. Treaties and sovereignty bind with the soil we stand on, the air we breathe, and the water that cleanses and nourishes all.

Treaties

Of the hundreds of treaties made between the United States and indigenous nations, some two dozen were made between the United States and Oregon Indians. According to Article 6 of the United States Constitution, "all treaties made, or which shall be made, under the authority of the United States, shall be the supreme law of the land; and the judges in every state shall be bound thereby, anything in the Constitution or laws of any State to the contrary notwithstanding." And just as the Constitution is still valid, so too are the treaties the United States made with Indian tribes.

The Congress of the United States implemented a policy of removal, using treaties to continually move Indians farther west, away from non-Indians. This mid-nineteenth-century policy manifested in Oregon as the removal of native peoples from prime lands to reservations.

After the initial treaty-making period, confiscation of tribal land occurred unlawfully, and in a number of cases, legal disputes over these lands have yet to be resolved. This also occurred a century later during the termination era. Yet, despite the federal termination policy of the 1950s and '60s, a vast amount of the country's resources is still reserved under treaties between the United States and the tribes, which means that the tribes own resources both within and outside of their reservation boundaries. Off-reservation, treaty-secured property includes water, hunting, fishing, gathering, and grazing resources. Other laws protect sacred sites, burial grounds, archaeological property, and items of cultural patrimony. Oregon tribes own agricultural, forest, rangelands, and mineral rights; they have the potential to develop and own solar, wind, and geothermal assets; and they are owed millions of dollars in overdue lease payments by the federal government.

However, until tribal people were able to exercise their sovereign rights to self-governance, they couldn't put that wealth from land and natural resources to work for them. A decade after receiving U.S. citizenship in 1924, many tribes began pushing for self-determination. The 1934 Indian Reorganization Act (IRA) formalized the establishment of governments by tribal members as a means of reducing federal authoritarianism in favor of self-governance. My grandparents told stories of this time and considered tribal government of great importance. They told me that people gathered to compare and debate all aspects of the formal realization of governance, including the ancient prerogatives of sovereignty. For instance, the people of the Warm Springs reservation decided that the Warm Springs tribal government possessed only the powers given to it by the people, and that women were equal citizens under its constitution. (In the United States, women had the right to vote at the time, but still, to this day, are not guaranteed equal rights under the Constitution.) Although not universally embraced, the IRA was the tool used by many tribes in Oregon and elsewhere to actualize a distinctive, modern nationhood to direct and determine their futures.

While most of our neighbors are fuzzy on the concept of sovereignty, many share a common respect for the U.S. Constitution. Sovereignty is important for everyone: we are all residents of counties, states, and the United States, and each of these entities possesses varying degrees of sovereignty. Since the late 1980s, when the tribes began developing successful gaming enterprises, Indian tribes as economic and sovereign entities emerged from the shadows of public consciousness; however, plenty of misinformation still accompanies the nonnative population's new awareness of their presence. The vital and ongoing presence of native communities in Oregon enriches the lives of all, whether through political changes or increased community funding.

Contributions to Local Economies

School districts across Oregon are eligible for federal funds based on the number of Indian students enrolled. For example, near the Warm Springs reservation, the Madras School District has a memorandum of agreement with the tribe and receives, in lieu of property taxes, about $2.5 million annually in federal Impact Aid. Title VIII of the Elementary and Secondary Education Act of 1965 (amended as the 2001 No Child Left Behind Act) allocates these funds. Impact Aid grants help educate federally connected children, including the children of members of the uniformed services and children who live on Indian lands, among others. Title VII of the act, which fulfills the federal government's unique and continuing relationship with and responsibility for the education of Indian children, gives about $250,000 each year to the school district. And the Johnson O'Malley Trust Fund, enacted in 1934 to enable Indian students living on reservations to attend local public schools, provides nearly $100,000 each year in supplemental funds for the Madras School District. These federal monies for local school districts would not be available without the presence of the children of Warm Springs.

Another example of the tribes' positive impact on local communities involves the federal fish and wildlife restoration dollars that the Umatilla tribe (as well as the Warm Springs, Burns Paiute, and other Oregon tribes) leveraged for the improvement of watersheds that extend beyond reservation boundaries. In the past two decades, because of its commitment to bringing back the salmon, the Umatilla tribe has brought tens of millions of dollars into northeastern Oregon—money that is spent in the community on employment, construction contracts, and the purchase of goods and services.

Despite tribal contributions to the broader Oregon community such as these, tribal casinos remain the most public face of Oregon tribes. All nine federally recognized tribes in Oregon now run gaming facilities, though different tribal casinos have had different levels of financial success. The most recent—since June 2004—is the Coos, Lower Umpqua, and Siuslaw tribe's Three Rivers Casino in Florence.

In early 2005, the economic consulting firm EcoNorthwest issued a study of the benefits Oregon receives from tribal casinos. Based on 2003 economic data, the study found that tribal gaming businesses "directly supported approximately 5,328 jobs and $192.4 million in wages and benefits for workers … and indirectly generated another 5,640 jobs and $156.5 million in income for workers in other sectors of Oregon's economy." In total economic output, tribal gaming generated over a billion dollars in Oregon in 2003, while "state and local government collected over $42.6 million in taxes" and saved "nearly $7.1 million in public assistance costs through greater statewide employment" thanks to the casinos. The economic benefits of casinos for nearby areas and for the state as a whole have made the tribes significant players in Oregon's business, public policy, and cultural spheres.

The gaming facilities that have been in operation for more than a few years have enabled tribes to make improvements for their memberships—some on only a small scale, but others on a larger

Sixty-five miles southwest of Portland and only twenty-five minutes from the coast, the Grand Ronde tribe's Spirit Mountain Casino is Oregon's most profitable gaming establishment. With its payroll and purchase of goods and services, the casino contributes more than $50 million annually to Oregon's economy. Photo courtesy of Smoke Signals, *the Confederated Tribes of the Grand Ronde.*

scale. The authors of a recent Harvard University study reported the benefits of gaming to Indian country. They acknowledged that the real reason for economic progress was self-determination. According to the report, "self-rule brings decision-making home, and local decision-makers are held more accountable to local needs, conditions, and cultures than outsiders."

A 2002 study of the Coquille tribe's economic impact on the Coos Bay/North Bend and Coos County area found that annual countywide sales from construction, wholesale purchases, real estate, and services that involved the tribe's Mill Casino and Hotel "exceeded $44 million in a typical calendar year." Coquille tribal businesses account for one in every twenty-eight jobs in the county, and charitable contributions have exceeded $500,000 since the Mill Casino opened. In 2001, the tribe established the Coquille Tribal Community Fund, which awarded twenty-two grants totaling $210,000 to nonprofit groups in its first two years.

EcoNorthwest conducted the Coquille study and a similar one for the Siletz tribe in 1998, finding that through its business activities, the Siletz tribe supported 1,493 full-time jobs (nearly one in eleven) in Lincoln County and contributed $9.1 million in wages to workers in the county, while adding an additional $10 million to the economy.

Through its economic activities, including the Wildhorse Resort and Casino, the Umatilla tribes have created more than 1,000 jobs since 1992 and currently employ 1,041 people, 49 percent of whom are non-Indians. Their total 2002 payroll of $30 million circulated throughout the local economy for an estimated economic impact of $168 million.

The Cow Creek tribe and its Seven Feathers Hotel and Casino

Resort provide an annual payroll of about $35 million to the community, and its philanthropic arm has provided nearly $5 million since its inception in 1997. Its grants, as of spring 2004, have been distributed to 425 nonprofit organizations in the tribe's seven-county service area.

The Grand Ronde tribe contributes to the state's economy mainly through its Spirit Mountain Casino, and together the tribe and the casino are one of the largest employers in the mid-Willamette Valley. According to the tribe, more than $31 million is pumped into the local economy annually through Spirit Mountain Casino's employee payroll, and the casino spends more than $32 million annually in vendor goods and services, $23 million of that in Oregon. Casino employees pay more than $3 million each year in state and federal income taxes. Spirit Mountain Casino has an annual net direct economic stimulation to the state of more than $29 million. The tribe's foundation, the Spirit Mountain Community Fund, has contributed $30 million in charitable giving to more than three hundred and fifty groups in an eleven-county area.

Even tribes without significant gaming revenues, such as the Burns Paiute, Klamath, and Warm Springs, bring jobs and dollars to both their tribal members and their neighbors. The Confederated Tribes of the Warm Springs Indians have a complex of economic enterprises that provides revenue streams from hydroelectricity, Forest Stewardship Council–certified timber products, ecotourism, recreation, sports, and fishing, to name a few. The Warm Springs tribe is also the fifth-largest employer in central Oregon.

Diversity Is Essential for Plentitude

Economic health makes it possible to begin to reconcile the past and bring into the present the fairness espoused by Americans. Ideas regarding "other peoples," however, still have to change. For successful trade, one has to know about "other peoples." Decades ago, those involved in American business learned Japanese customs when Japan became a major economic force. Today, China is touted as the next new market. Economic health, and the struggle for it, can catalyze cultural tolerance and test adaptability.

Most, if not all, Oregon tribes want to be part of the global economy, yet the tribes struggle against a global corporate monoculture and stand instead for multiculturalism. They want to retain their authenticity and right to live as indigenous peoples, which requires communication and education on a global scale. The tribes have made strategic spending decisions—made possible by better economic times—to generate interest in and develop sensitivity toward Indian people. They have both contributed to and built their own museums, interpretive centers, and schools to help promote the understanding of American history and culture from their perspective. Nixyaawii Community School on the Umatilla reservation, which opened in 2004, has a mandate to reinstate native language and cultural mores into the local education system, a curriculum change that has helped reduce recidivism when introduced in other native schools.

The Oregon tribes bring different values, new ideas, and new energy to the table. In 2004 the Umatilla tribe and Columbia Energy Partners joined forces to build a 104-megawatt wind-power project in northeastern Oregon. The Burns Paiute tribe is also developing plans for wind energy. Internationally certified as an environmentally responsible business, the Warm Springs Forest Products Industry is exploring the manufacture of biomass products using, and thus reducing, waste materials. Most Oregon tribes collaborate with the Affiliated Tribes of Northwest Indians to develop and promote their cultural centers, art shows, casinos, powwows, recreation and RV facilities, and other appropriate tribal tourism venues to draw regional and international visitors.

Tribes support entrepreneurship within their own memberships by encouraging and financing small businesses. Such investments extend beyond reservation borders as small-business owners engage in the purchase of goods and services from their surrounding communities.

Many industries move throughout the globe leaving damaged lands in their wake; the tribes stay in the homelands they have used and maintained in good health since the beginning of memory. To

Traditional Maori greetings are exchanged between Wanna Davis, a member of the Maori delegation, and Doug Hatch, council member of the Siletz tribe, during a Procession of the Nations held at Willamette University in Salem, Oregon. The Maori people of Aotearoa/ New Zealand visited Oregon to open the 2005 art exhibition "Toi Maori: The Eternal Thread" at the university's Hallie Ford Museum. The Grand Ronde and Siletz tribes helped sponsor the Maori visit. Photo courtesy of Sam Beebe, Ecotrust.

restore the whole, tribal members ask for both economic and environmental health from their leaders. For some, the necessary wisdom is contained in what tribal cultures often refer to as "natural law," and in lessons derived from centuries of observing one place that have been handed down through demonstrated practice, story, or song. A simple set of axioms for tribal people calls for vigilance for the improving and protecting the well-being of one's people and never forgetting what one has. These are among the values and practices that account for our survival and guide our plans for an abundant future.

Tribes from the Willamette Valley are currently looking to develop property near Keizer from lands returned by the Chemawa Indian School. The school bought these lands with the money earned by generations of Indian student labor. The Umatilla tribe monitors the nearby Hanford Nuclear Reservation, seeing that all the processes are evaluated and safe. What misfortune touches Umatilla affects those downriver, too. As a result, Warm Springs supports the Umatilla when needed. Such collaborative leadership worked in the past and is another example of the old ways still guiding us. Our tradition of cooperation also recognized seniority over place. For instance, fishing places along many of Oregon's rivers were owned by families who had seniority or priority use rights to those locations. Others could net or spear fish there too, but not without the consent of senior users. It was, and is, respectful to acknowledge this protective and orderly custom.

As economic need compels reconnection among tribal peoples, it also compels connection with nontribal peoples to conduct business and build a future. Our tribes need to make strategic moves that require accepting and managing diversity.

Pictured here are Grand Ronde and Chinook tribal members on the last day of the "Paddle to Elwha," a twelve-day, more than two-hundred-mile journey from the Squaxin Island Tribe in Washington to Port Angeles, Washington. So far Grand Ronde is the only Oregon tribe to paddle in this event of more than seventy canoes from tribes in Alaska, British Columbia, and Washington. That may change as other Oregon coastal tribes are also experiencing a revival in canoe culture. Bobbie Mercier, a Grand Ronde language specialist, is pictured front center. Photo courtesy of Smoke Signals, *the Confederated Tribes of the Grand Ronde.*

Thinking there may be some lesson from our tribal past, I asked my maternal uncle Louie Pitt about the challenges of diversity: "How could so many kinds of Indian people have lived together in the Northwest and not have been at war somewhere at any given time?" He answered, "You could not be outright suspicious of your neighbor. Customs dictate gathering and harvest of food with the proper attitude of peace and harmony. Still one could not let anyone be vulnerable. When you had business nearby in the root fields or some sort of business with your neighbor, you kept an eye to the side on your precious people who were gathering.

"You watched for what worked well with others, traded for it in commerce, and in trading, explained the ideas behind the making. Differences were respected, and any disharmony was a distraction from essentially productive work."

From that and other teachings, I gather that respect for our neighbors is also respect for our future. We have been here from the time of creation and will endure. Never give up. Always listen to your elders. Protect the land for your children's children. Our challenge lies in how we cooperate and interact with the ancient system and the modern infusion of popular culture and commercialism.

From my understanding, the older complex of tribes included many, and they were generally tolerant of new citizens. With distinctive languages and cultural practices, it would seem that getting along would have been harder. This interest in the "new" was a prevalent attitude in precontact times, stemming from trying to keep up with one's neighbor, the tribe "next door." But the tribal narrative of contact with the Russians, the Spanish, the British, and finally, the "Bostons" (as Columbia River natives called the Americans) is complex, cataclysmic, and even gritty. This "grit" rubbed delicate areas of our humanity, as during the commotion of change, mistrust, and misunderstanding accumulated. Patricia Limerick, a University of Colorado historian, says in her book *Something in the Soil* that skirmishes and relations between tribal people and newcomers came not from newness but from "a lot of water under the bridge." Ultimately, there came a point when each realized they could no longer exploit the other. Conflict ensued from relationships, not simply from ignorance.

Of course, there were major rifts in cultural understanding. Much of the initial trade was forced, and the Europeans did not understand the elaborate protocols of the trading system kept along the rivers. Another factor in early misunderstandings was the abuse of indentured workers by the colonial newcomers who brought them to these shores. The Chinese, Hawaiians, Russians, and others who landed here in Oregon also played roles in these conflicts.

In the 1700s, the Russians brought Aleut men to our coasts to hunt for valuable sea otter pelts. Nearly a million otters were extirpated during this period in the northeast Pacific. The Russians captured and held hostage Aleut women and children to coerce the Aleut men to hunt for the foreigners' profit.

Later, British fur companies such as the Hudson's Bay Company allowed marriages between their men and local native women. Building families and gaining in-laws eased some of the tensions, but the children of these intercultural couples went to separate schools, and as adults these children held particular "stations" within the company. Individuals like Ranald McDonald, a Scotch-Chinook and an early Oregon emissary, demonstrated the intrepid brilliance of Oregon's original peoples. As the first teacher of English in Japan in the middle of the nineteenth century, Ranald shared his global knowledge in trade and customs with his captors: At that time, the Japanese forbade foreigners in their country on punishment of death, but because of his assistance, they let Ranald go rather than execute him. Revered in Hokkaido today, he died, unknown, on the Colville Indian Reservation. Today his life is commemorated in Ranald McDonald Grave State Park near the Kettle River in Washington and on a granite tablet (inscribed in Japanese and English) at Fort Astoria Park in Astoria, Oregon.

Cultural differences caused great social stresses during the early trading days, but these tensions motivated change. The boom of new trade materials and the exposure to new values affected native cultures, and most of the adjustments were attempts to make life easier. Horses and guns brought mobility and more influence to the owners. The ready adaptation of the indigenous cultures of Oregon in the early years is comparable to the tribes' recent accomplishments in natural resource management, government-to-government relations, and economic development. To become static and singular meant failure for business and isolation and stagnation in terms of social development. These are valuable historical lessons from the standpoint of the state's indigenous peoples.

Oregon's tribal governments provide long-range planning and tangible solutions that take into account their members and their neighbors. "You are borrowing from your children's children when using natural resources," Old Chief Joseph, a Nez Perce whose homeland was northeastern Oregon, advised. "Think for year after year, for a far away ahead." In tribal oratory, I have heard leaders say that our ancestors maintained that same mind-set during critical times, making decisions for what is now our present generation. Making allowances for others, sharing responsibility, and honoring all in the process are other qualities of great leadership. Kathryn Harrison, a great-grandmother and the former chair of the Grand Ronde tribe, often stressed that the strength of the tribal council was in its collaboration. She follows in the tradition of Oregon's Sarah Winnemucca, who traveled to Washington, DC, repeatedly to appeal to Congress on behalf of her people, the Paiute. All demonstrate great care and concern for their tribes' future.

A Native State of Mind

Warm Springs Chief Delvis Heath emphasized, "Do not put us all in one basket. We are all unique." In that sense, each Oregon tribe has its own purpose, determination, and skill sets. Each tribe has its own systems, history, governance, and diplomatic relationships with other tribes. Each belongs to a place and has the important responsibility to care for and protect that place.

Indian Country Etiquette

Each tribal nation in Oregon makes its own decision on how best to balance community and tradition while providing visitors with enjoyable and educational experiences. However, in an effort to avoid misunderstandings or violations of our customs, we ask that visitors follow basic procedures for conduct. In doing so, we can ensure the protection of our sacred and ceremonial areas, including the preservation of historical artifacts. Traditionally, our people are hospitable and generous; however, spiritual teachings, sacred ceremonies, and burial grounds are not openly shared with the public.

We are proud of our teachings and our heritage. These have been passed to us by our ancestors, and represent thousands of years of our individual histories. Your patience and understanding of our traditions and cultures is appreciated.

- Please be attentive to signage, and obey our individual tribe's rules and regulations.

- Alcohol, weapons, and drugs will not be tolerated.

- Please respect the privacy of residential communities.

- Ask before photographing or recording an individual, event, or activity.

- Do not pick up or remove artifacts or objects.

- Burial grounds and religious ceremonies are sacred and are not to be entered.

—*Courtesy of Affiliated Tribes of Northwest Indians/Economic Development Corporation*
www.atnitribes.org

Intimate family responsibilities, lineal knowledge, and claims pass on to new generations through oral traditions. Individual strength of character is essential in learning the oral traditions that preserve place-based knowledge. Oral knowledge, both in a historical sense and where it concerns tribal use in "usual and accustomed" areas, is crucial to legitimize tribal claims of knowing and using these lands for millennia. Confronted with the considerable crises of our time, we find that there is too much generalized information and too little holistic content in land management. To know this land better, we must look to the old stories and see how long "time immemorial" really is. Warm Springs and Klamath oral literature, for example, provides explicit detail about the eruption of twelve-thousand-foot Mount Mazama volcano, which happened seven thousand years ago, forming Crater Lake.

Coquille members Don Ivy (foreground) and Law Irwin are carving out an old-style dugout canoe made from a large and hard-to-find Port Orford White Cedar. Photo courtesy of Coquille Indian Tribe.

Look closely at the rivers: the Columbia, Willamette, Rogue, Umpqua, Coquille, Coos, Klamath, and others. Historically, rivers were the easiest way to travel. People preferred to live near the source of life—the water and its fish. As the nexus of ancient international trade, routes provided by the rivers and their contours pulsed and expanded in all directions. Over time, trading alliances extended tribal awareness and interactions beyond the present political borders. The Columbia River crosses the international Canadian border to end at Astoria, Oregon, where the river flows into the Pacific Ocean. The Columbia Basin covers a tremendous area and diverse geographies. People thrived because of the familial bonds and tribal alliances that they developed across large geographic areas in what are now the surrounding states. Tribes created boundaries based on various usages, as activities overlapped in many places. People could visit relatives in an area outside their own territory during particular gathering seasons and be safe.

All tribes spoke Chinuk Wawa (Chinook Jargon), the lingua franca of the Pacific region. Many place-names like *Multnomah*, *Clackamas*, and *Gresham*, and other words like *Skookumchuck* ("powerful water") and *potlatch* ("to give," and the name of the traditional gift-feasts) are the result of its usage across the region. Tribal native-language speakers say the land creates and retains the indigenous languages as a fact. Many anglicized place-names still indicate the ethnogeography of place. Tamástslikt Cultural Institute began mapping native place-names for the Lewis and Clark commemoration (2004–06), and the number of native names is extensive and growing. The original peoples' languages evolved from the land and its spirit.

In 2000 the Siletz tribe founded the Elakha Alliance to focus attention on the health of the nearcoast marine ecosystem. (*Elakha* is "sea otter" in Chinuk Wawa.) The alliance is made up of tribes, science organizations, nonprofits, and educational institutions. The sea otters were hunted and trapped into extinction along the Oregon coast in the early 1900s, and their absence has altered the coastal ecosystem. Sea urchins, once eaten and kept in check by sea otters, began to flourish, eating away the kelp forests that blanketed the waters near the shore. The reduction in kelp forests has exposed fish to predators and decreased the overall productivity of the coastal system. Scientists are finding that the absence of kelp has even changed the kinetic energy of the waves near the shore. The kelp forests lack their keystone species, the sea otter. Members of the Affiliated Tribes of the Northwest Indians, and subsequently the National Congress of the American Indians, passed resolutions in support of the Siletz tribe's initiative to work toward restoring the sea otter population to its previous numbers.

Tribes tend to look deeply and methodically into their homelands. The Coquille tribe, which sponsors and organizes Changing Landscapes, an annual cultural preservation conference, takes participants on field trips like the one along the Coquille River in 2003, where unusual fish traps were in view. These forays into local areas provide real-life examples as one learns about traditional natural resource management. Guides discuss native plants used as medicines and foods on forest walks, while experts in traditional ecological knowledge show how sites were carefully tended as natural gardens over periods of years. Many of the participants on these field trips look for and tend the plants used in basketry.

Indigenous cultures and practitioners of indigenous knowledge can confirm and reflect our shared human resilience and creativity. Art embedded with cultural information and a specific worldview, such as ceremonial regalia and baskets, helps to pass on ancient technology. The movement to form an Oregon Basketweavers Association started at the Coquille tribe's cultural preservation conference, springing from the growing interest in making new baskets and visiting the old masters. The association's practitioners have located the places where basket materials grow and have learned to gather them using traditional methods. Reverence for the natural materials, the process of tending the new growth, the collection and preparation of the mature plant fibers, and the finished basket completes the full circle of respectful activity. These strands of tradition are passed along by the many different weavers of the older generation to the younger basketweavers of today.

Cayuse-Nez Perce beadworker Maynard White Owl Lavadour, whose experiences exemplify this tradition, said, "My grandmothers taught me everything I would need to know. They said to share this knowledge and not be stingy." As Maynard now teaches his craft, grandmotherly mandates that included a multicultural openness have improved his critical thinking, helped him interrogate his own assumptions, exercise social imagination, and use creative problem solving. A person of leadership in our tribes will epitomize what he or she wants others to become, without force, simply by example and sharing how to become proficient. This means having to hold in mind one's own interest and the larger community interest at the same time.

In the same vein of generosity, the Umatilla tribe's Tamástslikt Cultural Institute preserves and documents traditions and practices, and in doing so makes a unique contribution to Oregon's cultural heritage. The institute, on the tribe's reservation near Pendleton, hosts evolving exhibits and programs, classrooms, a conference room, a multipurpose theater, photo archive, research library, and safe storage for family heirlooms. In addition, it features presentations about traditional life that include storytellers and contemporary artists of the three confederated tribes of the reservation. Many of these artists are nationally renowned and involved in the Umatilla's other cultural institution, Crow's Shadow Institute of the Arts.

Walla Walla artist James Lavadour and a group of supporters founded Crow's Shadow Institute of the Arts in 1992. Located on the reservation, this nonprofit arts facility brings technology, instruction, and cultural exchange to Native American artists. Artists have access to and receive instruction from both indigenous and non-native art professionals from around the world. The facilities include a large printmaking studio, computer graphics lab, and photography darkroom, as well as an extensive library and private studio space. It is one of the first community centers devoted entirely to culture and art in the Pacific Northwest and provides a unique venue for community involvement.

On the Warm Springs reservation, the Museum at Warm Springs serves as a living legacy of culture. Opened in 1993 after years of planning, the museum's permanent collection of treasured artifacts, historic photographs, murals, graphics, and rare documents is a dynamic, comprehensive chronicle of tribal history. The changing exhibition gallery provides a flexible venue for the ongoing exploration of every aspect of the Native American experience. This twenty-five-thousand-square-foot, $7.6 million facility, located along U.S. Highway 26 near Warm Springs, houses the single largest collection of Indian artifacts under one roof in the country. Both the museum's remarkable architecture and its exhibition design have been recognized for their excellence.

Making peace with our past is not easy when mainstream America makes decisions that profoundly affect our lives. One of those decisions involved human remains uncovered in 1996 along the Columbia River near Kennewick, Washington, on U.S. Army Corps of Engineers land. The nine-thousand-year-old skeleton, called "the Ancient One" by tribal people and "the Kennewick Man" by others, created a furor that pitted a group of academics against the region's tribes. Shortly after the discovery, the Corps announced its intention to turn over the remains to five tribes under provisions of the Native American Graves Protection and Repatriation Act (NAGPRA). Soon a small group of academics filed a lawsuit against the federal government to prevent the transfer and won. The eight academics argued constitutional and statutory rights to conduct extensive studies on the remains irrespective of NAGPRA, and openly theorized the man was not Native American but Caucasian, though the skeleton's approximate age placed the man on the Columbia River in a time before nonnative peoples had arrived. The tribes intended to bury the Ancient One as a matter of respect, as they do all human remains.

Another story of making peace with our past comes from the era when fishing villages and sacred sites along the Columbia River were flooded by hydroelectric dams. The Smithsonian Institution partially returned human remains taken from Memaloose ("burial") Island to the Wasco/Wishram tribes in 1994. The petition took many years of paperwork and careful consideration of spiritual protocols by the Wasco/Wishram people, who are now part of the Warm Springs and Yakama tribes. The tribes have no traditional ceremonies for reinterment, because until recent times, our relatives' graves remained undisturbed. The mass grave is in concrete at the Wishram Cemetery, simply so our ancestors will not be disturbed again.

The Confederated Tribes of Warm Springs created the Museum at Warm Springs to serve as a living legacy of their three tribes' cultures. Its beautiful architecture harmonizes with the landscape and tribal values such as reverence for water, the natural environment, and the legacy of their ancestors. Both The Museum at Warm Springs and Confederated Tribes of the Umatilla Indian Reservation's Tamástslikt Cultural Institute house permanent collections of artifacts, historic photographs, murals, graphics, and rare documents as dynamic chronicles of tribal history and culture. Other Oregon tribes are planning to build museums or similar institutions to protect their cultural patrimony and tell their unique stories. Photo courtesy of the Museum at Warm Springs.

Cultural Heritage Centers and Museums

Here is a sampling of the museums and cultural centers that feature native arts. Many of our tribes are currently developing museums and heritage centers to preserve traditions and to display artifacts for the education and benefit of future generations. See tribal websites for updates.

- Confederated Tribes of Grand Ronde. Cultural heritage display located in the Spirit Mountain Casino. www.grandronde.org

- Siletz Tribal Cultural Center. Artifacts and historical documents are stored and displayed at the Siletz Tribal Cultural Center. www.ctsi.nsn.us

- The Museum at Warm Springs. The museum was conceived of and created by the Confederated Tribes of Warm Springs to serve as a living legacy of our culture. www.warmsprings.biz/museum

- Tamástslikt Cultural Institute – Umatilla Tribes. The Institute includes world-class exhibits, a museum store, the Kinship Café, the Coyote Theater, and meeting spaces available to the public. www.tamastslikt.org

- The Coquille Tribal Library. An extensive amount of information on the Coquille Indian Tribe as well as other tribes of southwest Oregon. www.coquilletribe.org

- Four Rivers Cultural Center and Museum. The museum exhibits trace the settlement patterns of the Northern Paiute Indians. Exhibits also include artifacts from many other Northwest tribes. www.4rcc.com

- Columbia Gorge Discovery Center & Wasco County Historical Museum. Indian heritage exhibits include a one-of-a-kind basket collection and Lewis and Clark archaeology. www.gorgediscovery.org

- Portland Art Museum. The museum's Native American collection is remarkable for both its depth and diversity, consisting of objects crafted by more than two hundred indigenous groups from throughout North America, including prehistoric, historical, and contemporary works of outstanding quality. www.portlandartmusuem.org

- Hallie Ford Museum of Art, Willamette University. The museum's permanent collection includes Native American art acquired in the 1940s as well as a basketweaving display housed in the Confederated Tribes of Grand Ronde Gallery. www.willamette.edu/museum_of_art

- High Desert Museum. "By Hand through Memory," a permanent exhibit, brings to life a seldom-told story of resilience and spiritual strength among Native Americans of the Columbia River Plateau. Featuring the Doris Swayze Bounds Collection of basketry and beadwork from the Plateau Indians. www.highdesertmuseum.org

Life off the Reservation

Indigenous peoples from other places also live here in Oregon. There are Dine, Lakota, Pueblo, Yaqui, and Hawaiian peoples, among many others. If you were to list all the tribes and indigenous peoples here, it would include peoples from most of the North and Central American continent and the Pacific Rim. In the urban areas where 89 percent of Oregon's native people live, you may also experience another type of native identity some call pan-Indianism.

Pan-Indianism, or the intermixing of Indian cultures through shared or common activities, has its roots in boarding schools of the late 1800s and became more widespread with the federal Indian relocation policy of the 1950s that moved many families to urban centers for training and jobs. After acquiring training and education, some Indians stayed in urban areas to find employment in their fields. Transitioning to urban life and trying to retain their cultural identities as Indians created a need for urban Indian community centers. Portland boasts one of the first urban Indian centers in the nation, and the same energetic leadership started the first alcohol and drug treatment center in the country to use Native American healing practices, such as the sweat lodge.

With the encouragement and support of the tribes and native communities, the state's system of higher education is increasingly accommodating the needs of Indian students on campus. Most colleges have a native student program to aid in student retention and support. A retention program often is simply an office where Indian students can meet with advisors and one another. In one recent year, the University of Oregon's program resulted in a reduction in the native dropout rate from more than 50 percent to only 2 percent.

Members of the Confederated Tribes of the Umatilla Reservation have been participants in the Pendleton Round-Up since its inception in 1910. They have an even larger role in Happy Canyon, the nightly pageant, dance, and games that officially started in 1916. Left: Former Happy Canyon princesses riding in the Westward Ho! Parade during ninetieth anniversary of Happy Canyon. Pictured are, far right, Caroline Motanic Davis, first-ever Happy Canyon Princess from 1952, and others from the left, Sandy Craig, Toni Minthorn, Nancy Minthorn, and Katherine Minthorn. Photo courtesy of Confederated Umatilla Journal.

Thanks to the generosity of individuals, the tribes, and foundations, as well as the persistence of students and native alumni, Native American longhouses are now part of the campuses at Oregon State University in Corvallis, the University of Oregon in Eugene, and Portland State University—the latter two opened in 2003. Southern Oregon University in Ashland provides a Native American Student Union. As of 2007, Lane Community College in Eugene has broken ground on its campus longhouse.

Nevertheless, no institution of higher learning in Oregon, public or private, offers a major in Native American studies. Oregon State University and the University of Oregon offer majors in ethnic studies, which includes Native American courses, and Portland State University and Southern Oregon University offer minors in Native American studies. Lewis & Clark Law School in Portland and the University of Oregon School of Law offer several Indian law classes, while Willamette College of Law in Salem offers one class. An Indian Law Summer Program at Lewis & Clark Law School offers six different courses on the subject. The Department of Fisheries and Wildlife in the College of Agricultural Sciences at Oregon State University has a long-standing and successful record working with tribes, tribal organizations, and Native American students. Also, in support of tribal efforts, the Central Oregon and Hermiston Agriculture Experiment and Extension Centers are currently studying the effects of stream and riparian area management on water quality and salmon recovery in the Umatilla River and its tributaries. The Native American Teacher Education Program at Eastern Oregon University in La Grande encourages American Indians and Alaskan Natives to become teachers and consider plans to return to their communities or teach in areas with high native student enrollments.

Leon Matthews from Chemawa Indian School plants a tree as part of a reforestation project inside Oregon's Opal Creek Wilderness area. The project is a joint effort of Ecotrust, the Opal Creek Ancient Forest Center, and the school. This Indian boarding school, which the BIA started in the 1870s as an elementary school focusing on vocational skills, operates now as a high school for native youth from Alaska to Arizona and is located near Salem, Oregon. Photo courtesy of Craig Jacobson, Ecotrust.

Over the course of a decade, the University of Oregon Native American Initiative forged closer relationships between the tribes and the academic community in order to integrate Native American subjects into the university's research and teaching. The Department of Anthropology has made efforts to "align the field more directly with the interests and needs of native peoples." Some of the important programs that are part of the initiative include Native Language Preservation, Native American Literature, the Center for Indigenous Cultural Survival, and the Southwest Oregon Research Project.

In 2000, the Portland Art Museum opened a new wing, the Grand Ronde Center for Native American Art. Its seven thousand square feet of exhibition space displays 375 works of art, drawn from virtually every major cultural group in North America. Former Native American arts curator Bill Mercer conceived the art installations, and Clifford LaFontaine designed the space. The Grand Ronde tribe, along with their Spirit Mountain Community Fund, has donated more than a million dollars to the museum since 1997. In 2005, the museum opened the exhibit *People of the River*, the first major collection of middle to lower Columbia River tribal art ever shown. It was accompanied by a catalog describing the exceptionally rare, distinctive, and unique art of these tribes from precontact to the early twentieth century. These objects and this style truly are not seen anywhere else in the world.

Political Gains

It was a historic occasion for the tribes of Oregon when Governor John A. Kitzhaber signed Executive Order 96-30 on May 22, 1996, which officially recognized state-tribal government-to-government relations. The governor's actions followed the lead of President Bill Clinton's 1994 Executive Order 13084 to all federal departments and agencies, clarifying their responsibilities to consult with tribes, government-to-government, before making decisions or taking actions affecting the tribes.

Several years later, the 2001 Oregon Legislative session took the relationship of Oregon tribes and the state a step further by codifying Executive Order 96-30 in Senate Bill 770: "Oregon law also requires state agencies to develop and implement policies to include tribes when state agency policies and programs affect tribal interests." Agencies are required to have a key contact for state-tribal relations, promote communication with tribes, and conduct positive government-to-government relations. The bill also obligates agencies to provide certain training, annual summits, and annual reports to the governor and the Legislative Commission on Indian Services on state agency interactions with tribes. Training, summits, and reports have occurred as required since 2001; and by most accounts, the state has improved its relations with the tribes.

As for other major legislative pieces on the state level, the Geographic Name Change Act, which called for the eradication of derogatory or demeaning words in place-names, provided a basis for new understanding and respect. Its passage required the state to change all geographical names with the word "sq—" in them by the year 2005. Women from the Umatilla, Warm Springs, and Burns Paiute tribes first spoke out against the use of this term, the origins of which are in dispute, but which was used by European Americans to disparage and demean Indian women. "It is never too late to right a wrong," said Senate Democratic Leader Kate Brown, who sponsored the bill. "We must acknowledge the painful and derogatory history of the word 'sq—' It is only right. We may not be able to change our past, but we can certainly improve our future." Assigning new names is a collaborative responsibility shared among local communities, neighbors, and counties.

Tribal elders from throughout the state and a few younger people who speak their native languages testified on behalf of the proposed Indian Language Act. The 2001 legislation allows tribes to develop a written and oral test for an American Indian Language teaching license, so that teachers can include native languages in their classroom curricula.

Termination: There and Back

American textbooks generally exclude the U.S. policies of tribal termination and restoration from our country's history. (Chapter 11, "Federal-Indian Relation," and chapters about the individual tribes further describe Termination and its consequences.) In summary, the U.S. government "terminated" federal trusteeship of roughly 3 percent of the country's Indian population. Oregon Indians suffered disproportionately, with termination of sixty-two tribes and bands. In the 1950s, the federal government abolished tribal governments and their laws, condemned reservation tribal lands, auctioned large tracts to the highest bidder (excluding tribal members from the auctions through difficult bidding terms), and canceled health, housing, and educational programs.

Even though many thought the purpose of the termination legislation was simply liberation from federal management of tribal affairs, the true result was devastating to tribes, as they lost federal recognition of their sovereign status when they were terminated. A decade later, tribes began to work to restore their status as federally recognized entities. All the terminated tribes and tribal confederations in Oregon were eventually reinstated: the Confederated Tribes of Siletz won restoration in 1977, followed by the Cow Creek Band of Umpqua Indians in 1982, the Confederated Tribes of Grand Ronde in 1983, the Confederated Tribes of Coos, Lower Umpqua and Siuslaw Indians in 1984, the Klamath Tribes in 1986, and finally, the Coquille Tribe in 1989.

These tribes are carefully rebuilding their security and sovereignty through gaming revenues and subsequent economic diversification. With only small pockets of their formerly vast holdings restored, tribes are also purchasing former lands. The Siletz, Klamath, and Coos, Lower Umpqua, and Siuslaw tribes have recouped little to none of their homelands, which encompassed some of the most desirable property in their given areas. A small but important portion of the Siletz's homeland came back to tribal ownership. The Chinook Winds Casino Resort now stands on that key property in Lincoln City. After Termination, the federal government sold most of the forest land that made up the reservation to private industrial forest owners. The federal government now owns less than 10 percent of the Siletz watershed.

The Klamath Tribes have yet to successfully win back any significant portion of its former 1.2-million-acre reservation lost as a result of termination. The government sold the reservation, mostly forest land, to private timber interests, and the rest became the majority portion of the Winema National Forest and a smaller portion of the Fremont National Forest. Senator Mark Hatfield knew these lands were unique and therefore led their transfer to federal ownership and some measure of protection.

Since restoration, the Klamath Tribes have worked to reclaim their land base, and in the interim, see it properly managed and brought back to health after the negative impact of destructive timber-cutting practices and overhunting. Eventually, the tribe brought a mismanagement suit against the Forest Service to save what remains of the once complex pine forest and the animals dependent on it. After winning in federal court, the Klamath Tribes and the Forest Service entered into a 1999 memorandum of agreement concerning future management. Talks and negotiations ensued, only to have these land and forest issues eclipsed by the water and salmon battles that erupted in the Klamath Basin in 2002.

Essentially, water is sparse and overallocated in the Klamath Basin. As a result, people and fish vie for the same water. When pictures of defiant farmers turning irrigation spigots back on and thousands of dead and dying salmon in the river suddenly made front-page news in 2002, the conflict entered the forefront of national politics. Once the water crisis was national news, returning the forests to the Klamath Tribes received less public consideration. Individual property rights groups, however, who had inflamed the water controversy in pursuit of their own agendas, now joined others to oppose the tribe's proposals for forest conservation and tribal reacquisition of the land. Meanwhile, because water has been allocated for irrigation at the expense of fish, downriver tribes—the Yurok, Karuk, and Hoopa—protested the devastating loss of tens of thousands of chinook, endangered coho, and uncounted steelhead and sturgeon. All the while the U.S. Bureau of Reclamation denied any responsibility in the matter. But the Klamath Tribes persist. Talks regarding the return of six hundred and ninety thousand acres of national forest land are expected to continue with the Bush administration.

Out of any of these groups, it is the Klamath Tribes that will remain to recover the forest and rebuild the economy for the benefit of the people. Oregon Governor Tom McCall recognized the tribe's role when he wrote in his 1958 book, *A Reintroduction to the Indians of Oregon*: "Nor should it be forgotten when plaudits are distributed that the Klamath Indians have in effect been subsidizing the economy of Oregon since 1913. … The sustained yield of the forest plan kept a steady pace, even though a faster cutting rate would have meant greater immediate income for the Indians than they realized under sustained yield." In early 1953, during a period of growing national prosperity and optimism, the Klamath Tribes were one of the most successful and economically self-sufficient tribes in the United States.

Without the forest, the Klamath Tribes still contribute about $25 million per year to Klamath County's economy in the form of payroll, direct expenses, and goods and services. The tribes are now writing "The Plan for the Klamath Tribes' Management of the Klamath Reservation Forest" with forest scientists K. Norman Johnson and Debora Johnson of Oregon State University and Jerry F. Franklin of the University of Washington. The plan is central to the tribe's goal of regaining its historic reservation. Ecotrust, a Portland-based environmental organization that collaborates with Indian tribes and Canada's First Nations, provides a layperson's version of the greater plan and treatments in *Klamath Heartlands* by

Edward "Ted" Wolf, which was written with tribal input and authorization. Although the return of the reservation will take an act of Congress and support from the nontribal community, the Klamath Tribes' quest exemplifies the will of the terminated tribes to regain lost ground and work toward a future that provides benefits for all.

For the Coos, Lower Umpqua, and Siuslaw, the nonnative settlement of Oregon initiated years of uncertainty. Some settlers physically removed Indian families and then moved into the very homes these native families had built. The U.S. Army removed some Indians for their protection but when they returned to their lands they found them occupied by white settlers. A very small land base of less than ten acres is all that remains of the Coos, Lower Umpqua, and Siuslaw homeland. Now the 720 tribal members mostly live in the Coos Bay-North Bend, Eugene-Springfield, and Florence areas. The tribes plan to reclaim lands for a larger reservation.

Recently, U.S. Senator Gordon Smith introduced a bill on behalf of the tribe—the Coos, Lower Umpqua, and Siuslaw Restoration Amendments Act of 2003. This legislation began the process of reacquisition of a small portion of the original ancestral territory of forested land (sixty-three thousand acres). At present this bill has not garnered the support of the executive branch. In the meantime, the tribe and state came to an agreement on a casino, which, along with a proposed entertainment center, is only one part of the tribe's economic plan to benefit not only tribal members, but also the larger community, which has suffered in the absence of once-thriving timber and fishing industries.

Salmon Restoration and Marketing

The salmon is a principal Northwest cultural icon. As we share a sense of its importance, salmon provides a common denominator for Oregonians. Its presence, or lack thereof, is also an indicator of watershed health. Management of salmon is inherent in the tribes' cultural mores, which are practiced by fishing families and supported by the cultural and religious centers of tribal life. Organizations like the Northwest Indian Fisheries Commission in Washington and the Columbia River Inter-Tribal Fish Commission (CRITFC) respond, at the behest of member tribes, to critical salmon issues and management of the river systems held in common with the non-Indians of the region. In the 1960s and '70s, strong Indian communities encouraged tribal innovation and intertribal cooperation. These two organizations were among the results of those times. While in-

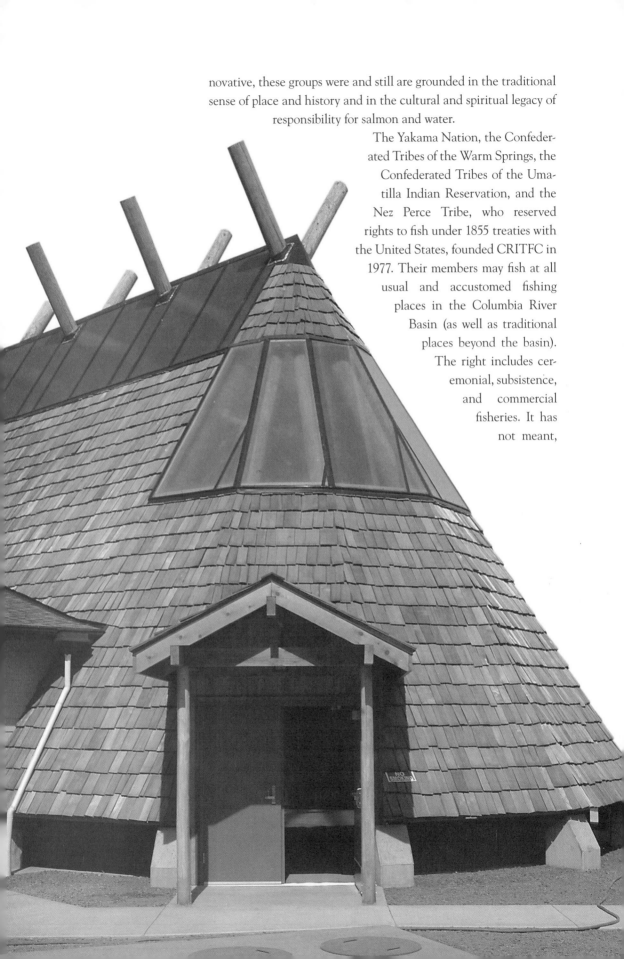

novative, these groups were and still are grounded in the traditional sense of place and history and in the cultural and spiritual legacy of responsibility for salmon and water.

The Yakama Nation, the Confederated Tribes of the Warm Springs, the Confederated Tribes of the Umatilla Indian Reservation, and the Nez Perce Tribe, who reserved rights to fish under 1855 treaties with the United States, founded CRITFC in 1977. Their members may fish at all usual and accustomed fishing places in the Columbia River Basin (as well as traditional places beyond the basin). The right includes ceremonial, subsistence, and commercial fisheries. It has not meant,

however, that these usual and accustomed places will remain undisturbed, as recent history on the Columbia River amply demonstrates.

With the construction of numerous hydroelectric projects on
the Columbia River, which began in the 1930s, the tribes lost major
fisheries, including Celilo Falls, a fishing and trading mecca for more
than twelve thousand years. After making do for decades while
waiting for fishing access to be reestablished, many tribal fishers now
harvest salmon at fishing sites built more recently by the U.S. Army
Corps of Engineers. CRITFC promotes direct-to-the-public sales at
these sites along the Columbia to help tribal fishers maintain their
traditions and supplement their incomes. The fish market in this
program is quite different from the trading and sales in the ancient
Columbia River fisheries at the Great Cascades, the Long Narrows,
and Celilo Falls—fisheries that provided the family livelihood for an
entire year.

Currently, CRITFC encourages fishers to participate in marketing through the Fisher-Chef Connection, a project of the Chef's
Collaborative. Along with Ecotrust, CRITFC is working on a value-
added product for tule fish with the Food Innovation Center. Tules
are low-end, white-fleshed fish commonly left over after market.
Being able to make a value-added product would potentially boost
income for fishers later in the year, after the fishing season is over.
Successful fisheries also have broader local and regional economic
gain: The Columbia River Inter-Tribal Fish Commission estimates
that for every ten dollars generated by fish sales, as much as seven
dollars is contributed to local economies.

The tribes at Warm Springs and Siletz work diligently on recovering the many species in their respective river systems. For the
Warm Springs this means tribally enhanced riparian zones, unprec-

The volcanoes in our stories moved and lived before our human presence. They made way for the contour of skyline. The river shifted this way, left its mark. It made

a way for us. Coyote walked here and made this so in this time's beginning. Songs are sung through our lives and are a part of how we follow. There is a difference here.

We dream. We know our bodies are made of all these elements. On this land we are all motion. We age. Society changes. New people arrive. Old people leave. Memory stays.

—Elizabeth Woody from "Recognition of the Maker"

Celilo (*Wyam*) Root Feast and Salmon 2005

Loss of Wyam caused pervasive sadness, even in celebratory events. The old Longhouse is gone. The Wyam, or Celilo Falls, are gone. Still courage, wisdom, strength, and belief bring us together each season to speak to all directions the ancient words. There is no physical Celilo, but we have our mothers, fathers, sisters, brothers, and our children bound together for all possible life in the future. We are salmon (*Waykanash*). We are deer (*Winat*). We are roots (*Xnit*). We are berries (*Tmanit*). We are water (*Chuush*). We are the animation of the Creator's wisdom in Worship song (*Waashat Walptaikash*).

edented enlargement of the buffers around streams, and restoration of naturally spawning spring chinook in Shi-tike Creek and Hood River. However, the most dramatic story is the Umatilla Basin Salmon Recovery Project, a long-term effort by the Umatilla tribe. The tribe began this salmon recovery project in 1980 to return water and salmon to the Umatilla River. This effort defended 1855 treaty rights and overcame water-use conflicts between Indians and non-Indians. The tribes here worked hard to simultaneously protect the local economy, which is dependent on irrigated agriculture, while putting water and fish back into the river.

The Northwest Power and Conservation Council, Bonneville Power Administration, Oregon Department of Fish and Wildlife, Oregon Water Resources Department, and the U.S. Bureau of Reclamation partnered in the Umatilla's salmon-recovery effort. The project piped water directly from the Columbia River into the area's irrigation systems rather than taking it from the Umatilla River. Irrigation continues, while water also flows in the river for fish, fish habitat, and fish migration.

The project's success brought salmon back to a river they had been absent from for seventy years. It also managed to do this while avoiding litigation. The dramatic return of all salmon species origi-

The spirit of the "Place of Echoing Water upon Rocks" is not silent. We care for the river and the life of traditional unity, the humble dignity, and purity in intention—wholeness. Ultimately, we restore life with our attention and devotion. Each hears the echoing water within.

The leader speaks in the ancient language's manner. He speaks to all in Ichiskiin. He says, "We are following our ancestors. We respect the same Creator and the same religion, each in turn of their generation, and conduct the same service and dance to honor our relatives, the roots, and the salmon. The Creator at the beginning of time gave us instruction and the wisdom to live the best life. The Creator made man and woman with independent minds. We must choose to live by the law, as all the others, salmon, trees, water, air, all live by it. We must use all the power of our minds and hearts to bring the salmon back. Our earth needs our commitment. That is our teachings. We are each powerful and necessary."

All lift their hands palms open and upward to acknowledge and recognize the speaker's truth: the presence of the Creator's strength is among us and inside us. The words enter the greater and expansive essence of living earth. We are land. We are water. Our passion is the fire in our home's hearth. We all exchange the same air in exclamation. We are all one.

—*Elizabeth Woody*
Spellings courtesy of Arlita Rhoan and Dallas Winishut,
Confederated Tribes of Warm Springs, from River of Memory *(2006)*

---

nally found in the Umatilla River Basin has allowed fishing seasons for Indians and non-Indian sports fishers. Another benefit is that tribal staffers have become active members of the regional technical committees that address fish, wildlife, and other environmental issues.

Now the Umatilla tribe is tackling recovery of the Walla Walla Basin with the same commitment to including the interests of the larger community that depends on this watershed.

In the last two centuries, indigenous people and their cultures accommodated the needs of the United States and adapted. Although many native people were able to stay at home and isolated, our communities must not remain completely self-absorbed. A genuine citizen of native descent takes a passionate position with long-term goals that extend beyond a single person's lifetime. If a tribal community does not educate the larger world, greed and more superficial aspects of postmodern life can overrun their lives.

The tribes are the elder nations. The native-run organization, nonprofit, corporation, or community group conveys professional observations, information, and volumes of wisdom based on older, time-tested systems. With native peoples truly included, possibilities unfold for their neighbors in the urban centers, the reservations, the state, and the nation.

When researchers asked Yukon elders, our resilient neighbors to the far north, to define "development," they said it was spirituality. As citizens of Oregon, we should start this new century with the same goodwill shared among its native peoples, the first Oregonians. If human development is truly spirituality, this may be the greatest exchange yet to come.

Powwows and Events in Oregon

The public is welcome to attend the powwows and many tribal celebrations throughout the year. Most powwows feature native dancers and drumming, traditional crafts, and wonderful food. Call ahead for exact dates and times, which can vary from year to year at the whim of Mother Nature.

Burns Paiute Tribe

- Reservation Day Powwow. Second weekend in October in Burns, Oregon. This is the day the tribe celebrates its social recognition by the United States government. Events include traditional games and a feast.

Coquille Indian Tribe

- Mill-Luck Salmon Celebration: Second weekend in September at the Mill Casino Hotel, North Bend, Oregon. (541) 756-8800 x420

Cow Creek Band of Umpqua Tribe of Indians

- Land of Umpqua Discovery Days: Third weekend in June in downtown Roseburg, Oregon. This local community event is supported by the tribe. Attractions include entertainment, exhibits, arts and crafts, food, and more. (541) 673-3352

- Canyonville Pioneer Days: August 25–28 at Pioneer Park in Canyonville, Oregon. This local community event is supported by the tribe. Attractions include logging contests, entertainment, parade, bed races, and food. (541) 839-4452

Confederated Tribes of the Grand Ronde Community

- Veterans Powwow: Second weekend in July in Grand Ronde, Oregon. Honors all tribal and nontribal veterans. (503) 879-5878

- Spirit Mountain Stampede. Father's Day weekend (June) in Grand Ronde, Oregon. (503) 769-8853

- Annual Competition Powwow. Third weekend in August in Grand Ronde, Oregon. One of the largest powwows in the Northwest. (503) 879-2037 or (800) 422-0232

The Klamath Tribes

- Annual Return of *c'waam* Ceremony: Held each year after the first snow in March (Mother Nature sets the date), in Chiloquin, Oregon. Attractions include traditional dancing and drumming, a traditional feed, releasing of a c'waam into the river, and other ceremonial practices. (800) 524-9787 x159

- Southern Oregon Memorial Day Powwow and Rodeo: Held Memorial Day weekend, each year, in Klamath Falls, Oregon. Attractions include rodeo, competition powwow,

powwow, and arts and crafts. The powwow and rodeo are held each year at the Klamath County Fairgrounds, in Klamath Falls, Oregon. (800) 524-9787

- Klamath Tribes Annual Restoration Celebration: Fourth weekend in August in Chiloquin, Oregon. This annual event marks the anniversary of the federal re-recognition of the Klamath Tribes. Attractions include rodeo, powwow, fun run, softball tournament, arts and crafts, food, and more. Everyone is invited to attend our Drug and Alcohol Free Celebration. (800) 524-9787

- Annual New Year's Eve Sobriety: Held New Year's Eve each year, in Chiloquin, Oregon. This event encourages family and friends to bring in the New Year without drugs and alcohol. Attractions include Indian dancing, drumming, a free feed, door prizes, friendly games, arts and crafts, a huge raffle, and more. Everyone is invited to attend. (800) 524-9787 x147

Confederated Tribes of the Umatilla Indian Reservation

- Wildhorse Powwow: First weekend in July at the Powwow Grounds, Wildhorse Resort and Casino, Umatilla Indian Reservation, Pendleton, Oregon. (541) 278-2274

- Celebrity Poker and Golf Tournament: Second weekend in August at Wildhorse Resort and Casino, Umatilla Indian Reservation, Pendleton, Oregon. Celebrities will play poker, golf, or both with participants who register for this event. (541) 966-1510

- Tamástslikt Cultural Institute Birthday Celebration—Tribal Art Show and Twilight Parade: The third weekend in August at Tamástslikt Cultural Institute, Umatilla Indian Reservation, Pendleton, Oregon. Attractions include a parade, a tour to watch spawning salmon, pony rides for kids, and much more. (541) 966-1977

- Pendleton Round-Up and Happy Canyon Pageant: Second full week in September in Pendleton, Oregon. Attractions include rodeo, dress-up parade, Westward Ho! parade, Happy Canyon Night Show, Round-up Foundation, Memorial Golf Tournament, Mainstreet Cowboys Show, Native American Tribal Encampment, arts and crafts, and children's rodeo. (800)457-6336

- Indian Summer Cruise-In and Performance Swap Meet. Second weekend in October at Wildhorse Resort and Casino, Umatilla Indian Reservation, Pendleton, Oregon. Swap meet attracts classic car buffs from California to the Canadian border. Free and open to the public, it offers everyone a chance to see the cars and obtain hard-to-find parts. Prizes are given in competitions for the best show cars. (541) 966-1977

- Wildhorse Hot Air Balloon Bash: Third weekend in October at Wildhorse Resort and Casino, Umatilla Indian Reservation, Pendleton, Oregon. Features an annual flying competition between pilots from throughout the West. Some three dozen colorful balloons brighten the skies over the Pendleton area at the foot of the Blue Mountains for three days of flying. (541) 966-1977

Confederated Tribes of Siletz

- Nesika Illahee Powwow: Second weekend of August in Siletz, Oregon. Events include dance competition, crafts, and food at one of the largest powwow events of the year. Visit the Siletz Cultural Center and the Nesika Illahee Powwow on Government Hill in the town of Siletz, follow Highway 229. (800) 922-1399

- Siletz Restoration Powwow: Third Saturday in November at Chinook Winds Casino, Lincoln City, Oregon. Celebrating Siletz Restoration Evening Social Powwow. (541) 444-2532

Confederated Tribes of Warm Springs

- Lincoln's Birthday Powwow: Second weekend in February at the Simnasho Longhouse in Warm Springs, Oregon. This traditional event is a celebration of sovereignty and includes a contest.

- Pi-Ume-Sha Treaty Days Powwow: Last weekend of June. Commemorates the signing of the 1855 treaty. Events include rodeo, softball tournament, endurance horse race, and golf tournament. Vendors will feature arts, crafts, and plenty of food. Contest dancing and drumming is held throughout the weekend. (541) 553-1196

Columbia River Treaty Tribes

- Celilo Village Longhouse Salmon Feast. Usually held the second weekend in April in Celilo Village, Oregon. Open to the public.

—Thanks to Affiliated Tribes of Northwest Indians/Economic Development Coporation

Chapter 2

Burns Paiute Tribe

BY MINERVA T. SOUCIE

The Wada Tika band of Northern Paiute Indians, known today as the Burns
Paiute Tribe, is descended from an ancient band of Paiutes whose territory
stretched the length and breadth of central and southeastern Oregon. The
traditional lifeway of the Northern Paiutes is described in Chapter 4, "The
Great Basin." Suffice it to say, the Wada Tika, like other Northern Paiutes,
covered great distances each year to gather food and to visit and trade with
other Paiute bands or with the Klamath, Shoshone–Bannock, and Umatilla.
The ability to move freely over large landscapes was vital to Wada Tika survival.

The First Contacts with Non-Indians

The Wada Tika's first contact with non-Indians occurred when fur trappers came into the Harney Valley in search of beavers. At first, the Indian people avoided the foreigners, but soon they became concerned, as more and more of the strangers appeared in the country the Paiutes had always regarded as their own. At first, the Indians encountered the intruders during their food-gathering travels, but by the nineteenth century, the Paiutes found that their camas fields had been fenced off by the new Harney Valley cattle barons, threatening their traditional way of life.

The Question of Land

By the 1860s, the Indian people knew that they and the government must try to reach some agreement about the land. With more settlers moving into the country and the military roaming the hills, the leaders knew they had to make decisions so that their people could have a place where they would be safe. Among the Paiutes who negotiated for land were Egan, Oits, Gshanee, Ponee, Tashego (Pasigo), and Weyou Wewa. Pasigo (the Burns Paiute believe that the old records misspelled Pasigo's name as Tashego)—whose Indian name means "blue camas" and whose English name was Peter Teeman—was the last chief/leader of the Wada Tika. He died in Burns in the 1940s.

The bands also wanted an area where they could maintain the old gathering and hunting ways, but the settlers pressured the government to give their cattle more room to graze. On September 12, 1872, by executive order, President Grant established the 1.8-million-acre Malheur Reservation, and most of the Paiutes were encouraged to move onto it and start to live like "civilized," that is, European American, people. The children started school, and the men began farming or learning carpentry skills.

The boundaries of the new reservation, however, had scarcely been set when they were changed, further reducing the traditional territory that the Paiutes had used in their seasonal round. Those first changes took place between 1872 and 1876 in response to pressure from settlers, who wanted use of the reservation's grazing land. Later, when gold was discovered in the northern portion of the boundary, the reservation was again reconfigured by Congress.

Life on the Reservation

Life on the reservation was far from happy, for it put an end to the traditional Paiute lifeways. Some of the leaders were dissatisfied because their people were not allowed outside the boundaries of the reservation to hunt and gather food. Oits, a medicine man, was also angered by the arbitrary treatment of his people by various Indian agents. These agents and the military watched Oits closely because they feared his influence among the Paiutes and thought that while he was doctoring his people, he was trying to recruit some of them to go to war against the whites.

When the Bannocks, who had decided to try and rid the land of the newcomers so that life could return to normal, came to the Paiutes and sought their help, dissension was already affecting the tribe, and many members were easily persuaded.

The Bannock War

Although most Paiutes did not participate in the Bannock War of 1878, they suffered from it nevertheless. Many were killed in their sleep or attacked by troops in their camps, innocent women and children were captured and tortured, women were raped by soldiers, and men were killed or tortured. My great-grandmother was a young woman during the Bannock War and was taken to Fort Boise, where women were violated by the soldiers.

During the winter of 1879, the Paiute leaders surrendered after Chief Egan was beheaded on Battle Mountain in the Blue Mountain range by Umatillas, who—along with Warm Springs scouts—had been hired to help the U.S. Cavalry. Ironically, Egan had been on his way to ask for help from the Umatillas, whom the Paiutes regarded as friends. To prove that Egan was dead, a Umatilla cut off his head and delivered it to the cavalry in a burlap sack. News of the death brought the Bannock War to an early end. Although Bannocks had started the war, the Paiute people suffered the greatest losses.

Removal from the Reservation

At war's end, the Paiutes were rounded up like cattle and moved to Fort Simcoe, Washington, in January 1879—a journey that killed many. The men walked two by two in iron shackles; the women and children rode in wagons. Babies were born and died on the trail, while the elderly froze before they reached the Columbia River.

This was the outcome of the Bannock War for the Wada Tika. Those who survived spent many years in Washington, where they were treated badly by the Yakama Indians. Subsequently, many of the Paiutes escaped and made their way back to the Harney Valley, enduring many hardships to reach their homeland.

A People without a Home

In 1883—while most of the Wada Tika were still at Fort Simcoe or Fort Vancouver, where some, including Oits, had been moved—the government returned their Harney Valley reservation to the public domain, giving as one reason the fact that "there weren't any Indians living on the Reservation." However, even before the land was opened to public use, settlers were running cattle and homesteading within reservation boundaries.

In 1887, at Fort Simcoe, the remaining Paiutes were asked if they wanted to return to Harney County. Many, being suspicious, opted to remain where they were—or to go onto other reservations such as Warm Springs, Fort McDermitt, and Owyhee in Nevada. Many others moved to Duck Valley and settled in the area of Miller Creek. Oits was one who went to live at Warm Springs.

Of the Paiutes returning to Harney County, each head of household received 160 acres as part of the

This is one of the earliest known photographs of the Burns Paiute people. The photo was taken on the area that is known as Old Camp around 1924–25. This was the site of the city dump that the Paiute's cleaned to build their homes. While Old Camp was being built, the Paiutes lived in tattered tents and teepees. Photo courtesy of the Burns Paiute Tribe.

1887 Allotment Act. In all, 115 Paiutes had a bit of land returned to them on which to live and try to grow food. They lived in wooden houses that the men built from milled timber brought from the sawmill in a nearby forest. The Indian men built the structures using the carpentry skills they learned while at Fort Simcoe.

The soil on the allotments, however, was alkaline, and the land was covered with sage and scrub brush. Without any water for irrigation, farming on it was bound to fail. As a result, the few families who had returned settled into a lifestyle dependent on the community of Burns and surrounding ranches for their survival. Many Paiutes hired on as ranch hands and washerwomen in Burns. People who did not have homes on the allotments lived outside of town in makeshift tents alongside the city dump in a community called Old Camp. Without a homeland, they lived in very poor conditions and endured the hostility of the townspeople. They managed to live as traditionally as their ancestors had. Their language and cultural knowledge intact, they subsisted off the land, hunting and gathering for survival.

Many elders lived out on the allotments before Old Camp was created. The last standing house was on allotment 49, which fell to the ground in 1978. My great-grandfather, John Camp, built the two-room house on allotment 49 and lived there until his death. My grandparents, George and Mabel Beers, raised their family on that allotment in the early 1920s. They moved from the allotment when Old Camp was established. Grandfather Beers tells stories about other Indians stopping at allotment 49 to get water and rest before continuing into Burns on buckboards (horse-drawn carriages). Social card games were played outside in the shade. Later, small bird points were found near the porch, where John Camp had chipped and sharpened them—evidence that traditional hunting continued throughout allotment times.

Unexpected Help

In the 1920s, life began to improve for the Paiutes when a Cherokee Indian man by the name of Strongheart learned of their situation and arranged to have surplus army tents brought to Old Camp to replace the tattered tents and brush wickiups the Paiutes were living in. Father Huel, a German priest from the local Catholic church who was a trusted friend of the Paiutes, gave them spiritual guidance and later helped them find justice for the 1.8 million acres taken from their tribe in the 1880s. Because the Indian people respected

Father Huel, they asked him to be their main spokesman during the meetings that were held regarding the Malheur claims. Indian stories speak of his being told to leave the church by townspeople because he helped the Paiute people. Later he moved away, and the Paiutes have always wondered what happened to their friend.

In 1928, the Egan Land Title Company gave up ten acres of land, which was the city dump, for the Paiutes to live on. The Indians cleaned the city dump to make way for twenty two-room homes. The Indian men cleaned the garbage, drilled a well, and built a school and a community building, which was funded by the Bureau of Indian Affairs (BIA). The local Catholic church constructed a small church in 1932. The church and the school were later moved to the more permanent village site, called New Camp, which was erected in 1935. Indian children were not allowed to attend public school during this period; the reasons stated were tuberculosis and glaucoma. Theresa Guinee was one of the teachers. She remembered the names and birth dates of the students and would bake them birthday cakes, even into adulthood. Paiute people still remember her as a special lady.

The Paiutes began to use teepees after the 1880s. Before then, the Paiutes lived in brush huts called wickiups, sometimes covering them with canvas. Photo courtesy of Oregon Historical Society, #OrHi41248.

A few families allowed their children to attend Indian boarding schools at Chemawa near Salem, Oregon; on the Warm Springs Reservation in Warm Springs, Oregon; at Stewart near Carson City, Nevada; and at Fort Bidwell, California. Many of the children ran away from school, while others stayed for years without coming home. Sometime in the 1930s, two young girls ran into the hills and hid when they were told that the following morning they would be taken to a Portland Catholic girls' school to prepare to become nuns. (The school was St. Mary's Academy and College, which later became St. Mary's Academy and Marylhurst University.)

INDIAN TRAPPERS CAMP.

Many Indian parents did not want their children to be taken from them to go to school in foreign places. Children who returned from the boarding school did not speak their language as much, and some quit speaking Paiute altogether.

In the 1930s, life started to change. In 1934, the BIA presented the Paiute people with a plan for a new kind of government under the Indian Reorganization Act. After meetings and discussions, tribal elections were held and the Paiute people adopted the plan. A business committee was formed, made up of five men who would be the governing body for the Indian community, managing the tribe's business and other affairs.

In 1935, the National Industrial Recovery Act brought hope that Paiute people would have land they could call home. The act allowed them to purchase 760 acres of marginal lands from the Brown family, 300 of which were developed into farmland, while the rest became homesites and rangeland. The tribe repaid the loan from the BIA with money earned from leases on the 300 acres that produced crops. The BIA held the land in trust. Indian men planted the crops and did the harvesting, and homes were built adjacent to the farmland. A Paiute couple, Bertha and Pete Quiver, were especially known for working the land.

It was during this time that New Camp became the new home for the Paiutes. Twenty-seven houses were built; the first to be completed was a home for George and Mabel Beers. Paiute elders talk about the move from Old Camp to New Camp, and how they sold their old homes for fifty dollars so that they could buy furniture for their new homes. A few Old Camp houses can be seen in the town of Burns today, a reminder of the lifestyle that our grandparents knew.

Paiute people were employed during this period as ranch hands and as loggers and brush pilers for Edward Hines Lumber Company, a timber harvesting company in Seneca, Oregon, that was the largest employer in Harney and Grant counties. Seneca became a home to some Paiute families, and many who lived there as children still recall the close community of mixed nationalities where Indian people were accepted as neighbors. Retired logger Chester Beers was the last Indian person who moved from Seneca to Burns in the 1970s.

Indian men were part of the early days of the Harney County rodeo and parade, wearing their eagle headdresses and beaded clothing. A Paiute cowboy, Billy Pete, was a rodeo buckaroo known for always wearing a large black hat. Many of the Paiutes owned horses and rode whenever possible. During the Civilian Conservation Corps (CCC) days, several Paiute men formed baseball teams and traveled to Diamond, Oregon, or to Alkali Lake to play the CCC teams. Later, Jimmie Louie, a Paiute man, organized a group of Indian boys who performed Indian dances for the Burns community during the annual parade, at special events, or when visiting dignitaries came to town. Later on, a Paiute woman, Rose Carlson, taught the girls how to do the round and rabbit dances.

During World War II, many Paiute men went off to fight while some remained to work in the woods. Other families worked hoeing beets and hops in Ontario during the summer and picking potatoes in Central Oregon in the fall. A few Indian families also sheared sheep for local ranchers and sometimes traveled out of the area as far as Wyoming and Montana to do this work. Because Paiute people needed to feed and clothe their families, they moved where the jobs were. They did the work that migrant workers perform today.

Children attended the Indian school at New Camp until 1948, when they were finally allowed to attend public school in Burns. Clifford Sam was the first Paiute Indian to graduate from Burns Union High School.

After the war, men returned to their jobs as loggers for Edward Hines and lived much like their white neighbors. They returned to Burns each weekend to keep their ties to their Indian way of life. The majority of the Paiute people lived at New Camp, while a few elders remained at Old Camp.

Life began to improve slowly in the 1950s, which brought more changes. Clifford Sam was one of the first young men to be sent to fight in the Korean War, and he returned home safely years later. In 1956, the BIA Relocation Program sent young people off to large cities outside of Oregon to become plumbers, welders, secretaries, or factory workers. Some did not stay for more than a year, returning home to talk about city life and the hardships they encountered. Eventually all of the adults returned home to our community with new job skills and new families.

The BIA built a longhouse at New Camp that—although it was called the dance hall—was the Paiute community center. This was the hub of Paiute activity. Many elders remember the Christmas parties and dances held there. Plaza Kennedy was in demand on weekends to play his accordion for the young people. Those who were children then remember happy times eating hot dogs and receiving used toys and gifts at Christmas time from Father Egan (who wore his cowboy boots). Later on, the building burned down and was never rebuilt. Today there is a new community gazebo sitting on the site.

Electricity was installed in most houses, but Indian homes lacked running water and indoor plumbing until around 1966. One

Indian home had a television in 1958, and neighbors would come by to watch the shows.

Meetings about the Malheur land claim were held at the old schoolhouse during the 1960s. Paiutes came from other bands to discuss the wrongs that were done to their ancestors and the old reservation. These meetings were called by representatives of the various bands and held at Burns and Owyhee, Nevada. Later these discussions materialized into a claim and finally a settlement: The Paiute people received compensation at 28¢ to 40¢ an acre for land from the old reservation that included prime ponderosa pine. In 1969, people who could claim ancestral ties to the original five chiefs were given $772 each. Many people still have appliances that they purchased with their share of the claim monies.

When war was declared against Vietnam, our young people were drafted out of high school once again to be sent to a foreign land to fight. Floyd Teeman, Russell Barney, and Ronnie Teeman were some of the young men who served their tours and returned safely.

In 1968, tribal members organized themselves into a working group and drafted the Burns Paiute Constitution and Bylaws. The membership voted to adopt this governing document, which became the law of the land. The constitution and bylaws for- malized agreements between

To help support their families, many Paiute women worked as washerwomen in the town of Burns. Photo courtesy of Minerva Soucie.

the tribe and the BIA, allowing the tribe to receive grants and contracts from the BIA. Discussions also led to resolutions supporting the creation of a reservation for the Paiute people. The group worked with Congressman Al Ulman, who sponsored the bill on behalf of the Paiute people.

The committee selected me and Charlotte Teeman to seek support for the resolution. We both laugh about the days in November 1969 when we went to speak at the National Congress of American Indians at the old Davenport Hotel in Spokane, Washington. We addressed delegations of Indian leaders from across the country, asking them to endorse the creation of a land base for the Paiute people. Conference attendees gave their support, as did the Affiliated Tribes of Northwest Indians and local organizations in Harney County.

The Paiute Tribe was officially recognized on October 13, 1972, when President Nixon signed a bill creating a mini-reservation of 770 acres. Without a home base for a hundred years, the Paiute finally had one. Being recognized brought good things to the Paiutes. For one thing, the tribe became eligible for broader federal funding, some of which was used to hire school counselor Richard Miller. Rena Beers was employed as the first community health representative. Cecil Dick was trained as a police officer. A small administrative staff, consisting of tribal secretary Lorraine Teeman and general manager Charlotte Teeman, handled the affairs of the tribe. An enrollment committee was formed to start the process of enrolling Paiutes into the tribe.

Planners were busy developing new homes and a new community center, which were completed between 1975 and 1978. Oregon's GI Bill program, which provided assistance to veterans, funded most of the new homes.

The tribal constitution was revised in 1988 to reflect the changes needed to do business as a tribe. The governing body, now called the tribal council, changed from a five-member committee to a seven-member council. This allowed them to handle the affairs of the tribe in a more timely and efficient manner.

The tribe entered into an employment agreement, called the Human Resources Program, with the U.S. Forest Service's Ochoco National Forest. Under this agreement, tribal members would be trained by agency personnel to become contractors and/or employees of the Forest Service after they gained experience. The tribe hired Indian crews to do office work and to work out in the woods doing a variety of jobs, such as fence building, water structure improvement, tree maintenance, timber marking, and stand examination. This agreement allowed many Indian people to be hired as temporary and, years later, as permanent employees, and was eventually phased out as employees were trained and hired into the workforce on a routine basis.

The tribe and the U.S. Forest Service—with funding from the BIA—also developed the Summer Youth Opportunity Program, which allowed young Paiute students to work for the Forest Service as summer help. As teenagers, many of our people gained experience in archaeology, data collection, firefighting, botanical surveying, and other skills. Many went on to have careers related to their summer youth employment with the Forest Service. It was a successful program because it allowed our young people to make career decisions before going to college. This program continued into the 1990s.

From the 1990s to the present, the Paiute community continues to experience growth, not only in terms of population, but also in programs, services, and community relations.

The Lutheran Church opened the old Catholic church on the reservation in March 1990, and worship services began again after many years. Reverend Gene Luttman served the congregation until his retirement in June 2002. Now the congregation is served by Reverend Ann Scissions, a Rosebud Sioux, who was installed as the new pastor on September 12, 2004.

A new health facility was built and dedicated in August 1996. The facility has one or two doctors who come from a local clinic to provide services twice a week for Indians and other people in our community, allowing tribal members to visit the on-call doctor and tribal nurses without having to go to town.

Also in 1996, sixteen new Housing and Urban Development (HUD) homes were constructed. New homes provide housing for our growing families and for Paiute people who want to return to the reservation. Homes are still being constructed today, but only a few at a time. Many of the original homes built in 1936 are still in use and kept in good shape by the elders who live in them; many do not want to move into new homes.

Tribal council began casino talks with the state government in 1995. Three years later, in August 1998, a small casino started operating at Old Camp and was coined the Old Camp Casino. While it continues to operate on a small scale, employing tribal members and people from the local community, it is one of the larger employers in Harney County. A recreation park was recently added to the casino.

The tribe was a significant player in changing the name of Sq— Butte, located on nearby Bureau of Land Management (BLM) lands. Paiute women felt that a derogatory term had been assigned to a

In the 1940s, Ada Smoke Capps was photographed tanning buckskins. Photo courtesy of Minerva Soucie.

prominent land feature. After many meetings and debates, the tribe and the BLM convinced the Oregon Geographic Names Board to replace the name. In May 1996, the state approved the change; however, the sign on Highway 20 was not replaced until the summer of 2002. Today it is called Placida Butte, which was its name in the early 1900s.

After two years of discussion, a memorandum of understanding was signed in November 2000 with the Malheur National Wildlife Refuge to safeguard human remains. This agreement guarantees the protection and return of our ancestors to their homeland, setting guidelines for the agency and the tribe when remains are found. The tribe reinterred several remains to a site on the refuge. The Burns Paiute Tribe was the first in the state to draw up a memorandum of understanding for Indian burials, which became an urgent matter when human remains began coming to the surface because of fluctuating water levels. The Harney County Chamber of Commerce honored me as Woman of the Year in 1990 for my role in negotiating the agreement with the state and my local cultural preservation efforts generally. It was a significant honor for a Paiute woman to receive this award.

In the summer of 2001, Chief Egan's remains returned home to the Burns Paiute Tribe from the Smithsonian Institution in Washington, DC. A reburial ceremony was held and his remains went back to the earth. His head, which had been collected by the military, sat in a vault for more than a hundred years until it was returned. The tribe has since brought back many other remains from other parts of the country for homeland reburials.

In 1995, the tribe received funding by the Bonneville Power Administration, initiating its active participation in the Columbia

River Basin Fish and Wildlife Program. Under this grant, the tribe acquired two parcels of land. The first was the Logan property. Logan Valley was a major Paiute hunting and fishing location that was culturally important to our Paiute ancestors and part of the old reservation. The Paiute Tribe can manage the property for its traditional fish, wildlife, and botanical values. The second land acquisition was the Jones property, which belonged to State Representative Denny Jones. Because it was along the route our Paiute ancestors used to travel to Idaho, it was also culturally significant and included a major waterway where our people erected fishing campsites and harvested salmon in days past. Combined, these land acquisitions total 8,260 acres.

This has made the Burns Paiute Tribe a significant player alongside other surrounding land managers—the U.S. Forest Service, BLM, and local ranch owners. In May and June of 2001, the Burns Paiute Tribe dedicated the two parcels, inviting tribal representatives from the Northwest and dignitaries from Washington, DC, to join the celebration.

In September 1999, the Burns Paiute Tribe set aside 6,500 acres of traditional root-gathering grounds called the Biscuit Root ACEC (Area of Critical Environmental Concern, a designation under the National Environmental Policy Act), which the tribe continues to use. The tribe provides input into area management with the goal of protecting the plant resources from overuse or ground disturbances, such as the gravel pit that destroyed one of the major root-gathering campsites some years ago.

In May 2001, three members of the Burns Paiute Tribe (Herbert Hawley, Amos FirstRaised, and I) gave testimony to the Oregon legislature about returning salmon to the tribe after a hundred-year

Nepa Kennedy demonstrates how she makes chokeberry patties in the old way. Photo courtesy of Marilyn Couture.

absence. A bill was approved directing the Oregon Department of Fish and Wildlife to return on a yearly basis five hundred pounds of surplus salmon to tribal members. This was a significant victory for the Paiute because salmon was a major part of their diet before the Bannock War and before dams were built on the Columbia and Snake rivers. Tribal history speaks about Paiute women using fishing baskets to catch the salmon and drying racks lining the rivers and streams.

In August 2001, the Burns Paiute Tribe played a major role in the creation of the Steens Mountain Management Area in southeastern Oregon, and today tribal members are part of the advisory board. This area was a major homeland for some of the people, and now they are able to provide insights and recommendations on the mountain's management, which has long been denied them.

My mother, Bernice Beers Teeman, was my basketweaving teacher when I was a young woman. Now I'm passing that knowledge on to others, especially to the next generation. Photo courtesy of Minerva Soucie.

Language classes for Paiute students began in October 2001 on the reservation. Instructors were hired to work with children after school. The U.S. Forest Service awarded the tribe a grant to publish booklets on plant and animal names and related information in both Paiute and English. Work is continuing on recording stories, legends, and word sounds, and finding a library to house the information.

Cultural classes also began on the reservation for the Paiute children under a Weed and Seed grant, a federal program focused on helping kids stay in school and out of trouble. I taught the children to make Indian baskets and Betty FirstRaised taught beading. The students and the instructors give public demonstrations at schools and county fairs and to government agencies. Both the beading and basketmaking classes have been successful in keeping the children informed about their culture and off the streets. Recently, the Indian community needed a tutor to help students with their homework. Mr. King, a local teacher, stepped up to work with the Indian students after school. With supplemental efforts like these, our students have made significant academic gains in the public school system.

One of the first Paiute students to graduate from college was Twila Teeman, in 1995, with a BS in nursing from Eastern Oregon University. In 2000, Vanessa Dick received her college degree from

Oregon State University. She was followed by her sister, Naomi Dick, who graduated from the University of Oklahoma in 2001, and Diane Teeman, who graduated from the University of Oregon in 2002 and is continuing her studies in the university's graduate program. These are major accomplishments for the students and the Burns Paiute Tribe. These women serve as role models for our youth. These days more tribal members attend college.

Since 2000, Paiute high school students have also made academic strides. In spring 2003, Tommy GhostDog was the first Paiute to be inducted into the National Honor Society since Brenda Dick earned that honor fifteen years before. Continued academic progress by our youth means that in the future, educated tribal members will have the ability to manage our land and resources.

The current tribal enrollment is 334 members; our numbers continue to increase as more Paiute people find their way home. The tribal blood quantum was changed several years ago to allow persons to enroll with the tribe who are of Paiute–Wada Tika band blood.

The Burns Paiute Tribe has nine tribal departments: administration, education, health, social services, cultural and heritage, fish and wildlife, environmental, housing, tribal police and courts, and the Old Camp Casino, which is a separate entity. The tribe has a professional staff working to provide the best service to the membership. Our young tribal council members come to the table with fresh insights, thoughtful solutions, and experiences gained off the reservation, which make them better decision-makers for the Paiute people and the community. This combination has made the Burns Paiute Tribe a successful group of Indian people.

In June 2003, the Burns Paiute Tribe won an award from the Portland-based nonprofit SOLV for having one of the cleanest communities in Oregon.

Our people have come a long way from the Malheur Reservation days and Fort Simcoe. With our Paiute language and our cultural teachings intact, we can continue to live as our ancestors did, but in a new world that requires us to learn and adapt. By remembering the challenges our ancestors endured for us and the generations yet to come, we will continue to better ourselves as Indian people.

Chapter 3

The Confederated Tribes of the Coos, Lower Umpqua, and Siuslaw

BY HOWARD P. ROY

The Coos, Lower Umpqua, and Siuslaw remain in touch with a rich, traditional culture and value system of living harmoniously with the earth. Tribal members say that the good way of life has sustained our people since time immemorial. The practice of songs, dances, regalia-making, basketmaking, canoe construction, toolmaking, crafts, and beliefs has sustained our way of life for thousands of years. Tribal members believe that the old lifeways have great value and seek to pass them on to succeeding generations. The elders teach these values to the children through oral history lessons, instruction, and participation in cultural activities.

Ancestral Lands and Languages

The Confederated Tribes of Coos, Lower Umpqua, and Siuslaw Indians trace their ancestry through time as the aboriginal inhabitants of the south-central coast of Oregon. Archaeologists have secured radiocarbon dates in the Lower Umpqua ancestral area of one of the oldest sites in coastal Oregon. This site on the western shore of Tahkenitch Lake is approximately eight thousand years old. In this excavation lay the nearly complete skeleton of a whale. Tribal people lived in the village when the lake was an arm of the sea. A nearby excavation on the North Spit of the Umpqua River has yielded artifacts more than three thousand years old, including one of the oldest houses on the Oregon coast.

The tribes' historic homelands extended from the densely forested slopes of the Coast Range in the east to the shoreline of the Pacific Ocean in the west, from Tenmile Creek (Lane County) in the north to a point halfway between the mouths of Whiskey Run and Cut Creek in the south, a vast region of some 1.6 million acres. Tribal ancestors lived in an area characterized by moderate and generally comfortable temperatures and abundant natural resources. These included fresh and saltwater fish, shellfish, wildlife, and a variety of edible plants.

There were three distinct languages spoken among the Coos (Miluk and Hanis people), Lower Umpqua, and Siuslaw. The Miluk language was spoken on lower Coos Bay and on South Slough, as well as along the coast south of the mouth of Coos Bay. The Hanis language, closely related to Miluk, was spoken on the rest of Coos Bay, the Coos and Millicoma rivers, and along Tenmile Creek (Coos County) and Tenmile Lake. The Siuslaw and Lower Umpqua Tribes spoke dialects of a mutually intelligible language that is often referred to today as Siuslawan, although in their own language it is known as *wa'as*. The Lower Umpqua people lived from Tenmile Creek to the Siltcoos River, including all of the Smith River Watershed and much of the lower Umpqua River Watershed. The Siuslaw people lived from Siltcoos River to Tenmile Creek (Lane County) in the north, including all of the Siuslaw River Watershed. All of these languages are part of a larger language family known as Penutian. Most of the other Penutian languages are spoken in Oregon and California.

Traditional Villages and Social Life

The ancestors lived in villages along rivers, estuaries, and the coast. Most people in a village were related. Their primary dwelling was a cedar plank house. Historically, people dug shallow pits in the ground and erected a pole frame. They fixed a notched log at the entryway to provide access from the interior bench lying immediately inside the house to the activity area and hearth floor below. The roof frame consisted of notched poles set approximately six to eight feet apart. The poles and frames supported a roof and walls of cedar planks, each overlapping and providing good runoff for the rain. They split out planks by driving elk antler wedges into cedar logs using stone hammers. To smooth and shape the planks, the men used adzes tipped with sharpened stone.

Inside the plank house was a fire pit for each family; the fire distributed heat throughout the building. Smoke left the plank house through a hole at the crest of the roof above the cooking hearth. The roof beams doubled as a place to hang fish and meat.

Other structures were built around the plank houses. Windbreaks were placed so people could work comfortably on basketry, cooking, and other projects out of the wind. A storage shed, or *maqmii*, was often nearby, where most tools, basketry materials, and other projects were stored. There were also large semi-subterranean sweat lodges where men and boys gathered. Women and girls used smaller sweat lodges that could be built entirely above ground.

Personalities and skills of the people in the village played a large part in the internal politics and social structure of the tribe, but the overall social structure was based principally on wealth and class distinctions. Villages tended to be autonomous, and each had its own headman, who was usually the wealthiest individual. Wealth was measured in canoes, quantities of baskets, dentalium shells, woodpecker scalps, large obsidian blades, abalone shells, gray pine nuts, and clamshell beads. Generally, the headman was obliged to use his wealth to benefit all, and in return, villagers brought him food and

Plank Houses

The traditional cedar plank house holds a special meaning for modern tribal members who gather in the plank house on the reservation in Coos Bay. In this plank building, the tribes hold traditional dances and healing and naming ceremonies, and host social gatherings.
A tribal member recently said that when approaching the plank house in the evening, the glimmer of light from the fire within dances across the doorway. The familiar sound of tribal voices emanates from within the building. Your hand grasps the solid cedar door as you enter. You are entering a world filled with heritage, culture, and traditions that are thousands of years old. The ambience within the plank house mentally and spiritually bonds you to Mother Earth and past generations' lifeways and culture.

gifts. The wealthiest families typically made the rules and decided the outcome of disputes. Wealthy men often had multiple wives, canoes, plank houses, and one or more slaves. Commoners had their freedom, but not much wealth or status, and they had limited authority in the resolution of disputes. A commoner's power to make decisions was limited to trivial matters. The important life decisions were generally reserved for the wealthy or the village headman.

In 1858 an army officer photographed a Lower Umpqua plank house near the river mouth. Several Indians, held prisoner by the federal government at Fort Umpqua, stand near the building. Photo courtesy of the Cow Creek slide program.

Toolmaking was an important and critical skill. Stones such as chert were also used to make cutting and scraping tools. Men used elk and deer bone and antler to make wedges and scraping tools of many sizes. They used these woodworking tools to fashion bows, arrows, spears, parts of traps, and digging implements. Antler wedges were used to split planks from cedar trees and logs. Cedar, like the redwood logs that sometimes drifted onto the beach, had a straight grain that readily yielded to the force of several wedges driven at intervals along the log. Sometimes the men constructed a scaffold and broke planks loose from living cedars. Until recently, an ancient cedar stood near the Siuslaw River, still bearing the scars of such plank cutting. Other tools included polished bone and antler scrapers, and awls useful for dressing leather and making clothing.

Games have always been an important part of tribal social life. Tribal ancestors played many stick games, including *lamtalam*, which was highly popular. *Lamtalam* used four sticks, two marked with female designs and two marked with male designs. Players held the sticks in one hand and threw them like dice. They based scoring on the combinations thrown. Pastimes also included *shinny*, a kind of field hockey played on a large beach or field with sticks and a ball made of huckleberry root. The goal was an upright stake with the bottom half buried in the ground. The stakes were approximately two to four inches in diameter and of various lengths depending on the availability of wood. Two teams, made up of an equal number of players, tried to move the ball toward the stake at the opposite end of the field by hitting it with sticks. There were no boundaries or fouls. Players scored goals by hitting the opponent's stake with the ball. *Lamtalam* and *shinny* continue to be enjoyed by current generations of Coos, Lower Umpqua, and Siuslaw Indians.

Tribal youth participated in spirit quests. These rites of passage allowed them to come to terms with their spiritual values and to obtain a spirit helper. The quest involved fasting, praying, dancing, and waiting at a secluded location. The individual gained a heightened sense of the natural world, and the experience connected people to the Creator in ways that fostered physical, spiritual, and social health. Often during the quest, an individual gained a song or basketry design that became a legacy to share with family and pass on to the next generation. In the 1930s, tribal elders were able to recall and sing numerous spirit-quest songs they had heard as children. Spirit quests continue today for some as a means of spiritual help.

People often visited other villages. This provided the opportunity to trade goods. These visits also presented opportunities for people from different villages to meet, share culture, and form bonds.

Fishing, Hunting, and Gathering

In years past, permanent villages of plank houses were located near abundant supplies of fish and shellfish. During the summer and fall, people moved to seasonal hunting, fishing, and gathering camps away from the year-round villages. Shellfish, salmon, and eels (lamprey) were the main sources of protein. (Lampreys are slender eel-like fish that our tribes and most Northwest tribes refer to in English as eels.) Camas, bracken fern, and myrtle nuts were the main sources of starch. Women and men had different, but equally important, roles in obtaining food and other resources.

Historically, women were the primary gatherers. They gathered shellfish from the mudflats and rocky intertidal areas. They gathered plants and dug roots as sources of clothes, food, medicine, cordage, and basketry materials. They picked berries such as salal berries, huckleberries, salmonberries, and blackberries. They dug bracken fern rhizomes and collected and ground myrtle nuts. Camas bulbs were a staple starch, much like flour. Camas was dug at meadows, such as those near Whiskey Run and at Burton Prairie on the North Fork Coquille River. Large meadows of camas grew in lowlands along the Coast Fork of the Willamette, just east of the upper Siuslaw country. Camas grew in a similar fashion at Camas Swale in the Umpqua Valley and at Camas Valley at the head of the Middle Fork Coquille River.

Men built weirs to trap fish. They drove wooden stakes into the mud and wove in a lattice of limbs. As the tide rose, fish swam over and around the weir seeking food or their spawning route. When the tide went out, the fish were trapped behind the weir and were cut off from the main channel. The men also used dip nets to catch fish at low tide. Sometimes they installed funnel-shaped basket traps at the weirs. With prongs at the entrance, the traps permitted the fish to swim in but made it difficult for them to swim back out.

Traditional upriver fishing techniques used fish dams in shallow water to corral fish so they could be easily caught with a leister spear or dip net. Men cut deer or elk bones to size and fashioned them into barbed hooks for deep-water fishing. Eels were another good food source. The ancestors knew when the eels were coming from the influx of mayflies covering the river late in the spring. They caught eels using a gaff made from a sharpened elk bone attached to a length of ocean spray shoot. Eels were most often caught in woven eelpots. Being poor swimmers, eels entered the woven pots to hide during the daylight hours on their migration upriver to spawn.

One of the most popular summer fisheries of the Coos tribe was at Smelt Beach between Gregory Point and Yoakam Point. In July, August, and September, smelt use the coarse sands at this beach for spawning. The men of the tribe thrust A-frame nets into the waves and then dumped on the beach a host of small fish that the women and children gathered up for cooking or for drying on racks in the sun.

Seals and sea lions were hunted near the shore and in the estuary margins. These animals were mainly used for the large amounts of oil that were rendered from them and then preserved in bags made from sea lion stomachs. Dried meat, fish, and berries were mixed with seal oil to make the meal more rich and palatable.

The men hunted big game by stalking with bows and arrows, digging pit traps, or lying in wait near water holes, game trails, and bedding areas. Hunters formed a line and walked through the forest to flush game. This technique drove the deer and elk toward hidden pits that were usually six feet wide, six feet deep, and six to eight feet long. The hunters had buried sharpened stakes in the floor of the pit and covered the pit with foliage. The deer or elk would step on the foliage and fall in.

People, including those who were fluent in other languages, journeyed to trade for goods. These trips provided access to goods, such as acorns from the Umpqua and Willamette valleys and obsidian from the quarries in central Oregon and beyond. Acorns are more palatable than myrtle nuts, and obsidian was prized for making projectile points, knives, and wealth-display blades. Trading with other tribes created a welcome exchange of food, baskets, hides, furs, seeds, and shells.

Canoes

Canoes were an essential part of tribal life, required for travel, fishing, trading, war, diplomacy, and ceremony. Men made canoes from cedar and redwood logs. Canoes were shaped on the outside first and then turned over, and the inside was removed through a process of burning and splitting or adzing the log down to a thickness of about two finger widths. The canoe was generally built on a scale of one foot wide to eight feet long. Usually, paint for the canoes was made from salmon eggs, saliva, and red ochre (mercuric oxide) from sites such as the Siuslaw tribe's quarry at Cook's Chasm north of Heceta Head. Canoes passed from one generation to another, as they tended not to deteriorate since they were made of cedar and redwood, both of which are resistant to rot. The men carved paddles from hardwoods, such as oak, ash, and yew, and sometimes from softwoods, such as cedar and fir. Some ceremonial paddles used in marriages and sacred salmon ceremonies were also made of cedar and had intricately carved designs. Although a more aesthetically pleasing wood, cedar was generally not strong enough for the rigorous, everyday use required of a paddle.

Two main styles of canoes were used traditionally. One was the high-prow canoe, which was the dominant style to the north. These canoes were known as *aluudaq* in the Coos Bay and Siuslaw-Umpqua languages. This style of canoe was usually purchased from Chinook, Tillamook, or Alsea people. The other canoe style was the shovel-nose; it was made in the tribes' territory and in the rest of southwestern Oregon and northwestern California. In the two languages spoken on Coos Bay, Hanis and Miluk, this style of canoe was called *maxmax*, and in Siuslawan it was called *sixai*.

One observer of an old canoe (probably an *aluudaq*) wrote: "Her bow and stern were considerable elevated, and were carved in the semblance of some unknown monsters, while the gunwales, instead of retreating canoe fashion, would be outwards." The first recorded encounter between the tribes and Europeans was in 1792; it described a canoe paddling out from the Umpqua River to greet the ship *Columbia Rediviva*, with its occupants offering meat in exchange for trade goods such as iron axes and copper.

Basketry

Basketry was, and remains, an especially significant tribal skill. Basketry had many uses. Hats were twined from spruce root with patterns created by overlays of bear grass and eelgrass. Burden baskets were made for carrying large and heavy loads. Baskets stored seasonal foods for use throughout the year. Those made from conifer roots could be woven so tightly that they could carry and store water. Our ancestors preferred to make water storage baskets and drinking cups from cedar roots, as they thought water from these vessels tasted better. Meals could be cooked in a basket by filling it with water, adding rocks heated by fire, and then adding food.

The traditional weaving style of the central and southern Oregon coast people is twining basketry. The weavers used awls made of bone to tighten the twined stitches. In Coos, Lower Umpqua, and Siuslaw basketry, women have made wide use of spruce root, cedar root, tussock (for soft containers), and hazel. Other traditional basketry materials include fir and other conifer roots, tules, cattail, bulrush, fiber stems from fireweed, saltwater sedge, juncus rush, eelgrass, willow, and cedar bark. White bear grass and black eelgrass were commonly used in overlay patterns.

Dyes were obtained from alder bark (red), hemlock bark (brown), and chittam bark (yellow). The color black was achieved by burying the materials in black mud. During the era when the federal government sent children to boarding schools, traditional crafts such as basketry were discouraged and nearly vanished. Stunning works did survive, however, because European and American collectors valued basketry as art. Agnes Ruth (Lockhart) Sengstacken of Coos Bay collected 223 examples of tribal weaving, clothing, and weaponry between 1872 and 1921. Her collection, never exhibited, is preserved at the Phoebe A. Hearst Museum of Anthropology at the University of California at Berkeley. The Sarah Magee Collection is housed at the Coos County Historical Society. The Museum of Natural History at the University of Oregon in Eugene holds another collection, and the Western Lane County Historical Society at Florence, Oregon, has a small collection, including works given by tribal member Marge (Drew) Severy.

Basketweaving continues as a major cornerstone in our tribal culture. Our ancestors believed baskets had spirits of their own. They were more than useful vessels or objects of art, and many basketweavers teach this message today. A basket pattern identifies the weaver by the family design and reflects the woman's origin.

Contact with Europeans

Affirming elements of tribal self-governance and sovereignty, Congress passed the Northwest Ordinance in 1787. The ordinance contained a section articulating federal philosophy in Indian affairs. It read:

> The utmost good faith shall always be observed towards the Indians; their land and property shall never be taken from them without their consent; and in property, rights and liberty, they shall never be invaded or disturbed, unless in just and lawful wars authorized by Congress; but laws founded in justice and humanity shall from time to time be made for preserving wrongs being done to them, and for preserving peace and friendship with them.

The first documented contact between Americans and our tribes occurred on April 10, 1792. John Boit, a seaman aboard the *Columbia Rediviva*, noted an encounter with Native Americans on the south-central Oregon coast, probably members of the Lower Umpqua tribe. Boit wrote:

> Abreast a small inlet in the land [Umpqua estuary], which had some appearance of a harbor. Hove to for some canoes that were coming off. These Natives talk'd a different language from any we had ever before heard. Their Canoes had square stems and the blades of the paddles oval. We puchas'd of them many fine Otter Skins for Copper and Iron. They had some raw Buffaloe in the Canoes, which they offer'd us for sale, and greedily devour'd some of it, in that state of recommendation. I'm fearful these fellows are Cannibals. Mr. Smith, 2nd Officer was sent in the Cutter to look for an harbor but was unsuccessful. Bore off and made sail.

In July 1827, Alexander Roderick McLeod of the Hudson's Bay Company led a brigade south along the central coast of Oregon and passed through the homeland of the Siuslaw and Lower Umpqua Indians. McLeod traveled overland, crossing Heceta Head, and, starting on July 16, camped on the banks of the Siuslaw. Some of his party traveled south along the shore by canoe. On July 18, McLeod wrote, "… did not go but three miles when I perceived three Canoes under sail coming forward I accordingly returned to the entrance of the River Saestecau [Siuslaw] to meet them. The canoes passed safely over the bar." McLeod continued, "We erected our Camp at the entrance of the River Saestecau it is about three hundred yards wide at ebb tide and would be a very deep strong current, several Indians collected about our Camp in the evening, it is with difficulty that we can converse with them for none of the Tribe were acquainted with the Chinook dialect."

In 1828, Jedediah Smith, an American mountain man and shareholder in the Rocky Mountain Fur Company, traveled with his men north from California, trapping furs and trading along the way. Smith's party camped uneventfully at Coos Bay near a Coos village, crossed the estuary with horses and furs, and continued north to the Umpqua River. A dispute arose between the Americans and the Lower Umpqua Indians. Subsequently, officials of the Hudson's Bay Company thought the conflict arose from inappropriate advances of Smith's men toward Indian women or the alleged theft of an ax by a young Indian man who was then killed. Whatever the cause, on July 14, 1828, the Lower Umpquas retaliated and killed fifteen of the nineteen men in Smith's party. Dispatched by Hudson's Bay Company officials to check into the matter, McLeod arrived on the estuary with a brigade in October. He reported finding eleven skeletons at the site and with Smith, who had survived the attack, spent several days visiting villages between Coos Bay and the Siuslaw to recover furs, journals, horses, and other property belonging to Smith.

For the next twenty years, southwestern Oregon remained wholly an Indian land. The only intrusion was Fort Umpqua at the mouth of Elk Creek, a site east of the territory of the Lower Umpqua Indians. This, the southernmost Hudson's Bay Company post in North America, became a trading center for the Indians of the region seeking to exchange furs for knives, beads, hatchets, cloth, blankets, and other goods. However, contact brought more than commerce. Epidemics of European diseases, to which our ancestors had no resistance, spread through our villages, striking the first of many blows, which almost led to the destruction of our tribes.

Dispossession of Our Homelands

In 1846 Great Britain and the United States signed the Oregon Treaty. The United States assumed sovereignty over the Pacific Northwest. In 1848, Congress passed the Organic Act, creating Oregon Territory. The law affirmed the Northwest Ordinance and observed that nothing in the act "shall be construed to impair the rights of persons or property now pertaining to the Indians in said territory so long as such rights shall remain unextinguished by treaty between the United States and said Indians." Without any treaties, however, Congress in 1850 passed the Donation Land Act, which by 1855 led to more than 9,200 land claims to 2.6 million acres of Indian lands in the Pacific Northwest. Several of those claims were within the tribal territory of the Lower Umpqua and Coos Indians.

On August 17, 1855, the Siuslaw, Lower Umpqua, and Coos Bay Indians, along with the other coastal tribes, signed a treaty. The signatories included forty-eight Coos, eleven Lower Umpqua, and fourteen Siuslaw men. The northern and southern boundaries between the individual coastal tribes and bands were not delineated, and the eastern boundaries were, by default, set at the western boundaries of treaties previously concluded with tribes to the east. The treaty ceded extensive amounts of land but provided for a reservation, goods, and annuities. The tribes waited in vain for ratification of the treaty. The Senate ignored the agreement. The lands of the tribes were stolen in violation of the "utmost good faith" affirmed in the Ordinance of 1787 and the Organic Act of 1848.

In October 1855, hostilities resumed in the Rogue River Valley between Indians and settlers. In February 1856, war broke out on the coast at the mouth of Rogue River, and tensions were high. Although the Coos had never taken up arms in spite of widespread trespass and settlement on their lands, starting in 1853, they were told to assemble on the beach south of Empire City, then the county seat of Coos County. The Coos County Guard, a volunteer militia, held the Indians prisoner until the U.S. government concluded that the prisoners had to move north. Late in the summer of 1856, the Coos Indians were exiled, many leaving their homeland forever.

In August 1856, President James Buchanan, by executive order, created the Coast Reservation. It reached from Cape Lookout in Tillamook County to Tahkenitch Outlet in Douglas County. The U.S. government set up three administrative units for the Coast Reservation. The area from Siletz Bay north to the Nestucca was placed under the Indian agent at Grand Ronde; the central portion of the reservation was placed under the agent at Siletz; and the southern portion, known as the Umpqua (and later the Alsea) Sub-Agency, was placed under the agent resident at Umpqua City on the North Spit of the Umpqua River, about five miles south of the southern boundary of the Coast Reservation.

Agent Edwin P. Drew assumed authority for the Coos and Lower Umpqua people who were held on the North Spit of the Umpqua River. Fort Umpqua, the nearby Army post, had a company of soldiers to keep the Indians from returning to their homes south along the coast. In September 1859, the Commissioner of Indian Affairs ordered the relocation of the agency and the Indians under its charge to Yachats Prairie, nearly sixty miles north. On July 12, 1860, the agent reported 279 Coos and Lower Umpqua Indians living near Fort Umpqua and 181 Siuslaws living in their old homeland.

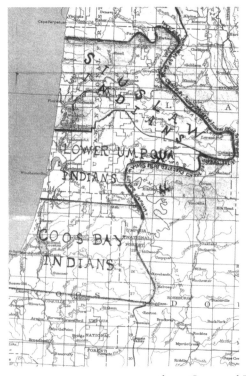

George Wasson presented this handwritten map of our tribes' ancestral territory to the Court of Claims in 1935. Drawing courtesy of the Confederated Tribes of the Coos, Lower Umpqua, and Siuslaw Indians.

Agent Linus Brooks reported in July 1862 that the Siuslaw Tribe resided near the mouth of the Siuslaw River. The Siuslaw continued their traditional lifeways but, under the instruction of Jean Baptiste Gagnier, a former trader at Fort Umpqua, they also learned to grow potatoes, corn, squash, carrots, and peas. Gagnier and his Indian wife lived among them. Brooks believed the Siuslaw to be harmless and peaceful.

On March 3, 1875, Congress opened the northern and southern units of the Coast Reservation for pioneer settlement provided that the tribes living in those areas agreed. The southern unit, administered as the Alsea Sub-Agency at Yachats, was the home to the refugee Coos and Lower Umpqua and also included the traditional homelands of the Siuslaw Tribe. On June 17, 1875, the Bureau of Indian Affairs held a council at Yachats to secure consent of the Coos, Lower Umpqua, Siuslaw, and Alsea tribes. The leaders vehemently opposed closing the agency because, without a homeland, they feared for the survival of their people and the fate of their children. Their years of arduous labor to clear the lands at the mouth of the Yachats River for farms were for nothing. Again, the tribes were to become an exiled people.

During the nineteen years of imprisonment at the Umpqua and Alsea sub-agencies, the tribal population had decreased by more

Chief David Brainard and tribal member Doug Barrett in West Coast tradtional-style canoe made by Brainard. Photo courtesy of the Confederated Tribes of the Coos, Lower Umpqua, and Siuslaw Indians.

than one-third. When released, the families walked south along the coast to their old villages, and they found the sites occupied by settlers who had built homes and fenced properties. The Lower Umpqua settled near the mouth of Smith River in the vicinity of Gardiner and at the North Spit. The Coos settled on isolated South Slough near the entrance to Coos Bay, at Jordan Cove on the North Spit of Coos Bay, at Tenmile Lakes, and throughout the Pacific coast.

The years after 1875 were ones of major adjustment. Adults found menial labor working on farms, cutting wood, washing clothes, and logging. By the 1890s, many worked at harvesting cranberries in the fall. The women continued to make baskets that they sold. The Indian Manual Labor Training School at Forest Grove opened in 1881 and was moved to Salem in 1883, where it became the Chemawa Indian School. Many of our children were sent to Chemawa. Some attended Greenville School at Fresno, California. The Bureau of Indian Affairs sent others, like Rose McArthur, a Lower Umpqua, to Carlisle Indian School in Carlisle, Pennsylvania. Boarding-school teachers forbade the use of traditional languages, spiritual observances, hunting, fishing, and gathering. The goal of these schools was to transform the Indian children into "civilized" farmers, carpenters, cooks, and seamstresses.

Congress passed the General Allotment Act in 1887. Among other provisions, the law permitted nonreservation Indians to file for public domain allotments. Starting in 1892, some members of the Coos, Lower Umpqua, and Siuslaw Tribes obtained trust allotments in their old homelands. Officials of the Siuslaw National Forest, however, blocked many of the allotments by arguing that the lands were not suited for agriculture. Thus, only a few allotments were made in the lower Siuslaw watershed.

Seeking Justice

The tribes kept their identity alive by meeting regularly and observing special celebrations throughout the year. In May 1917, the Coos, Lower Umpqua, and Siuslaw tribes formally and officially confederated and began electing tribal leaders after the deaths of Coos Chief Doloose (Chief Jackson) and Chief Bobbie Burns. A primary objective of the new council was to try to obtain land or payment for the lands stolen by the United States. After thirteen years of work, Congress passed a law waiving the sovereign immunity of the United States and permitting the tribes to sue in the U.S. Court of Claims. The litigation gained momentum in 1932 when elders gave their

Hanis Coos Chief Doloose Jackson was photographed in traditional regalia in 1905. Photo courtesy of Bandon Historical Society.

depositions through an interpreter in hearings held in North Bend, Oregon. The Court ruled on the case in 1935, and it rejected Indian oral testimony as hearsay and the unratified treaty of 1855 as evidence of aboriginal ownership. Tribal lawyers could not access the Bureau of Indian Affairs files, which had not yet been transferred to the new National Archives or to the privately held Hudson's Bay Company records held in London. Critical evidence contained in those files proving aboriginal ownership of tribal homelands was not considered. The court ruled that the tribes had "no right, claim, or title to any part of the coast of Oregon whatsoever." In 1938, the Supreme Court declined to consider the tribes' appeal.

Passage of the Indian Reorganization Act in 1934 had little impact on the Confederated Tribes except for the provision that the "trust" (tax-exempt) status of allotments was extended indefinitely. Indian policies during the New Deal, however, brought for the first time a "needs assessment" of the tribes and interest in securing a small reservation where tribal members could have a meeting hall, clinic, and site for processing traditional foods. In 1940, William G. Robertson and Louis J. Simpson, developers of the "New Empire" in west Coos Bay, deeded to the United States 6.12 acres for a reservation for the tribes. The federal government took the land into trust for this purpose. In 1940–41, the Indian Civilian Conservation Corps cleared part of the small reservation and with federal funding constructed a tribal hall in what is now west Coos Bay. The building became an important meeting place for the tribes and a symbol of the determination of the members to affirm their Indian identity.

When Congress created the Indian Claims Commission in 1946, the Confederated Tribes renewed their land claims case. The commission rejected the claim and declined to hear the matter or consider new evidence. It concluded that the Court of Claims had already judicially determined the matter. This was a devastating setback for the tribes.

Termination

On August 13, 1954, in spite of the strong objections of the Confederated Tribes, Congress passed the Western Oregon Termination Act. The tribes' opposition was so unwavering that when the federal government held termination hearings and conducted tribal voting in Siletz, Oregon, in 1947, the forty-six member delegation from the Coos, Lower Umpqua, and Siuslaw tribes were taken from the hearings and placed in a locked room under guard until voting was completed. Nonetheless, Congress applied the Western Oregon Termination Act to the Confederated Tribes of Coos, Lower Umpqua, and Siuslaw without ever providing them an opportunity to vote.

When the Termination law became effective in 1956, some eighteen months after enactment, the Bureau of Indian Affairs began issuing deeds to individual allotment owners. The allotments immediately became subject to county taxation. Many tribal members did not realize this or simply could not afford the taxes. Another problem was that many of the allotments had multiple heirs: it proved quite difficult or impossible to solicit each heir to pay his or her proportional contribution to the tax assessment. Allotments were lost by the county that foreclosed on the properties when taxes went unpaid.

The tribes' reservation property had a different fate under termination. On April 17, 1956, the city of Empire declared its willingness to accept the reservation and tribal hall for the use of the Indians of the Coos Bay area. The city, however, almost immediately leased the property for $230 per year to the U.S. Navy Reserve as meeting space. The lease provided no maintenance, which caused the 6.12-acre property and meeting hall to fall into disrepair. When the city of Empire merged with the city of Coos Bay, the tribal hall passed to Coos Bay jurisdiction. In 1972 Coos Bay tried to sell the land. Learning of the city's actions, the tribe contacted the Bureau of Indian Affairs to voice its objections. On January 8, 1973, the city

Above: The Tribal Hall in 1941 after framing construction was substantially completed in 1941. Right: Shown as it appears today, the Tribal Hall continues to be our members' primary meeting place. Photos courtesy of the Confederated Tribes of the Coos, Lower Umpqua, and Siuslaw Indians.

of Coos Bay yielded control of the hall to the Confederated Tribes.

Having regained Tribal Hall, the Coos, Lower Umpqua, and Siuslaw used the poorly maintained building for meetings during the 1970s. In the hall, the tribal council established the Willow River Benevolent Association, a manpower training program, which ran a store to distribute government commodities to tribal members; they also opened a small cultural museum. Although the reservation remained in trust, the Bureau of Indian Affairs provided neither assistance to the tribes nor repairs for the building. In 1973, the tribes sent Stephen Dow Beckham to Washington, DC, to talk to members of Congress about the tribes' terminated status and their unresolved land claims. Two things came out of these meetings: a bill to reopen the land claims case (that failed to pass Congress) and, in March 1976, the opportunity to testify before Task Force 10 of the American Indian Policy Review Commission. In those hearings, tribal leaders Russell Anderson, Bill Brainard, and Edgar Bowen, along with Beckham, laid out the consequences of termination and the importance of re-establishing federal recognition for the

Confederated Tribes. The testimony documented loss of allotments, the impact of the loss of federal services, and the condition of the reservation and its people.

Tribal leaders prepared to leave for Washington, DC to testify on behalf of the Confederated Tribes of Coos, Lower Umpqua and Siuslaw Indians Restoration Act of 1984. From the left, Brenda Brainard, Bill Brainard, Carolyn Slyter, Edgar Brown, and Donald Whereat. Photo courtesy of Muriel Brainard.

Tribal Recovery

On October 17, 1984, with the signing of P.L. 98-481, legislation introduced by Representative James H. Weaver and Senator Mark O. Hatfield, federal recognition of the Confederated Tribes of Coos, Lower Umpqua, and Siuslaw Indians was restored. Restoration undid the misguided and unjust policy of termination, but years of effort remained and still remain to undo termination's lasting effects. Restoration made federal services available to the Confederated Tribes. Equally important, restoration cleared the way for the Confederated Tribes to regain some of what was lost in 1855.

Today, the Confederated Tribes are the only federally recognized tribe in Oregon never to have secured a financial settlement or land restoration from the United States for the taking of ancestral territory. Since restoration, the tribes have mounted an intensive land recovery campaign focused on regaining the most culturally important lands, including acreage of federal forestland and ancestral village sites along the coast that are also held by the federal government. In 2003 U.S. Senator Gordon Smith introduced legislation that would restore 62,865 acres of the tribes' ancestral homelands.

In 2005, after more than twenty years of tribal efforts, the tribes succeeded in regaining ownership of the former military facility at Coos Head. This culturally significant headland at the mouth of Coos Bay overlooks part of the coastline of the tribes' ancestral lands. This area was returned to the Confederated Tribes by the federal government not as restitution for lands ceded in 1855, but to support tribal government programs.

The current services offered to nearly nine hundred tribal members are housing, dental care, health services, mental health counseling, educational services, employment assistance, natural resource management, cultural development and resource protection, realty management, transportation planning, law enforcement and tribal court services, and stable government. The tribes are creating new revenue sources to support these services. The Three Rivers Casino is the newest of our economic ventures. Located near the city of Florence, the casino opened in June 2004. It operates under a gaming compact with the state of Oregon and is regulated by the Tribal Gaming Commission. Expansion of the Three Rivers Casino and the construction of an events center and a ninety-three-room hotel began in April 2006 and is scheduled for completion in October 2007. The tribes will continue to diversify their economic base to provide revenue governmental services for future generations.

The tribes have adjusted to many circumstances over the centuries. We thank those who have had the wisdom, strength, persistence, and ability to survive the hardships. We honor and respect the Creator who brings all good things to our people.

Chapter 4

The Memory of a People

The Coquelles of the Southern Oregon Coast

BY GEORGE B. WASSON JR.

The Coquelle people have lived so many generations in their homeland environment and traditional hunting-gathering territories that the years have become too many to count.

As is true with other southern Oregon coastal people, the oldest stories of the Coquelle (the original name) tell about the creation of the world and its rearrangement to suit the needs of the people who were to come later. Mythical beings, such as Talapus (Old Man Coyote), told how the land was built from blue clay scooped from under the water and how that land was protected from wave action by lining the shores with woven mats and basketry.

The old stories relate firsthand accounts of the great floods and fires that repeatedly swept over the land from the west, often changing the geography significantly while scattering people and other animals far and wide.

The Coquelle Indians and the Cultural "Black Hole" of the Southern Oregon Coast

Because of the short time span from the beginning of daily contact between non-Indians and the native peoples of the southern Oregon coast to the demise of the native cultures' cultural, spiritual, and physical identity, very little descriptive data were collected and preserved for posterity. In 1931, T. T. Waterman wrote, "A number of ethnologists worked in this region, prior to the writer's advent … but relatively little concerning these groups has found its way into print."

Because of the thorough destruction of the village sand people's lifeways, only bits and pieces of their culture and languages survived. Consequently, I have adopted the concept of a cultural or ethnological "black hole" as a descriptive term for southwestern Oregon, where the surviving descendants have retained only a few relics of their indigenous culture. The Coquelles are a group from that "black hole" and are now looking at the bits and pieces of surviving knowledge about themselves in an effort to reconstruct, as adequately as possible, their lost and forgotten cultural heritage.

Coquelle Cultural Geography

For purposes of sociocultural identification, Coquelle tribal members are directly descended from people of the following geographical locations: villages at South Slough and Coos Bay, villages along the Coquille River, and coastal villages as far south as the Sixes River. Because of intertribal marriages, many members are also related to Umpqua, Coos, Siuslaw, Tutut'tni, Shasta Costa, Chetco, Tolowa, or other American Indian tribes. In the late nineteenth and early twentieth centuries, the common spelling was "Coquelle," pronounced "Ko-Kwel" as in tribal use today. The official name of the tribe is the Coquille Indian Tribe, but tribal members prefer to use "Coquelle" in deference to old tribal tradition.

The origin of the name "Coquille" has long been uncertain. However, the traditional pronunciation has been well documented by early ethnographers. Many tribal members (including this writer) grew up among old-timers who would accept no other pronunciation. It has been declared by early residents of the area that the accepted spelling was "Coquelle" until sometime in the early 1900s, when a group of white businesspeople launched a campaign to change the spelling to the French form, "Coquille." Bess Finley Wasson recalls that in the early 1900s, when she was a girl, a group of city supporters organized an annual civic event they called the Kokeel Korn Karnival.

In 1942 ethnologist John P. Harrington interviewed Coquel Thompson, an upriver Coquille, who said, "Mrs. Daisy Codding's statement that 'Coquille' always used to be pronounced by the whites K'ok'wel is correct. Only recently are people changing it to K'oK'il … This name is of Whiteman origin and has nothing to do with the South Slough word for bow."

More recent research by anthropologist Scott Byram strongly suggests that the original name "Kokwel" is derived from the Chinook Jargon word "scoquel," the once-abundant Pacific lamprey (*Lampetra tridentata*), which migrated annually in the Coquille River in great abundance. The eel was a major food source for the people and a most important trade good for the Coquille Indians. Byram says, "It seems reasonable that *Scoquel*, the word for eel, was used as a name by traders and Native people from other areas for the Coquille River and the people who lived in this valley."

Coquel Thompson was an important source of information about early Coquille life and myths. He was eighty seven years old when this photo was taken in 1937. Photo courtesy of Oregon Historical Society, #CN015067.

Languages and Culture

The dominant language of the lower Coquelles (along the coast from South Slough on Coos Bay and upriver to the present town of Coquille) was Miluk, originally identified as a division of Kusan. The Upper Coquelles spoke an Athabaskan dialect. However, because of intertribal marriage practices, as well as social and commercial interchange, most tribal members also spoke the languages of their relatives and neighbors.

Among the Coquelles, village and family life was patrilocal (upon marriage, women moved to the homes of their husbands), while family lineage was matrilineal (children belonged to their mothers' lineage). Thus women needed to know or learn the language of their husbands' villages if they were different from that of their fathers. In fact, women in general had to learn more than one language, and before marriage, young girls probably knew the several languages spoken by their mothers. Evidence of women's multilingual skills can be found in the number of multilingual female informants for the several linguists and ethnographers who collected language information from the Coos/ Coquelle area. My grandmother, Susan Adulsah Wasson, and her mother, Gishgiu (T'cicgi'yu), each spoke several languages and dialects fluently.

Along with Miluk and Athabascan languages, Chinook Jargon, the lingua franca of the Pacific Northwest, was used regularly by the Coquelles and their neighbors as far south as the Tolowas and Yuroks in northern California.

Social and political leadership among villages and extended-family bands was acknowledged through group deference to dominant wealthy headmen or shamans with especially prominent healing powers. Both men and women practiced shamanism, and all people were free to seek personal spiritual power from fasting, praying, and vision quests. Slavery was not unknown to the Coquelles, but was less common than among the more northern tribes of the Northwest coast.

Thus, Coquelle culture included elements from the Northwest coast (for example, wealth accumulation and a form of potlatch, or giveaway). Their dance forms, ceremonial clothing, and spirituality (including reverence for flicker feathers and redheaded woodpecker scalps) were related to their southern neighbors—the Tututnis, Chetcos, Tolowas, and Yuroks.

Coquelle Material Culture

The Coquelles have long been a strong mix of hunter, gatherer, fisher, and seafaring people. Their daily implements of clothing, ritual items, cooking utensils, and tools were fashioned from stone, wood, bone, antler, seashells, feathers, grasses, and other plant fibers.

White Cedar Canoes

Many Coquelle canoes were of shovelnose design, preferably carved from Port Orford white cedar. Special canoes with high prows were designed for oceangoing. Linguist John Peabody Harrington described the canoe made by my great-grandfather:

> The Coos canoe was made preferably of white cedar, but
> sometimes of red cedar. There was a Coos Indian canoe that
> a few years ago broke away and got crushed in a log jam. But

there is still one Coos canoe in existence, made by a man some 40 years ago for fishing on a small lake near his home, but made in true Coos style, though with modern tools. The maker has died but his son is there and uses the canoe.

George Wasson knows exactly how a Coos canoe is made. It has high bow and stern, and beveled gunwales, and no seats, only sometimes they tied a board across. The Indians sat in their canoes and old canoe Indians were bowlegged as one who rides horseback all the time.

A small fish weir like this would have been used to trap salmon. Photo by Edward S. Curtis, courtesy of Oregon Historical Society, #OrHi78267.

Legends tell that one such canoe carried a whole village of people across the Pacific Ocean to escape inevitable annihilation by a vengeful village of southern Tututunne. Many years later, people were found in Japan who could still speak the Coquelle Miluk language (see Roberta Hall in *The Coquille Indians: Yesterday, Today and Tomorrow*). Practically nothing more is known of these people beyond Hall's reference. Hopefully, scholars will someday be fortunate enough to explore and learn more about this intriguing story and the connection with Miluk speakers in Japan.

Basketry Materials and Production

The manufacture of baskets, nets, twine, and other woven materials was among the traditional industries of all Oregon coastal peoples. The Coquelle Indians and their close neighbors lived in a region with abundant resources for those weaving materials. The untimely decimation of the people and their traditional cultural practices destroyed much of the knowledge of the art and craft of gathering, preparing, and weaving. Yet, basketmaking continued for generations and is now seeing a resurgence.

The importance of basketry and woven materials such as twine, rope, mats, and wicker products in the cultures of the coastal people is strongly indicated in coastal creation myths. For instance, mats and baskets were used by two mythical beings in creating the world. Baskets were split open and laid out flat to protect the newly forming landmass from erosion by ocean wave action.

Annual Burning Practices

Certain basketry materials, such as bear grass and hazel, needed to be burned off a year before being collected and prepared for weaving. Each fall people would go to the mountains and set fires in the areas where the best grass and sticks were growing. When they returned the following summer, the bear grass would have grown into fresh clumps ready for harvesting. The hazel, however, needed to grow for another season after burning and was harvested the following spring when the sap started flowing again. Fire was also used to maintain prairies as habitats for deer and elk.

Elk Dogs from K'ammahss-Dunn Rancheria

Upper Coquelle informant Coquel Thompson related the following story to Harrington sometime in the early 1940s. The location of the village mentioned here is at Bullards Beach State Park on the Coquille River, just north of the town of Bandon, Oregon:

> My father bought two Indian male elk-dogs from K'ammahss-dunn rancheria at the mouth of the Coquille River. The Indians there raised these pure-breed of dogs known as "elk dogs." These dogs grabbed the elks by the hind legs and every time the elk started to run the dog would hold his hind legs. ... They told the dog to go after the elks: *dushleet-ch'uh* or *dushle-cheh*. Then you would hear the dog bark when he arrived where the elks were. You could tell the arrival by the kind of bark.

> The elk kept wheeling around with the dog biting high on his thighs and my father thus overtook the elk—[he then] shot arrows into him. As soon as the elk fell, the dogs bit him in the throat and killed him.

> My father paid Indian money (dentalia) the length of my arm worth maybe $100 for those two dogs. They were

A coastal woman gathering shellfish with a dugout canoe. Photo courtesy of Oregon Historical Society, #OrHi21058.

young, my father would not buy old ones, they were big dogs, with black and white color in spots. Those dogs were just like people, knew their names, they would sit down.

A Sacred Food from the Ocean

Surely there never existed a more spiritual and ritualized relationship between humans and fish than has flourished among the cultural groups of the Northwest coast and their beloved salmon. So special was salmon to the Coquelles (and other Northwest coastal people) that a highly sacred ceremony was performed upon the arrival of the first salmon. There was an obvious intent to pay honor and tribute to the salmon for returning again to the streams where the people could obtain them for food. A common and primary element of those rituals required that the bones of the honored fish be maintained intact. The flesh was cooked and shared with many people and eaten ritually with great reverence. The whole skeleton was then placed in the water with the head pointed upstream to ensure that the salmon would continue to multiply and return the next season.

The Legend of Old Man Coyote and the Fish Dam
Salmon fishing was done primarily in the streams, where weirs or fish dams were constructed to either catch salmon in basketlike traps or contain them in areas where they could be readily speared or dipped out by hand nets. Hence the setting for the following legend.

From Coquel Thompson, Harrington collected one of the most intriguing stories of Old Man Coyote. It told of a notable fish dam on the Coquille River, and how the place came to be called *Thet-Suh-wuh-let-Sluh-dunn* ("a place where two large round stones are located on either side of the water"). There was a riffle at this place on the Upper Coquille River, located somewhere around Myrtle Point at a broad stretch of gravel bar. There the Upper Coquelles built a fish weir and a salmon trap in July or August to catch the salmon that came in September. Made of willow stakes driven straight down into the gravel bottom, this sizeable dam spanned the full width of the river. The construction of this dam was obviously a great undertaking; it required an extensive communal effort to cut, sharpen, and pound the great stakes into place and to weave smaller branches between them to form a secure barricade fence that had to be rebuilt annually.

Such an enormous salmon weir always seemed to be of special importance to all the people along that river. Each coastal stream with a salmon run provided a reason to have such a structure, and the people who were dedicated and accomplished enough to build one that reached from shore to shore had reason to be proud. The larger the dam, the more prestige it bestowed on the builders.

No one seems to know where Coyote was coming from on the occasion recounted in this story, or just why, but he was poling his way upstream in his canoe along with his current wife, the former Mrs. Fish Duck, when his progress was halted by the enormous salmon weir. Coyote tried to push his way through but the structure was too sturdy. Of course, true to form, he became angry and vowed to smash through. So he went back downstream and loaded two large round boulders into the bow of his canoe and placed his wife at the stern. Even though he was pushing against the current, Coyote was determined to break through the barricade. His first attempts were too feeble, and he failed. Finally, in a fit of rage, he poled as fast and hard as he could and broke through. But just as he got to the upstream side, his pole slipped, and he lost his balance. The current threw his canoe back against the weir, flipped it up on end, catapulted the boulders out onto either shore, and

Old Man Coyote. Courtesy of Roberta Hall.

dumped Coyote and his wife into the water. Using *tamanawis*, the magical powers of his mind, Coyote brought the canoe up from under the swift current and quietly took his wife back downstream. That's why the place was called *Thet* (stones) *suh-wuh-let* (spherical) *sluh-dunn* (on opposite sides of the water-place).

"A Most Horrid Massacre"

Early on the morning of January 28, 1854, the Nasomah village of the Lower Coquille was brutally attacked and destroyed by a mob of forty miners from the nearby gold diggings at Randolph. Two of the main instigators were named Packwood and Soapy. A week later, special agent Smith wrote the following report:

> A most horrid massacre, or rather an out-and-out barba-
> rous mass murder, was perpetrated upon a portion of the
> Nasomah Band residing at the mouth of the Coquille
> River on the morning of January 28th by a party of 40
> miners. The reason assigned by the miners, by their own
> statements, seems trivial. However, on the afternoon pre-
> ceding the murders, the miners requested the chief to
> come in for a talk. This he refused to do.

The report goes on to say that a meeting was held and a courier dispatched to obtain the assistance of twenty more miners from nearby Randolph. Smith continued:

> At dawn the following day, led by one Abbott, the ferry
> party and the 20 miners, about 40 in all, formed three
> detachments, marched upon the Indian ranches and "con-
> summated a most inhuman slaughter," which the attackers
> termed a fight. The Indians were aroused from sleep to
> meet their deaths with but a feeble show of resistance;
> shot down as they were attempting to escape from their
> houses. Fifteen men and one [Sq—] were killed, two
> [Sq—s] badly wounded. On the part of the white men,
> not even the slightest wound was received. The houses of
> the Indians, with but one exception, were fired and de-
> stroyed. Thus was committed a massacre too inhuman to
> be readily believed.
>
> —*Peterson and Powers*

Similar slaughters and battles took place along the river and southern coast—some as part of the Rogue River Wars of 1856 and some as isolated instances before and after the wars.

Miluk Tales of Jedediah Smith at Coos Bay

This story was told by an old woman of the Coos Bay tribe who could not read or speak a word of English, and had not heard of Jedediah Smith or the North American Fur Trading Company. It was about July 10, 1828, that Smith's party reached Sunset Bay, where they were met by about one hundred Coos Bay Indians who talked to them in the Chinook Jargon and told them that they were within ten days march from the McLoughlin camp on the Columbia

British and American Hostilities
Complicate Relations among the Tribes

There is another obscure detail of historical relationships between the Hudson's Bay Company, the Oregon Indians, and the European Americans that seldom is discussed or noted. The rivalry between the British Hudson's Bay Company and the Americans took on vicious proportions as the Americans moved west and competed for the land and its resources. The native tribes were often told by Hudson's Bay Company personnel that the Americans were bad and the British good.

James G. Swan commented on that bitterness:

> I have remarked on the hostile feeling evinced toward Americans by the former employees of the Hudson Bay Company, and here was a circumstance to corroborate my assertion. Captain Scarborough was known to keep quite a sum of money in his house at all times. He charged an old Indian servant-woman, who lived with him, in case of his death, on no account to tell a Boston man [American] where his money was, but to deliver it either to the Hudson's Bay Company's agent at Chenook [sic] or some of their people up the river, alleging that the Bostons were very bad people, but the King George [British] people were honest and good.

It seems probable that the Umpquas, influenced by the McCloud Expedition and already ill-disposed toward the American expedition of Jedediah Smith, were easily aroused to attack his party. Upon further reflection, it is now clear that the Umpquas were subsequently ill-disposed toward Kitzenjinjn Galah-dah Luee because he protected the Americans while at Coos Bay. He would not attack and kill the Smith party as the uninvited visitor at their camp had requested. Shortly thereafter, a group of Umpqua men invited Kitzenjinjn to join them in an elk hunt somewhere just north of the Coos Bay in the southern Umpqua area. When they got him in the lead, the hosts attacked and killed the Coos chief by shooting many arrows in his back. Thus ended the life of Kitzenjinjn Galah-dah Luee, the most prominent Coos chief of the 1800s.

River. These were the first Indians Smith had met with whom he could carry on a conversation.

Early in the nineteenth century, white explorers, trappers, and missionaries began to come to the Pacific Northwest. In 1828 an angry group of Lower Umpqua Indians attacked the expedition of one early explorer, Jedediah Smith. An incident at Coos Bay that happened before Smith met the Umpquas provoked the attack. The story remains a part of Coquelle oral tradition.

In the summer of 1828, when the Jedediah Smith expedition made its historic trek up the coast of Oregon, word of its strange light-skinned people with hair on their faces and large four-legged animals that were neither deer nor elk spread rapidly up the coast. Those animals, it was said, also had curved flat blades of *chicamin* ("iron" in Chinook Jargon) fastened to the bottoms of their single rounded hooves to make them tougher and to help them endure the rough terrain. The hairy-faced men also carried "rock-throwing sticks," which they didn't have to swing but merely pointed at a target, which caused fire and smoke to explode as the stick threw a metal stone harder, faster, and farther than any of the Indians had imagined possible.

News of the slow and laborious progress of this awesome caravan had been carried up the coast to every village headman. One group, the Nasomahs, had sent word up to their Miluk relatives on the South Slough of Coos Bay. Those living at the mouth of the Coquille River were relatively few in number, and as the expedition finally approached the main village, most of the people had gone across the river to the north-side village.

Smith must have posed a formidable specter to the last of the fleeing villagers, for they paddled furiously to the other shore, smashed their highly prized *thlahkhoosa* ("canoes" in Miluk) to pieces and hid among the trees to watch in awe as the white men tore up the Indians' plank houses to make a raft on which to cross the tidewater.

What Smith and his men did next must have truly puzzled the Indians. Instead of following the well-established trail that led directly to South Slough, Smith took his weary group through the sand hills along the coast and led them into the worst terrain they had yet encountered in their long journey. At this point, the Nasomah people rushed to tell Kitzenjinjn Galah-dah Luee, the prominent Miluk headman at Sough Slough, who was so tall and robust that his name meant "elk skin robe would not meet all the way around the middle."

When told of the strangers in their midst, Kitzenjinjn responded with great military pomp and diplomacy, taking three hundred armed men dressed in their finest skins and feathers out onto the coastal headlands near Cape Arago and ceremoniously welcoming the astonished whites. The Indians escorted Smith and his men, along with their several hundred head of horses and mules, to South Slough, where they were duly ferried across to the village site and guided to a suitable place of encampment nearby. Family relatives have told me recently that Smith camped on the west side of South Slough at Battle Flat, now a part of Charleston, Oregon.

During the next few days, Smith and his party rested and enjoyed the abundant hospitality of the local people, who provided much food, and the two groups participated in extensive trading. The Indians were also introduced to the white method of boiling and eating dried beans—food that both fascinated and puzzled them and which led to a humorous situation years later, when they tried to prepare and eat coffee beans in the same way.

However, during this otherwise amiable interlude, some difficulties arose. For one thing, Smith was greatly annoyed by some of the more curious and meddlesome tribesmen who shot arrows into some of his pack animals, wounding and killing a few. Another incident that seemed unimportant at the time was to have a disastrous result.

An old man from a distant village who was visiting at South Slough on Coos Bay could not contain his curiosity about the strange habits of the white men. As was the common practice among European descendants, a cook in the Smith party had hung an elk carcass in a tree to age until it was suitable for consumption. The visitor, however, apparently felt that the meat was turning to a state that decent palates would not find edible and stuck his knife into the flesh to determine its degree of putrefaction.

Unfortunately, the cook discovered the old Indian and, thinking he was trying to steal the meat, rushed at him with a butcher knife, cutting off the Indian's ear and part of his nose. Thus marked, the Indian was disgraced beyond social acceptability, for to his people the severing of an ear—or worse yet, a nose—was punishment only meted out to a runaway slave or an adulterer.

When the insulted visitor rushed to Kitzenjinjn demanding that the Miluks attack the white men in retaliation for his humiliation, his complaint was rejected. The wise headman responded that the man had trespassed on the territory and possessions of those who were guests of the local people, and that those guests had diplomatic immunity in their own camp. The uninvited guest, he said, would have to suffer the consequences of his bold intrusion.

This response made the wounded man furious, and he stormed away from Coos Bay, raving about the hairy-faced intruders and vowing that he would have revenge. When he reached the Umpquas, he related his tale of mistreatment, which seemed to offer proof that the Smith party was not to be trusted and deserved punishment. The Umpqua chief gave the old man a hearing and was just about to turn him down, as did the chief and headmen of the Coos Bay tribe, when a half-dozen little boys, ranging between six and ten years old, came running into camp with their legs bleeding. They were curious about the pots and kettles and were looking around the camp when the same cook who had bounced out the old man lashed the boys with a black snake whip until their legs bled.

The old Indian pointed to the bleeding legs of the boys and said, "See what they did? They are bad people and ought to be killed." Thus, the mood was set among the Lower Umpquas for the arrival of Jedediah Smith and his expedition. When he and his men reached the Lower Umpqua, the Indians grabbed their war clubs and attacked the party of strangers, massacring them all except two, who jumped into the river and managed to make their escape. The Indians held their possessions and horses until someone from the Hudson's Bay Company came down and claimed them. History clearly details the near total destruction of those explorers and the events that followed. (See Stephen Dow Beckham in *Requiem for a People: The Rogue Indians and the Frontiersmen* and Nathan Douthit in *A Guide to Oregon South Coast History*).

Treaties and Land Claims

In 1855 Coquelle headmen signed a treaty with the United States government (the unratified Port Orford treaty of 1851 also identified several signatories as Coquelle Indians), which would have ceded tribal land to the United States in return for a reservation and various tribal rights. Congress failed to ratify the treaty. Instead, the U.S. Army herded the survivors of the Rogue River Wars of 1856 (and of earlier Army retaliations and village massacres by white miners) overland or shipped them up the coast by steamers to concentration camps at Reedsport and Yachats. Some were moved later to the Siletz Reservation, while many others died or ran away. In less than two years the people were gone, except for those few women who had taken white men for their husbands. The effect on the culture of the Coquelles and their close neighbors was devastating. Yet through all the years of languishing in seemingly total deprivation, bits and pieces of tradition and cultural spirit remained alive among the tribal survivors or were recorded for scientific posterity. A few anthropologists and historians recognized this unprecedented oblit-

eration and worked with knowledgeable elders to save or write something of the cultures, however small a segment.

A Life with a Mission

When he was a little boy, says George Bundy Wasson Sr., his grandmother Gishgiu took him up on the hill above South Slough and, gesturing broadly with her outstretched arm, told him, "All this land belongs to your *hiyas papas* (grandfathers). Someday, Chawtch (George), you get it back."

His life's work was set for him. Bundy went away in 1898 to the Carlisle Indian School, studied law, and played clarinet in the Carlisle Indian Band with John Philip Sousa, the guest conductor.

This schooling put him in a special position, and he spent the next thirty-plus years trying to organize all the western Oregon Indians into a concerted effort to obtain payments for the land. In 1916 George Bundy Wasson began investigating Indian land claims based primarily on broken or unratified treaties. For eleven years, he lobbied Congress and finally won permission to go to court in 1929. Historian Stephen Dow Beckham portrays "Bundy's quest" to right the wrongs against the tribes as follows. (Like the Wassons, many Coquelles were Miluk Coos as well as Upper Coquelle, and thus had the option of identifying as Coos and/or Coquelle.)

> The concern about injustice, legal rights, and land claims was voiced most clearly by the Coos, Lower Umpqua, and Siuslaw. These three tribes—operating as one unit since their treaty agreement with Joel Palmer in 1855—

pioneered in using the "system." Their efforts, which set a pattern for other Indian groups throughout the Pacific Northwest, began in 1916. In the summer of that year, George Bundy Wasson, a graduate of Chemawa and Carlisle, went to Washington, DC, to investigate the Indian land claim. Wasson had grown up on his mother's allotment on South Slough on Coos Bay. That trip began eleven lonely and frustrating years of lobbying by these Indians. Like other American Indians, they were prohibited by law from suing the United States government. To bring a suit for their land claims, the Coos, Lower Umpqua, and Siuslaw had to gain a special act of Congress. Not until 1929 did Congress pass the measure which permitted them to go to court. Case K-345, the lawsuit of the Coos, Lower Umpqua, and Siuslaw for settlement for land claims, took nine years to get a judgment in the Court of Claims. During all of the time between 1917 and 1938 these Indians had to pay for their own legal expenses. ... Each family that could gave $5 a month to help pay for George Wasson's trips to Washington, DC, and to pay for the work of the attorneys.

In 1931 George Bundy Wasson called upon the most knowledgeable members of the Coos and Coquelle tribes to provide evidence for aboriginal land claims. Beckham described the participation in those hearings:

George B. Wasson Sr., circa 1947, holding a Beaver Stick from the Coquille River found during land resource assessments for coastal Indian land claims. Photo courtesy of George Wasson Jr.

In 1931 Court-appointed clerks took Indian testimony in North Bend, Oregon. Seventeen members of the tribes spoke, several of them in their native languages. The aged James Buchanan was one who remembered much of what had happened. ... In 1875 he had spoken at the Yachats Conference and protested against the closing of the Alsea reservation. Now in 1931 he spoke again for his people and their land claim. Lottie Evanoff named the villages and fishing places. George, Maggie Sacchi, Annie Peterson, Laura Metcalf, Frances Elliot, and Mrs. William Waters spoke.

It was a losing battle from the beginning, but he could not stop working on it. It must have been as though his grandmother was standing alongside him urging him to "get it back."

His job was truly impossible. There were delays in Congress; committee meetings and hearings; lawyers, senators, and representatives to consult for the best time to make presentations; and documents and testimonies to locate and gather. Some Indians were negligent in turning in their pledged support funds for the enormous effort in Washington, DC.

Some tribal members back in Oregon became restless, claiming nothing was being done. The progress was too slow. They wanted land or compensation immediately. Some small tribes even attempted to hire their own lawyers, hoping to present their own separate cases to Congress. Indolence and divisiveness among the western Oregon tribes were as detrimental to the cause as was the sluggishness of the federal government.

To make his case, Bundy had interviewed the oldest living Indians. These elders told him the history of the people, who was related to whom, where they were born, the old customary fishing places, and much more. Federal officials, however, considered all the affidavits hearsay. Not understanding the significance of an oral culture, officials emphasized that Bundy had not been there when those activities and events happened, that he had simply heard about them from his elders. Bundy did not have access to records of the Hudson's Bay expeditions to the Coos Bay area in the early 1800s. Those privately held records might have been convincing enough, but he could not get to them. Hence the land claims case for the Coos, Lower Umpqua, and Siuslaw was lost.

Sometime in the 1940s, however, a strange man named John Peabody Harrington who worked for the Bureau of American Ethnology visited western Oregon and interviewed a few remaining old Coquelle Indians. (I say "strange" because Harrington was odd, according to his employers, the local Indians, and his ex-wife, Carobeth Laird, who authored a biography of Harrington confirming his eccentricity. One mere example: He was regularly observed bathing and swimming naked in a nearby slough of brackish water each morning, which appalled the Indian people who bathed privately—men and women separately—and in clean fresh water.)

Harrington interviewed Coquelles who had claims attached to the land claims case *Alcea Band of Tillamook, et al.* He was impressed with their information and remarked something like, "There is no doubt that these are the true descendants of the aboriginal occupants of their land." Upon hearing these simple words from an employee of the Bureau of American Ethnology, the Court of Claims granted the Coquelle claims on April 2, 1945—even though the Coos had already been denied. It is ironic that a few words from such a strange and idiosyncratic man as Harrington carried so much weight with the Court of Claims, particularly after George Bundy Wasson had amassed considerable, detailed evidence for the peoples' legitimate right to their homelands and failed to receive a favorable ruling. Alas, what really counted, apparently, was Harrington's European American ethnicity.

The Justice Department appealed the case, and on November 25, 1946, the United States Supreme Court overruled the appeal. The case was finally closed in 1950, awarding $1.20 per acre for 722,530 acres. Coquelle descendants were awarded an inheritance of $3,128,000. The final settlement was divided equally among eligible tribal enrollees. After numerous federal deductions, the remainder equaled approximately $2,000 per person. (After the Court of Claims' Coquelle decision, all of the Miluk Coos became eligible for inclusion in the Coquelle Land Claims, thus causing a division of many Coos members in the Confederated Tribes of the Coos, Lower Umpqua, and Siuslaw, which exists today: some Miluk Coos are enrolled in the Coquille Indian Tribe, and other Coos are enrolled in the Confederated Tribes of Coos, Lower Umpqua, and Siuslaw.)

Perhaps the tribal members were glad to get something at last for all they had lost by not having a treaty and giving up all of their land. It seems as though they believed that the end of their status as a legitimate Indian tribe was at hand. It surely seemed impossible to fight the federal government's efforts to destroy their Indianness and render them personae non grata, as had already been done to the Coos, Lower Umpqua, and Siuslaw.

Termination, Restoration, and Political Turmoil

On August 13, 1954, the Coquelles, along with forty-two other western Oregon Indian tribes, were effectively terminated by President Dwight D. Eisenhower's signature of Public Law 588, which made termination effective immediately. Even though they were a non-treaty tribe without federal recognition, the Coquelles were among those terminated and among those whose cultural losses became most evident. Ironically, as a federally recognized tribe after restoration years later in 1989, there came a whole new set of problems that compounded the cultural turmoil. Restoration required the establishment of a tribal council and adoption of a tribal constitution (which needed to be approved by the Bureau of Indian Affairs and Department of Interior), as well as the acceptance of federal dollars in the form of funding for new tribes.

Termination was not a satisfactory solution to the problems of American Indians and did not fulfill the obligations of the federal government to Indian people. Tribal members continued to communicate through a home-printed newsletter, and tribal leaders worked with Native American Program Oregon Legal Services attorneys Rod Clark and Michael Mason to reverse termination. Wilfred Wasson, eldest son of George Bundy Wasson, skillfully led tribal efforts to restore the tribes to federal recognition. A Coquelle delegation, accompanied by its attorneys, traveled to Washington, DC, to lobby and testify before the U.S. Congress. The Coquille Indian Restoration Act (103 Stat. 91) finally restored federal recognition to the Coquille Indian Tribe on June 28, 1989.

Contemporary Views of Coquelle and Oregon History

Early American settlers did not have to fight for the Willamette Valley. Those native peoples had been so severely decimated by the "fevers" of 1829–32—probably malaria and diphtheria—that their villages had become virtual ghost towns with scattered survivors stunned and in permanent shock. To the good fortune of those settlers, the remaining Indians were gathered up by the missionary Jason Lee and his helpers and put in what Stephen Dow Beckham referred to as "a virtual Indian death camp" (even though the residents were there as recipients of Christian charity).

On the coast in subsequent years, the southern Oregon Indians were herded to the concentration camp at Yachats. There was no Christian charity, only government agents. Yachats was nothing more than an extermination camp, and many of those people were the survivors of village massacres. This destruction might be understood as the Oregon Holocaust.

Merely 260 Indian people were accounted for, by virtue of their village headmen's signatures on the 1855 treaties, in southwestern Oregon. Another two thousand were dumped into the camps with them and were covered de facto under the terms of the treaties. The provisions guaranteed them by the treaties seldom arrived (or were too few to effectively divide among all who were starving). Fifty percent of them died of starvation in the first decade. Forced to live away from traditional fisheries, they had to use summer gathering practices year round. Some drowned on the ocean rocks while attempting to obtain mussels for food.

Most of those concentration camp secrets have never been told publicly, but several accounts of the wretched social and cultural clashes have been documented by some of the more assiduous ethnologists. With the loss of family and group integrity necessary for appropriate spiritual and social guidance, decadence and moral decay claimed many Indians. One ghastly account tells of a jealous woman punishing a woman from another tribal area who was an unpurchased wife of her husband. (As scholars Miller and Seaburg remark, "To be respectable a woman had to be purchased.") The unpurchased wife was pounced upon, beaten, dragged to the fire where her undergarments were ripped off, and sexually humiliated. In a second and similar incident, the offending woman was ultimately chastised with a burning firebrand.

Another seldom-told story is about a young Miluk woman brutally murdered by a drunken miner who was attempting to rape her. She managed to escape temporarily and ran down the beach to hide, but he caught up with her and was infuriated with her attempts to thwart his desires (he found her desperately stuffing sand into her vagina), so he killed her.

The tribe created this national prize-winning poster in celebration of the Coquelle's first commercial, organic cranberry crop in 1998. Photo courtesy of George Wasson Jr.

Gishgiu—grandmother of George Bundy Wasson and wife of Miluk Headman Kitzenjinjn Galah-dah Luee—ran away from Yachats, swimming around the major headlands. She walked the long sand beaches at night, all the way back to South Slough on Coos Bay. Living in a hollow log until discovered by her son-in-law, George R. Wasson, she was finally brought into her daughter's home, where she was hidden from the Fort Yamhill soldiers. There she lived out her life.

A Sketch of the Coquelle Tribe Today

The Coquelle Indian Tribe currently has about sixty-five hundred acres in twenty-four parcels in Coos County, Oregon. These sixty-five hundred acres, all held in federal trust, include a reservation with a community health center and tribal housing on a thousand acres in the Empire district of Coos Bay, the Mill Casino in North Bend, and fifty-four hundred acres of Coquille Forest Land, most of which is in the Coast Range headquarters of the Coquille River.

The tribe has approximately 750 enrolled members. Tribal enrollment is dependent on direct blood descendancy. An enrollment committee reviews all applications for new enrollment.

On September 13, 1991, the members adopted a tribal constitution consisting of legislative, executive, and judicial branches, and providing for ordinances, charters, and committees. The general council, made up of enrolled members who are of voting age, elects a seven-member tribal council composed of three general tribal representatives, officers—the chairperson, vice-chair, secretary-treasurer—and the chief. Council members serve three-year, staggered terms. The tribe functions on an annual budget of $7 million.

Among the current tribal business ventures are Heritage Place, an assisted living and Alzheimer's center in Bandon, and the Mill Casino and Mill Hotel located on the Coos Bay waterfront. Coquille Cranberries, with ten acres of cranberry bogs, is believed to be the world's largest producer of organic cranberries. ORCA (Optical Rural Community Access) Communications acts as a middle-mile, or secondary, telecommunications service provider, linking the local community with broadband, high-speed, fiber-optic networks throughout the state.

The tribe recently developed another large waterfront site adjacent to the Mill Casino in North Bend. Plans for growth and development are still under consideration by the Coquille Economic Development Corporation and the Coquelle Tribal Council. The tribe is the second largest employer in Coos County.

The tribe holds two main gatherings annually: the Salmon Bake and Restoration Celebration in mid-summer and the Mid-Winter Gathering in late January. These two events provide opportunities for the entire membership to be updated on the status of tribal projects and programs, and for the tribal leaders to gather input on pressing issues and concerns. Most important, these annual gatherings assemble the extended family of the Coquelle Tribe, bringing them together in a spirit of warmth and celebration, which resonates throughout Coquille culture.

Since 1997, the tribe has also sponsored an annual cultural preservation conference in May. Selected conference proceedings are published in *Changing Landscapes*. The diverse contributions— from historical Indian correspondence, the results of archaeological research, and traditional stories to articles on native Oregonians' relationships to the natural environment and more—reflect the contributions of participants. Members of academic programs, institutions, other tribes, federal and state agencies, private businesses, independent scholars, tribal members, and other interested persons are invited to deliver papers, participate in discussions and panels, and attend other presentations all related to native cultural, historical, social, and economic topics.

The Past Colors the Future

Just as the history of the holocaust of the Jews in Germany must be accurately and fully detailed, so must the holocaust of the tribes in southwest Oregon. Indications of the extensive variety of lost languages, myths, tales, and cultural traditions in the Pacific Northwest (and most particularly in southwestern Oregon) can be noted in the comments of linguist/ethnologist Melville Jacobs, which bear repeating. In one instance, he wrote:

> Northwest states, before 1750, had sixty to seventy Indian languages, two to three thousand bands, hamlets, or villages, and something under, around, or over two hundred thousand people. This hunting-fishing-gathering population could once have yielded a million or more versions of myths, smaller numbers of tales, and no one can estimate how much of other oral genres. ... Myths of most variable merit that have been collected over the region total less than a thousand and will never exceed that number. Tales amount to a few hundred, forever so. The bleak harvest is ... maybe one percent of what could have been obtained if the culture-bound, condescending, and racist invaders had had the slightest capacity to perceive merit in the heritages of non-Europeans. By the time anyone with such capacity went to work, native humiliation and extinction had erased almost everything. Folklore-oriented linguists ... arrived too late after the pioneers had trampled upon and destroyed the Indians.

By that time, most of the aboriginal myths and legends had been lost with the extreme decimation of the native peoples. However, among the meager collections of myths and stories from the people of the southern Oregon coast that remain are descriptions of floods, fires, earthquakes, and tsunamis reported in specific geographic locations. These and other stories are especially interesting, relating as they do to the earliest human knowledge of the world's creation and of other momentous geologic and environmental events.

Renewing Our Cultural History

To recapture the heritage of the Coquelles and their neighbors, this author, in 1995, led a team in a unique enterprise: the Southwest Oregon Research Project (SWORP). In two trips sponsored by the University of Oregon, the Smithsonian Institution, and the Coquille Indian Tribe, the SWORP team brought back more than a hundred thousand pages of historical documents, which are now housed at the University of Oregon's Knight Library and tribal archives in western Oregon and northwestern California. The SWORP archive contains materials of obscure, lost, or hidden information on our cultures, languages, history, and lifeways that have been separated from many of us. We need to renew those aspects of our culture for the sake of those who are to come later.

While the bones of our ancestors must never be put on display for public curiosity, I personally believe that we must at least know that those remains are indeed our ancestors. And though this is a contentious issue in the Native American community, I believe that scientific examination is how we must determine this. Just as we now rely on medical science to examine, operate on, and treat our bodies for improved health, so must we medically examine ancestral remains without substantial desecration or mistreatment. DNA and carbon-14 analyses are expensive but quite simple and relatively nonintrusive. Supporting and funding that vital research is imperative.

Gishgiu hoped young Chawtch could get the land back for her descendants and neighbors. Maybe she did not mean just the land. As she swept her arm broadly across the mountains up and down the coast, maybe she desired the unity of her people again. She was proud that her grandson was receiving a modern education. Surely she wanted him to learn and use all the education that the white schools had to offer. Today we must follow those same admonitions and take full advantage of our current educational and scientific opportunities. We must also look to our ancestors for help. If we do not know who and what they were, we cannot know who and what we are today.

Chapter 5

Patience and Persistence
The Cow Creek Band of Umpqua Tribe of Indians

BY STEPHEN DOW BECKHAM AND MICHAEL RONDEAU

In the Upper Umpqua watershed in Douglas County, Oregon, lives a tribe whose history mirrors the difficult relations between Indians and the United States. The story of the Cow Creek Band of Umpqua Indians is one of inequity, misrepresentation, tantalizing hope, deep frustration, triumph, and persistence. The tribe's ability to survive is testimony to unquenchable human spirit and determination to shape a better future.

The Land and Its Early Inhabitants

The Cow Creeks lived between the Cascade and Coast ranges in southwestern Oregon, concentrated along the South Umpqua River and its primary feeder stream, Cow Creek. This homeland was one of mountains, uplands, and valley floors—a place of beauty and challenge that sustained life but demanded work from those who called it home.

The prehistory of the Umpqua region is incompletely known, but archaeology confirms a deep timeframe for Indian presence in the interior of southwestern Oregon and suggests a way of life that changed little over the centuries. The archaeological record also confirms a use of the land extending from the margins of streams to the highest ridges, a tapping of both flora and fauna, and a technology typical of that of Indians elsewhere on the Pacific Slope.

Language

For centuries, Indian voices floated on the summer air and winter winds of the South Umpqua, and Indian names marked the land. Lakwal, or "Cow Creek" as the newcomers called it, flowed past the sleepy villages; the eels surged up the creek to the falls where the young men dived and wrenched them from the rocks; and Kwenta't, an ancient village, stood on Canyon Creek near the point where it cut out of the hillsides and entered the South Umpqua River. Rarely are these names used today. No one thinks in the cadences of words and sentence structures of the time-tested Takelman language, once common in southwestern Oregon.

The term "Takelma" was taken from "Da-gelma," meaning "those living alongside the river." Collectively these people were called the Rogue Indians, whose kinsmen to the north included the Grave Creeks and the Cow Creeks, bands sharing the same language but living in isolated stream systems to the south and north of the Rogue-Umpqua divide.

Traditional Lifeways

For many years the Cow Creeks followed a seasonal round that responded to nature's cycles and food sources. In the spring they hunted along the Umpqua River for ducks and geese, gathered shoots and greens in the meadows, and harvested the first salmon. By April they had access to the first berry crops, and within a month the men and boys began to harvest vast quantities of eels, which the women smoked and dried in the sun at places such as the falls of Cow Creek above Riddle or at South Umpqua Falls deep in the Western Cascades.

During the late spring and early summer, the women and girls worked their way through the river meadows and mountain uplands to harvest the bulbs of camas and Cat's Ears and to pick salmonberries, thimbleberries, and strawberries. Meanwhile, the men repaired brush fences on the ridges and anticipated the time when they would drive deer in a frenzied rush into the canyons through the narrow places where they had fixed their prized iris-fiber snares. These snares handily caught the deer, which played an important part in the Cow Creeks' diet and provided hides for their clothing. The men also flaked stone projectile points, hafted them on wooden spears and arrows, and carved yew wood bows, which they backed with sinew from the legs of elk and deer. Although these bows were resilient and useful, the snares proved even more efficient during the game drives.

By late summer the families had moved from the uplands to the high country, gathering at Huckleberry Lake, Abbott Butte, and elsewhere along the Rogue-Umpqua divide. There, they picked huckleberries, which they dried for winter use, and the men hunted for elk, deer, and bear. At night the old people sang and told stories, while the young people listened, looked up at the stars, and wondered about life. The old ones said that if they spied a falling star it meant the passing of a life and the arrival of a new soul among the humans.

As the nights began to chill and the prospect of rain set in, the people dropped down from the mountains, abandoned their temporary huts of limbs and reed matting, and took up residence in the permanent winter villages in the lowlands. As they returned, the women torched the fields to burn off the globules of sticky tar on the

The Work of Women

In the early morning the women would be out in the Kamass field provided with a basket—a cone-shaped affair wide open at the top, and swung across the forehead—a manner in which the Indians carried all their burdens and which left both arms free. Each [woman] would be armed with a kamass stick made of Indian arrow wood fashioned to a point at one end by burning and rubbing the charred wood off leaving the point as hard as steel.

—George Riddle, 1921

tarweed and, with beaters and funnel-shaped baskets, worked their way over the bottomlands to harvest the seeds. The men made certain that the fires burned out the forest understory, for then there would be an abundance of blackberries in another year, as well as good feed for the deer that grazed there.

In preparation for winter, the Cow Creeks constructed semi-subterranean lodges covered with planks or large pieces of bark and stored the gathered foodstuffs—acorns, hazelnuts, cakes of camas, tarweed seeds, smoked salmon, jerked meat, and dried eel. Their supplies also included the amber-colored balls of pitch from the tall "medicine trees" on Jackson Creek and upper Cow Creek—treasures that oozed from scars in the bark of ponderosa pines and provided medicine when the turn of seasons brought colds and chills.

In this manner, winter followed summer and summer followed winter in endless progression.

Early Contacts

During the first half of the nineteenth century, the Cow Creeks probably lived as they had for the preceding thousands of years. However, an early encounter with whites came in about 1819, when land-based fur trappers of the North West Company entered the Umpqua watershed and opened fire on the Indians, killing several of them. Then, in the 1820s, the Hudson's Bay Company inaugurated regular trade in the region and founded the "Old Establishment," a temporary post probably located near the mouth of Calapooia Creek. In 1836 the same firm built Fort Umpqua at the mouth of Elk Creek, north of Cow Creek country. This post assured a steady supply of trade goods to the Indians of the region—goods that included brass kettles, needles and thread, colorful trade beads, clothing of wool and cotton, blankets, and sea biscuits.

While relations between the Cow Creeks and fur trappers were generally good, a new chapter unfolded in 1846 when explorers opened the

Photo courtesy of Stephen Dow Beckham

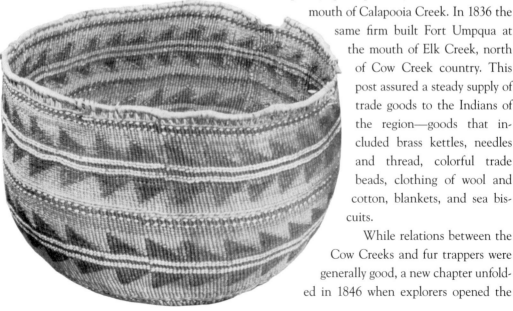

Applegate Trail and the flow of pioneers began in earnest. Tragically, this north-south trail, which bisected the Cow Creek homeland, soon became an artery of commerce and trouble for the Indians who lived there.

Part of the trouble came with the discovery of gold in the Sierra foothills of California in 1848, an event that sent tens of thousands of miners to the West Coast. In 1851 many of them had shoved north into the Klamath River watershed and begun laying out claims in the Rogue and Umpqua valleys. Then, in January 1852, the discovery of gold on Jackson Creek opened a new mining frontier, and within months, several thousand men poured into the Rogue, Illinois, and South Umpqua watersheds in a frenzied search for precious metal.

These events and others combined in the early 1850s to shatter the world of the Cow Creeks. With the gold rush came a rough, lawless element that lay siege to the ancient stream terraces where the Cow Creeks had their villages. Farmers filed for donation land claims on the meadows where the Indian women gathered seeds and dug for bulbs. And travelers passed regularly through the Indians' lands.

These incursions disrupted the Cow Creeks' subsistence patterns and cut deeply into their lives. The acorns they had once harvested were now eaten by hogs, and the camas that played such an important part in their diet was cropped by horses and cattle. The pioneers constructed split-rail fences and log cabins and ruthlessly forbade field burning for fear that their investments would be destroyed. The miners sent a flood of muddy debris down the rivers, which threatened fish runs, and the newcomers' firearms decimated both deer and elk. Before long the Cow Creeks and their neighbors were reduced to starvation.

Treaty and Warfare, 1853–56

In 1848 Congress created Oregon Territory through the Organic Act and acknowledged the validity of Indian land title. In so doing, it referenced the assurances of "utmost good faith" first articulated in 1787 when the Continental Congress set up a means for dealing with frontier lands. Between 1849 and 1853, however, the execution of good faith with Oregon Indians faltered as initial rounds of treaty negotiations led nowhere and the Senate failed to ratify any of the treaties.

The discovery of gold and consequent settlement of southwestern Oregon, however, persuaded Superintendent of Indian Affairs Joel Palmer to try a new treaty program. In September 1853, Palmer headed south to the mining region and stopped at Cow Creek, where he assembled a number of Indians. On September 19, he negotiated a treaty and secured the "X" marks of men who headed various villages of the Cow Creeks. In his diary, Palmer wrote, "Sealed the treaty with two bushels of potatoes."

The treaty called for the Cow Creeks to cede to the United States their entire homeland, approximately 720 square miles, for a price of 2.3¢ per acre. In return the United States promised a reservation, two houses worth not more than two hundred dollars each, and a plowed and fenced field of five acres. The Cow Creeks agreed to restore any stolen property they possessed, remain peaceful, and bring their complaints to a local Indian agent. This treaty and the one made with the Takelma in the Rogue Valley on September 10 were the first from Oregon Territory to become law. The Senate ratified the treaties on April 12, 1854, and on February 5, 1855, the president proclaimed them.

Treaty guarantees, however, provided no protection for the Cow Creeks, who soon became refugees in their own homeland. Settlers drove them from their villages, bands of self-styled "volunteers" from the mining communities preyed on them, and local soldiers—alleging various wrongs—murdered many and drove others into the hills.

Mi-wa-leta, a tribal leader, attempted to chart a course for his people. "That he always counseled peace and was able to restrain his people from going to war with the whites," recalled George Riddle, "we had ample evidence." Tragically, Mi-wa-leta and dozens of his people perished in a fever epidemic that decimated the population.

Terrible times ensued. When Palmer visited the Cow Creeks in the spring of 1854, he noted, "I found many of them wretched, sickly, and almost starving." The severe winter, competition with settlers for food, dislocation because of mining and land claims, new diseases, and aggression had dramatically altered their lives.

Henry Eld, an American explorer with a U.S. Navy expedition, sketched an Indian in 1841 standing by the South Umpqua River. Eld noted the use of Indian fire ecology on his trip through southwestern Oregon. Drawing courtesy of Beinecke Library, Yale University.

In the fall of 1855, the Oregon Volunteers provoked a renewed outbreak of the Rogue River Indian War. When that conflict spread north in October, Cow Creek Tom, a leader, faced the pioneers, reiterated the calamities that had befallen his people, and said that the survivors had decided to fight. The Cow Creeks left the conference and disappeared into the hills.

During the winter of 1855–56, the volunteers attempted to track down and imprison these Indians. Although they succeeded in assembling a bedraggled group on the temporary reservation in Cole's Valley on the Umpqua, dozens more began their long concealment in the mountains, occasionally coming down to the lowlands to raid for food.

Six months later, the U.S. Army entered the region and concluded the conflicts. Although the federal government rounded-up more than two thousand surviving Indians for removal to the Siletz and Grand Ronde reservations, scattered individuals and families still held out in the hills. Later, these "outlaw" or "renegade" Indians were hunted down by contractors hired by the Bureau of Indian Affairs (BIA).

In July 1856, the BIA estimated that more than one hundred Cow Creeks remained hidden in their old homeland. On April 20, 1864, a small band of Indians raided the isolated John Doyle farm on upper Olalla Creek, provoking the BIA and army to capture and remove more than a hundred Indians during a forty-day expedition to southwestern Oregon. As late as 1871, Superintendent Alfred Meacham wrote, "Another band is now being oppressed and driven by white men from place to place in a small tract of country about thirty miles by forty miles long, covering the head-waters of the Umpqua River, in southern Oregon." Meacham lamented that "at least, as original inheritors of the soil," these poor Indians had "a 'God-given right' to life, liberty, and the pursuit of happiness."

Cow Creek Treaty Provision, 1853

For and in consideration of the cession and relinquishment contained in article first, the United States agree to pay to the aforesaid band of Indians, the sum of twelve thousand dollars, in manner to wit: one thousand dollars to be expended in the purchase of twenty blankets, eighteen pairs pants, eighteen pairs shoes, eighteen hickory shirts, eighteen hats or caps, three coats, three vests, three pairs socks, three neckerhandkerchiefs [sic], forty cotton flags, one hundred twenty yards prints, one hundred yards domestic, one gross buttons, two lbs. thread, ten papers needles.

—Cow Creek Treaty, September 19, 1853

Patient Endurance

The surviving Cow Creeks retained a tenuous hold on parts of their old homeland—mostly those parts that had proven too marginal for farming. Some of the Indians had intermarried with French-Canadian fur trappers who had come to the region in the employ of the Hudson's Bay Company and lived on the edge of frontier society in Douglas County. Many of their cabins stood on the margins of small meadows above Tiller on the South Fork, near Drew on Elk Creek, or far up the main course of Cow Creek. There, the men hunted for elk and deer, and the women made leather gloves and jackets, which they sold in Canyonville, Myrtle Creek, and Roseburg.

The Cow Creek families lived close to the land. They planted small gardens, fished, hunted, and persisted in burning the hillsides until the Forest Service curtailed the practice early in the twentieth century. They also found seasonal work harvesting prunes, picking hops, or assisting in farm labor in the Umpqua Valley, and some of the men became placer miners, packers, and trappers.

Above: Eleanor Lee Dumont and her daughter Mary Agnes LaChance in the 1920s. Below: Rondeau School, 1910. Photos courtesy of Cow Creek archives.

Because they did not live on reservations, the Cow Creeks had only sporadic relations with the Bureau of Indian Affairs. However, in 1918 the elders decided to establish a tribal government and began to fight for a program of federal services, including better educa-

tion for their children. Perhaps the presence of the Roseburg Superintendency of Indian Affairs, an office that operated from 1910 to 1918 in Douglas County, inspired this determination.

Unfortunately, the results of their efforts were limited. Some children gained admittance to BIA schools, and the Grand Ronde-Siletz Agency entered a number of tribal families on the annual Indian Census Schedules from 1918 to 1940. However, the greater challenge was to seek introduction of a bill to permit the tribe to litigate over the taking of its lands in the 1850s.

Five times, the Cow Creeks secured such bills, largely through the assistance of Senator Charles McNary, and once—in 1932—their bill passed the House and Senate, only to be vetoed by President Hoover, who contended that the United States could not afford Indian claims litigation in the midst of a great depression.

Twenty years later, on August 1, 1953, their efforts were blocked when Congress adopted House Concurrent Resolution 108, a general statement that Congress would move as rapidly as possible to withdraw from long-standing relationships with Indian tribes. On August 23, 1954, Congress passed the Western Oregon Termination Act, which specified that within two years, the federal government would suspend recognition and services to every tribe and band in western Oregon.

An 1894 photograph of the Thomason children. Photo courtesy of Cow Creek archives.

The Land Claims Case and Federal Recognition

Although no longer federally recognized as a tribe, the Cow Creeks persisted in meeting, planning, and seeking their day in court. In 1979 they secured introduction of a bill to permit them to sue the United States, and on May 26, 1980, P.L. 96-251 passed. The law allowed the Cow Creek Band of Umpqua to file a complaint in the claims court in Washington, DC, over the value of their lands taken more than a century before. In this litigation, the tribe's counsel was Dennis J. Whittlesey, an attorney in Washington, DC.

As the Cow Creek case proceeded, the justice department filed interrogatories, secured depositions from tribal elders, and sought to

Jean Rondeau. Photo courtesy of Cow Creek archives.

discover the nature, extent, and value of the lands in question. In February 1984, before the case came to trial, the tribe and the government reached a negotiated settlement when the tribe agreed to a value of $1.25 per acre, or a total of $1.5 million for their lands as of 1855. By the rules of claims litigation, the tribe could secure no interest and no land. While the claims case proceeded in the court, the Cow Creeks pursued federal recognition and sought to overturn the termination law of 1954. On December 29, 1982, Congress did restore federal recognition to the Cow Creeks, enacting P.L. 97-391.

Once again, the Cow Creeks secured a direct relationship with the United States through the Bureau of Indian Affairs, but that relationship proved to be a mixed blessing. When the tribe proposed to vest its judgment fund in an endowment, the BIA opposed the move, demanding instead a per capita distribution. Although this was a long-discredited manner of handling judgment funds and was contrary to the philosophy of the Indian Judgment Fund Distribution Act, the BIA was adamant. Not only did it refuse to approve the tribal plan, it failed to bring forward its own plan during the 365 days provided by law. Thus, the Cow Creeks had no recourse but to turn, once again, to Congress. On October 26, 1987, Congress passed P.L. 100-139, the Cow Creek Judgment Fund Act, a statute that wrote into law the tribal plan. The Cow Creeks vested their entire judgment fund of $1.5 million in an endowment from which they would draw, on an annual basis, only the earned interest. These earnings were earmarked for economic development, education, housing, and elderly assistance.

Persecution of Cow Creeks

Although they may not be the possessors of enough political power to secure to them the consideration of local politicians, they, at least as original inheritors of the soil, have a "God-given right" to life, liberty, and the pursuit of happiness; and no race, however strong, under a Government claiming to be established on principles of "equal and exact justice," should be permitted to trample on and exterminate a race whose misfortune is to be "untutored and untaught."

—Alfred Meacham, 1871

Tribal Planning for the Present and Future

Since the 1850s, the Cow Creeks had always been keenly aware of their landless condition. Therefore, one of their most important actions following recognition and settlement of their land claims case was their 1984 purchase of twenty-nine acres adjacent to Interstate 5 at Canyonville, Oregon. On September 15, 1986, after two years of difficult dealings with the BIA, the Department of the Interior took the land into "trust." In 1990 the tribe purchased an adjoining sixteen acres fronting on the South Umpqua River.

The Cow Creek people, having endured the failure of the United States government to acknowledge the Treaty of 1853 and its provisions for a reservation, received no land in the settlement agreement of 1984. Using a portion of the Tribal Judgment Fund as collateral, the tribe's purchase of the twenty-nine-acre parcel of land, originally a thirteen-unit motel and trailer park, would eventually become the site of one of the tribe's major economic development projects.

In 1991, after several unsuccessful attempts to gain financing for a small bingo hall on the Evergreen Property, the tribe succeeded in securing an $825,000 federal loan through the BIA's Direct Loan Program. The tribe, having no specific experience in bingo management, found it prudent to enter into a management agreement with British American Bingo (BAB). The tribe's successful partnership with BAB provided the experience needed to assume full tribal management of the bingo hall within three years.

This photograph of an elderly Indian man ("Cushion Creek Charley"), taken in Northwestern California, shows the type of sweat lodge that was an important structure in each village. The lodges were almost subterranean, constructed deep into the earth. The men took a daily sweat to stay clean, have luck in hunting, and cure illnesses. Photo courtesy of National Anthropological Archives, Smithsonian Institution, Washington, DC.

Shortly after the opening of the Cow Creek Indian Bingo Center in April 1992, tribal leaders negotiated the first tribal-state compact with the State of Oregon, enabling them to conduct Class III gaming activities within the bingo facility.

Over the next several years, the tribe completed several expansions to the original 9,600-square-foot bingo hall. The Cow Creek Indian Gaming Center evolved into the Seven Feathers Hotel and Casino Resort. The massive destination resort includes a casino, convention center, five food outlets, a sports bar, a cabaret-show lounge, hotel with Olympic-size pool, a spa, and gift gallery.

The modern Cow Creek Tribal Government Office houses all social, economic, culture, and natural resource programs, the health and wellness center, and also the meeting chambers for the tribal board of directors. Photo courtesy of Cow Creek archives.

The financial success of the gaming operation has enabled the tribe to begin building a tribal reservation and tribal economy, with diversification and land acquisition as primary targets for achievement. From 1995 to 2003, the tribe's land holdings were in excess of four thousand acres, all of them purchased. These parcels are all located within a twenty-mile radius of where the treaty was signed on Council Creek. Nearly half of all tribal lands have been taken into "trust" by the federal government, allowing these areas to become tribal reservation lands. An estimated $250,00 has been removed from the property tax rolls as a result of the "trust" process, however, this amount pales in comparison to Cow Creek's annual payroll of $56 million and annual charitable contributions of $1.8 million to communities within the tribe's seven-county service area. (It should be noted that Cow Creek tribal individuals do not receive any special tax exemptions. Tribal members who are homeowners pay annual property taxes and receive no payroll tax relief.)

Over the past 150 years, focus on maintaining a tribal community has continued. Although landless, tribal families retained ties with their homeland and have continued to uphold many cultural practices, such as their annual powwow at South Umpqua Falls and fall gatherings at the historically significant Huckleberry Patch on the Rogue-Umpqua Divide. Efforts to protect this most significant cultural resource continue to the present.

The Cow Creeks have maintained strong ties to the communities of southern Oregon and have developed government-to-government relationships with all levels of government. The tribe is committed to several cooperative agreements with state, county, and city governments, and has representation on county and city park boards, and regional investment and industrial development boards, as well as receiving special appointments by the state's governor to various committees and boards. Additionally, the tribe is very active in local chambers of commerce, historical societies, hospital foundations, and, of course, civic and philanthropic organizations such as Rotary, Optimists, United Way, and March of Dimes.

Relationships with federal agencies have been a constant with the tribe. Prior to the official Federal Recognition Act, various tribal leaders had a long history of individual involvement with many of the congressional delegation at the state and national levels. Additionally, various tribal members had ongoing relationships with the Forest Service regarding cultural resource issues.

A prerequisite to the success of the Cow Creek Band of Umpqua Tribe of Indians has been the strength and stability of tribal government. This strong and stable environment did not come about without some controversy. In the late 1980s, the tribal government was engaged in various legal disputes within the tribe and the Bureau of Indian Affairs. Despite these challenges, the tribe's mission "to uphold Tribal Government, protect and preserve Tribal history, culture

South Umpqua Falls remains a place of spiritual and cultural significance for the Cow Creek. In the summer, an annual powwow is held here and cultural practices still occur on seasonal basis. In the fall, tribal members gather nearby to pick huckleberries and enjoy the end of summer. Photo courtesy of Cow Creek archives.

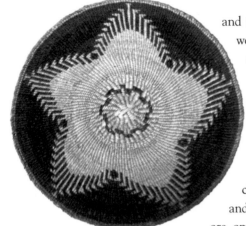

Susan Nonta Thomason wove these mats in the 1850s or 1860s. Individuals owned their basket designs, but some elements were shared with other basketmakers. Photo courtesy of Cow Creek archives.

and the general welfare of the Tribal membership, as well as to provide for the economic needs of the Tribe and its members through land acquisition and business development" has indeed prevailed.

The Cow Creek tribe is governed by an eleven-member board of directors; each director is elected to four-year terms by the general tribal membership. The primary officers of the board include chairperson, vice-chairperson, secretary, and treasurer, who are appointed by the remaining members of the board of directors each year. The Cow Creek Tribal Board of Directors is exceptionally stable. In 2004 the board had an estimated 175 combined years of service and experience in tribal government.

The Cow Creeks do not consider the Seven Feather Hotel and Casino Resort a personification of who they are; although it is the tribe's most public activity, it is just one of many things they do. Through its tribally chartered corporation, Umpqua Indian Development Corporation, the tribe conducts research, development, and management of all economic ventures. The following is a brief summary of tribal businesses.

Creative Images

Creative Images is a printing and design firm with a state-of-the-art, full-color digital press. The business has been expanded to include video production, web design and maintenance, and commercial photography, and has a full-time media buyer.

Hospitality Division

The Valley View Motel is within one-eighth mile of the Seven Feathers Resort and consists of eleven units with beautiful views of the South Umpqua River.

The Riverside Motel is located one-quarter mile from the Seven Feathers Resort on six acres of wooded land located between Interstate 5 and the South Umpqua River. The Riverside has thirteen units equipped with kitchenettes.

Canyonville Cubbyholes Storage Units

The Canyonville Cubbyholes are storage units that are located across the street from Seven Feathers Hotel and Casino Resort. There are 205 mini storage units and a home for an on-site manager.

Seven Feathers Truck and Travel Center

The Seven Feathers Truck and Travel Center is a premier travel plaza, serving both travelers and the local community. This complex is located across from the Seven Feathers Hotel and Casino Resort, on the west side of Interstate 5, and consists of a 24-hour restaurant, con-venience store, deli, drivers' lounge, private showers, arcade, public scales, and tire repair shop.

Umpqua Indian Foods

Umpqua Indian Foods is located in downtown Canyonville, roughly one mile from the Seven Feathers Hotel and Casino Resort. The business produces six flavors of beef jerky, hot dogs, polish dogs, pepperoni, salami, and hamburgers.

Agriculture Division

The Tribal Agriculture Division operates under the name of K Bar Ranch and is currently managing approximately twenty-five hundred acres. The operation is primarily beef and hay production but is considering crop diversification.

Umpqua Indian Utility Cooperative

The Umpqua Indian Utility Cooperative (UIUC) was formed by the Cow Creek Band of Umpqua Tribe of Indians to provide electricity to tribal businesses. Power is purchased directly from the Bonneville Power Administration (BPA) and distributed to Cow Creek tribal locations. The UIUC is the first tribally owned cooperative in the Pacific Northwest to contract directly with BPA.

Among the tribe's enduring strength has been continuity of leadership, at both the tribal chairperson and the tribal board of director level. Sue Shaffer, tribal chairperson for more than twenty-five years, expressed her philosophy and gratitude to tribal members in this statement: "The Cow Creek Band of Umpqua Tribe of Indians focuses on supporting families and children through job creation, and furthering economic diversification for the tribe and the communities of southern Oregon. Our tribal members have not deviated from their mission of building strong people capable of facing the coming tomorrows."

Chapter 6

The Confederated Tribes of the Grand Ronde Community of Oregon

BY BRENT MERRILL AND YVONNE HAJDA

While the ancestors of the people who today comprise the Grand Ronde tribal community came from all over western Oregon and beyond, most were from the Willamette Valley and the upper Rogue River and its tributaries. They included a few Lower Chinook-speaking Clatsops and Chinooks from the lowest few miles of the Columbia River and the adjacent coasts; Upper Chinook speakers, who originally lived along the lower Columbia from the Lower Chinook area up to The Dalles, on the Clackamas, and on the lower Willamette; and a few Klickitats, possibly from southwest Washington or east of the Cascades, Tillamooks from the northern Oregon coast, and Northern Paiutes from northern Oregon and Nevada.

From the Willamette Valley came speakers of three Kalapuyan languages and several dialects: Northern, consisting of Atfalati (now called Tualatin) and Yamhill; Central Kalapuyan, including Santiam, Luckiamute, Ahanchuyuk, Chepanefo, Chelamela, Winnefilly, Mohawk, Tekopa, Calapooia, and others; and Southern, or Yoncalla, Kalapuyan. From the slopes of the Cascades came two groups of Molalla speakers representing seven dialects throughout the Cascade range, and from several interior valleys adjoining the Yoncallas came speakers of Upper Umpqua and other Athabaskan languages. In addition, there were speakers of Takelma, a Penutian language related to Kalapuyan, who lived mainly in the upper Rogue River and Cow Creek area, with groups of Athabaskan speakers interspersed. From the same general Rogue River area came some Shasta speakers. In addition to their native languages, many of these Indians—especially those from northwest Oregon—also spoke Chinuk Wawa (commonly known as Chinook Jargon), and a few knew English and French. In addition, many of the French-Indians, men and women who had Hadanausanee (Mohawk, Chippewa, Iroquois) ancestry who worked for Hudson's Bay Company also moved to Grand Ronde with their local Oregon Indian spouses.

As many as twenty-seven tribes and bands can be traced to the Confederated Tribes of Grand Ronde. Most families now are descended from more than one tribe or band. In 1856, when the cavalry rounded up more than three hundred Indians and forcibly moved them to the base of Spirit Mountain in the Yamhill River Valley, these native peoples represented as many as forty bands. Once there, they joined the Yamhill tribal people who were already living on what became the Grand Ronde Indian Reservation.

Overleaf: For a time, the reservations were parceled out to various churches to oversee. At Grand Ronde, Belgian missionary Father Adrien Croquet established a Catholic presence in 1860 and arranged for a group of nuns to operate a boarding school. Photo courtesy of Oregon Historical Society, #CN022572.

Events That Led to Creation of the Reservation

The story of how vast Indian lands in Oregon were appropriated for white settlement is told elsewhere (Chapter 11, "Federal-Indian Relations"). Those actions led directly to the establishment of reservations on and near the central Oregon coast. Joel Palmer, who became superintendent of Indian affairs in 1853, proposed that a reservation for all western Oregon Indians be established on the central coast, on land that had not been settled, was seen as poor farming country, and was separated by mountains from the settled Willamette Valley. This plan was approved, and in 1854 and 1855,

Palmer proceeded with treaties with Willamette Valley and coastal Indians. The United States was to pay annuities in exchange for the land and was to furnish what the Indians might need if they were to learn to live like white people, including a permanent land base, health care, education, and security against further aggressions by white people.

The treaty with the Umpquas and Kalapuyas—some of whom had been moved to the upper Umpqua—was ratified in 1854, as was one with the Shastas. The Molalla treaty was ratified in 1855, and so was one with the Kalapuyas and Confederated Bands of the Willamette Valley. The treaties with the Tualatins of 1854 and coastal tribes in 1855 were never ratified, but by executive order in 1855 the Coast Reservation was established in their territory anyway. The new reservation encompassed about a third of the Oregon coastline (more than one million acres), fifty miles north and fifty miles south of Yaquina Bay, extending about twenty-five miles inland. It included sixty-nine thousand acres at the northeast corner that became the Grand Ronde Reservation.

The Indians who signed the treaties received none of the promised compensation and were forced onto the reservation. While the Rogue River wars in southern Oregon continued, Indians from the Rogue and Umpqua were marched north by the U.S. Army, beginning on February 23, 1856.

U.S. military personnel appeared in the villages, giving the native people only a few minutes to pack their belongings—whatever they could carry. Today, tribal elders question the timing of the forced relocations. They ask why the move, 265 miles north, took place in February. They say if the military had waited until the spring, which was just three to five weeks away, the trip would not have been so harsh and deadly. They wonder if the real goal was attrition.

During their month-long trail of tears, these Indians—being herded like cattle—suffered from disease, exposure, and attacks by white vigilantes. They crossed rivers and streams and climbed hills and mountains, many barefoot and others carrying children and old people. The journey took 33 days and covered the 265 miles from Table Rock in southern Oregon north to Grand Ronde. The procession of 325 Indians, 106 cavalry members, and their horses, cattle, and dogs would have stretched for over a mile as they made their way up the Applegate Trail.

On the journey, eight people died and eight babies were born. The Indian agent in charge of the relocation wrote in his diary account, with pride, of arriving in Grand Ronde with the same number of Indians that he started with.

The general did not consider the consequences of losing eight people. Tribal people passed on their family traditions and histories as part of an oral system of acquiring knowledge and understanding. Relying on writing and reading, European Americans kept journals and written family accounts, while tribal people shared their family accounts from person to person, generation to generation. When those eight people died on the way to Grand Ronde, they took with them their family histories. One of the stories that survived related to this period is that of Hattie Sands. Hattie, as a young girl hid in a beaver dam from the volunteer militias while her family was killed. Hattie walked to the Grand Ronde Reservation from southern Oregon in bare feet.

In November 1855, with the Rogue River wars almost over, other people were sent north by steamship. These Indians from the southwestern part of Oregon were located around the Siletz and Yamhill River agencies. The Yamhill Valley or River agency was the original name until confirmation of the reservation. Siletz Reservation was confirmed by Congress in 1855, while Grand Ronde was not confirmed until 1857, yet they were settled at the same time. In 1857, once Grand Ronde was granted reservation status, two-thirds of the Rogue River Indians were moved to Siletz, leaving an official count of 267 Rogue Rivers at Grand Ronde. Peaceful Kalapuyan Indians from the Willamette Valley were also moved to the Grand Ronde agency. The Clatsops and Tillamooks of the northern coast, without ratified treaties, and those already on the central coast were left where they were at the Salmon River settlement. By 1858, the population at Grand Ronde was about twelve hundred.

Removal to and Creation of the Western Oregon Indian Reservations

Reservation	Created	Indians Moved There	Comments / Tribes
Table Rock Reservation	November 15, 1854	Spring 1854	Rogue River, Chasta, Scotons, Grave Creeks
Headwaters of the Yamhill River Indian Reservation		November–December 1855	Originally called a "Temporary reservation" or "Grand Ronde Encampment" or "Yamhill River Reservation." Became Grand Ronde
Reservation			and located in the northern corner of the coast reserve.

Coast Reservation	November 9, 1855		For the Coast, Umpqua and Willamette Valley Indians, 2/3 of Rogue Rivers in May 1857
Grand Ronde Reservation (officially)	June 30, 1857	June 30, 1857	1/3 of Rogue Rivers, Confederated bands of the Willamette Valley, Umpquas and Calapooias of the Umpqua Valley, Mo-lal-la-las or Molel tribe, Cow Creek Band of Umpquas, stayed at Grand Ronde.
Coast Reservation (Siletz Reservation)	December 21, 1865		Reduction of the coast reserve.
Alsea and Siletz (Coast reservation)	March 3, 1875		Reduction of the Coast reserve, Alsea was a sub-agency.
Salmon River (Siletz)	Summer 1877	Summer 1877	Alsea sub-agency Closed, Settlement resettlement to Salmon River, associated with Siletz but people petitioned to be part of Grand Ronde.[1]

[1] *Annual Report of the Commissioner of Indian Affairs to the Secretary of the Interior for the Year 1877, Washington GPO 1877, pp 169–170. Southern Oregon Digital Archives.*

Life on the Reservation

The gathered Oregon tribes represented different cultures and different languages yet when the cavalry made its round up in 1855 through northern Nevada, northern California, and southern Oregon gathering all Indians they encountered, they did not take these cultural and political differences into consideration. Some of the tribes were traditionally warring tribes who had chosen not to live near each other. They spoke different languages and had different forms of leadership. Only the trade that many brought with them, Chinuk Wawa, gave the people a common form of communication.

Early life on the reservation was extremely hard. After surviving the forced relocation to the sixty-nine-acre reservation in Grand

Ronde, Indian people were forced to blend with other tribes with whom they may not have been friendly or familiar.

While the backgrounds of the different tribes and bands brought together at Grand Ronde were extremely varied, they did have some commonalities. For some tribes, the largest sociopolitical unit everywhere was a village, consisting of one or more households, each holding extended families related through males. For others, there were spiritual and economic regional associations that were quite extensive. An example of this is the political acumen of the Chinook leader Concomly, who strategized to marry wives from several different tribes, to solidify his political and economic relations over a vast region surrounding the Columbia River. Chief Concomly also married his many daughters to several tribal leaders as well as to leaders within the Hudson's Bay Company and Northwest Fur Trading Company to continue solidifying his position on the Columbia. For smaller tribes, the wealthiest household was likely to be looked to as the village leader. Family groups left these permanent villages during the season changes to collect resources in other places in a regular annual cycle. This type of seasonal resource collection is called a "seasonal round" and was practiced throughout the region. This was an activity that the Indians practiced for more than ten thousand years. (s 308–309.)

The early reservation was located among numerous forts; Fort Yamhill and Fort Hoskins especially were established to control access to the reservations. Indian people could not leave the designated area without traveling papers and white people could not enter the reservation. This was essential because the settlers continued to attack Indians even when removed and living peacefully in a remote reservation. Once the forts were no longer needed as military posts, they became what today are referred to as blockhouses. They were basically jails. Indian people were taken there if, for example, they tried to escape the reservation's boundaries. There they might be beaten and could be hung or shot for their transgressions. A century ago, the citizens of Dayton, Oregon, loaded the Grand Ronde blockhouse onto a wagon and moved it to their city park where it can still be seen today.

This policy loosened significantly as time went on, and many Indian families would leave the reservation to work in the agricultural fields of the Willamette Valley or in logging. Since there was little of no work at the reservation, and Indians were paid one half of the salary of whites, this was a necessary annual activity that constituted a continuation of seasonal gathering, and made the Indians the first migrant farm workers in the Pacific Northwest.

Throughout the latter half of the nineteenth century, reservation agents found it difficult to keep track of the Indians under their supervision because groups were relocated and people moved off and on the reservation—despite potentially severe penalties—to work for whites, acquire traditional foods, or visit relatives temporarily or sometimes permanently. As the reservation proved to not provide the services promised during treaty negotiations, some people also returned to their traditional homelands to live. At first fluctuations were especially large as groups were added or transferred to other reservations like Warm Springs, Siletz, Klamath, or Yakama. Later on, in the 1870s, reductions in the lands of the Coast Reservation uprooted many more, with some Indians from the coast and the Alsea agency moving to Grand Ronde, and others trying to homestead among the whites. Some joined small groups that had escaped or managed to avoid being swept off to the reservations; such groups were found even in the growing cities and in rural areas of southwestern Oregon where they established their own landless tribal organizations.

Portland newspapers in the 1870s reported on disturbances caused by Indians. One such incident, in 1872, occurred in "the Indian quarters" in Oregon City, where Indians had lived for "many years past." As the agent at Grand Ronde complained in his 1887 report, "There are several hundred Indians that belong to this reservation that are scattered over the country, but I have not any authority to bring them back." The large drop in population reported that year was not due to illness—though outbreaks of disease did reduce the number of people from time to time—but to the agent's decision to remove from the rolls the names of many people who had left the reservation and not returned. This was a practice among Indian Agents who continued to omit Indians from the annual Bureau of Indian Affairs census throughout the early part of the twentieth century.

Life on the reservation was difficult, as people settled down among strangers while trying to learn new ways of life in an unfamiliar land with inadequate means to do so. Victoria Howard recounted what she had heard of the move and the first months on the reservation:

On the following day they [the whites] killed cattle, they killed hogs, they brought them to them [the Indians]. In the same way also sugar, grease, potatoes, wheat flour and all sorts of things they came and gave us. Some of the old people would not eat it. They just cried, and the days following they were still crying. … Some of them would not have as their food the meat of cattle, even worse was pig which they would not eat.

We stayed there [at Dayton] for quite a while. The houses were sail houses [tents] which they constructed for us. They took them farther, where we are living now [Grand Ronde] … The Upper Umpquas, the Shastas, the Rogue River Indians, the Kalapuyas, the Yonkallas, they brought all of them to this place here.

At first they gave us just sail houses. Speedily we lived in log houses there. They were full of people. … Others had no houses, but later on they built small houses. …

It was quite some time before they assigned land to us. They moved some of them [Shastas, Rogue Rivers, Upper Umpquas] across there [to New Grand Ronde]. … Then they constructed houses for us [Molalas, Chinooks, Kalapuyas, Klamaths] here on this side [Old Grand Ronde]. …

Now they brought soldiers, they took care of us. Wherever we went, they gave us a paper. They stood on each side of the road, they held guns. Some ran away, they went back to where their home village was. Such persons got no land.
(Melville Jacobs, *Clackamas Texts*)

Until the Indians began to farm productively, much of their food had to be supplied by the government, or they had to find their own in the traditional way as best they could on the unfamiliar reservation. The idea that hunters and gatherers could be quickly retrained to be farmers was nearly disastrous for many of the Indians brought to the Grand Ronde Reservation. According to federal representatives, only those with ratified treaties were eligible for government help and security, and many Indians on the reservation had no such protection or aid. Because of the unratified treaties, funds were never appropriated on a regular basis, so in lieu of the promised payments and annuities, Indians had to rely on special funds and yearly appeals. Indian children were sent to on and off reservation boarding schools for their American education. There, the children were fed as for a time some of the treaty provisions applied directly to education. Indian people were regularly given passes to leave the reservation to get food—by salmon fishing at Oregon City as they used to do or working for white farmers in the Willamette Valley, commonly in hops or beans. At the time the treaties were signed in 1854 and 1855, tribal leaders wanted to be able to hunt and fish in areas they were familiar with, areas where they knew they could acquire their traditional foods: deer, elk, salmon, roots, and berries. (The 1853 and 1855 treaties did not reserve hunting, fishing, and gathering rights as had the unratified treaties signed in 1851 by tribes and Indian Agent Anson Dart. (See Chapter 11, "Federal-Indian Relations.") The agents, as previously suggested, would allow off-reservation hunting, fishing, and gathering to supplement inadequate supplies.

The efforts of fishermen and hunters to learn to farm were hampered by disease and weather, land not suited for the crops chosen, bad decisions by agents, and inadequate tools and supplies. The Indians at Grand Ronde, however, were strongly motivated to learn as fast as they could.

The first teachers at Grand Ronde had to communicate with their students in Chinuk Wawa, also known as Chinook Jargon. Their efforts to discontinue what one called "that barbarous" tongue were reinforced in 1887 when the federal government decreed that English would be used exclusively. Now the Grand Ronde and other tribes have developed programs to teach Chinuk Wawa to their children and other tribal members who want to learn. Photo courtesy of Oregon Historical Society, #CN022603.

Becoming Grand Ronde Indians

How did it happen that by the first decade of the twentieth century, these people from all over western Oregon had become a community calling themselves "Grand Ronde Indians" rather than "Molalas," "Clackamas," or "Rogue Rivers"? This was a long-term process, which started when they were thrown together in one place under a military regime that at first enforced segregation from the surrounding society. The situation made it necessary for people to cooperate in solving common problems and helped to create an "us against them" mentality. Coercive government policies undermined key elements of native society and promoted, if not compelled, the wholesale adoption of European American dress, habits and attitudes, religion, and language.

Just before the reservation period, not only villages but also whole tribes had come to have chiefs who acted as their representatives in dealing with government officials and representatives of other tribal groups. Depopulation, followed by population consolidation and treaty-making, made "tribes" and their leaders into salient social units. Those government officials who were responsible for negotiating treaties often directed a group of Indians to select a chief to represent them by signing a treaty. If and when native leaders were available, they were likely to be the ones chosen. On the reservation, thirteen Grand Ronde tribal groups censused between 1877 and 1899 averaged only between 35 and 50 people each, with the largest having only about 105 members. Each group at first had its own location on the reservation, making it much like an aboriginal village. In these local groups, people lived together in households of ten to fifty, as in the pre-reservation extended households. The chiefs continued to represent these groups in dealing with reservation agents and other officials, but within twenty-five years, the native political systems, with headmen and followers, lost much of their earlier functions and significance.

In some ways, hop picking served the same function for reservation dwellers as traditional trade centers like Celilo had before white settlers arrived. Beginning in the late 1880s, Indians came to the Willamette Valley from all over Oregon to harvest hops and have an opportunity to visit with distant friends and relatives. This photograph was taken around the 1920s. Photo courtesy of Oregon Historical Society, #OrHi65090.

During the 1870s and early 1880s, the Grand Ronde Indian Legislature governed the internal affairs of the reservation, choosing chiefs, writing laws, setting up courts, and appointing police. During its first five years, this body was

John and Hattie Hudson and some of their children are ready to market the baskets made by Hattie and her mother, Martha Jane Sands. Baskets made by women provided welcome extra income for many families. Photo courtesy of Oregon Historical Society, #CN22570.

made up of nineteen representatives of thirteen tribes, but in 1878, tribal representation was replaced by a division of the reservation into three precincts, each with three representatives.

The federal policy of allotting land to individual family heads was intended to break down Indian patrilocal extended families and tribes and to destroy their traditional relation to the land. It did so by emphasizing nuclear families, instilling a European American sense of property, and creating self-sufficiency. This process began only fifteen years after the reservation was established and, indeed, caused residence patterns to become more like those of the whites.

As a result, group activities of all kinds, from native ceremonies to Indian gambling to hop-picking, became keys to uniting the reservation population. Especially important in creating a new identity, however, were the marriages between members of local groups that—before the reservation's creation—had been widely separated. The early tradition of "marrying out" now created ties that helped to make the reservation people into one network of kin. Today, the tribe refers to itself as a family of families.

Indian agents complained about the fragility of Indian marriages and the extension of adoption and other forms of social kinship beyond the bounds of consanguinity. Polygyny (the practice of taking more than one wife), which was strongly disapproved of, disappeared early on, but serial marriages and socially defined kin ties continued. However, as the extended families broke down, marriage became a matter of personal choice rather than the result of a contract between two families, as it had been before the reservation was established.

By the early twentieth century, people who remembered life before the reservation were dying off. With them died the tribal languages, which, together with attachment to local territories, had been the foundation for tribal identities. After the 1950s, what remained was Chinuk Wawa, "the Grand Ronde language," which had become necessary during the first years of the reservation for communication among people who did not share a common language.

Cultural Changes

According to European American views of social evolution prevailing in the nineteenth century, Indians were savages who had to be civilized before they could fit into the larger society. Accordingly, Indian agents set up schools. At Grand Ronde, the earliest schools reflected the geographical division on the reservation between Indians from southwest and northwest Oregon: one school was for Rogue Rivers and Umpquas, the other for Kalapuyas and Clackamas. After the conclusion of the Rogue River Indian wars, when many of the Rogue River people were moved to Siletz in 1857, the division of the school population was no longer maintained.

These early schools were not particularly successful: teachers changed frequently, students were often sick or absent, and many older people viewed the schools with suspicion. A common idea was that they were responsible for outbreaks of disease. In fact, one shaman proclaimed that illness came from the trumpet blown by the teacher at the opening of the school, an act that spread disease over the camp like a mist. The teacher reported, "I was not such a monster as to sound it again, so the Indians 'still live.'"

At first, teachers had to communicate with their students in Chinuk Wawa. English made some headway, but in 1864 the teacher reported difficulties in inducing children to speak it, and in 1866 the new teacher said that although the boys could understand English, "they will use that barbarous jargon, the Chenook." Prohibiting the use of native speech in schools became official government policy in 1887.

Government officials, who equated Christianity with civilization, regarded native religions as particularly pernicious, and everything possible was done to stamp them out. In an attempt to stem the tide of poorly trained, avaricious, and badly motivated agents, the reservations were, in effect, parceled out to the churches, with agents chosen by various religious denominations. In 1860, before the policy went into effect, Father Adrien Croquet, a Belgian Roman Catholic missionary, had arrived at Grand Ronde, where he remained for thirty-eight years, well loved by many Indians and respected by whites (except some Protestants).

The year Father Croquet arrived, he wrote the superintendent of Indian affairs for permission to bring nuns to operate a school at Grand Ronde. The boarding school there was under the auspices of the Catholic nuns for some thirty-five years.

Father Croquet also opened St. Michael's Church in 1862. Ten years later, 650 of the 870 Indians at Grand Ronde were at least nominally Catholic. Unlike many officials who spent time at Grand Ronde, Father Croquet had no interest in acquiring land or otherwise profiting materially from his position. His concern for the welfare of the Indians, if not for their beliefs, did a great deal to ease their conversion to Western society.

In spite of the priest's efforts, however, native religions persisted at Grand Ronde, though decreasingly so as the years went by. Especially popular were the Warm House Dance and a variant of the Ghost Dance. The Indian Shaker religion, a Christianized reworking of native elements, also gained adherents, as did several Protestant groups. Shamans, though strongly discouraged by officials, continued to practice to some extent until after the turn of the century, but yearly the agents reported that their influence was declining. Even today, however, a few old people can remember being warned as children to stay out of the way of one old woman who was reputed to be an "Indian doctor."

In addition to adopting white religions, the Indians were expected to learn European American occupations. Besides farming for themselves and for local whites, the men found an important source of income in logging. The women often made baskets for the white market in styles unique to each maker.

Each July the Grand Ronde host a Veterans' Powwow. In 2005, after the grand entry and the posting of the colors, 272 veterans introduced themselves and the military branch in which they served. At the event, nearly five hundred Medals of Valor were handed out to the veterans. Courtesy of Smoke Signals, *Confederated Tribes of Grand Ronde.*

Although baskets made at the Siletz Reservation were extremely similar, today the baskets are easily identified when discovered in local collections and museum inventories because of their trademark designs. Elders in the tribe are currently able to identify the designs and associate a name with each basket.

Hop picking also deserves mention, for it offered not only a source of income but also a time of celebration rivaled only by the Fourth of July fairs. From the 1880s well into the twentieth century, Indians came from all over Oregon to pick hops in the Willamette Valley. To them the games, dances, and opportunities to meet with distant friends and relatives were as important as the pay they earned.

The Grand Ronde Community also initiated its own cottage industry in the making of Blackberry Jam, called "Gay Moccasin". Blackberries were picked by the children who sold the berries to a group of women at the Grand Ronde Community Center. There the jam was cooked and canned, then sold locally, mainly to railroad workers. The Gay Moccasin jars had labels and the industry continued into the 1980's with gifts of "Moccasin" Jam to Oregon Lawmakers.

Today, tribal members gather annually at local powwows, which, although largely Plains Indian in tradition and history, have been adopted by Northwest tribes as a time of celebration and family reunion-style gatherings. People get together and share salmon, venison, roots, berries, and salads made up of local, traditional ingredients. In the custom of seasonal hop-picking gatherings, traditional stick games are now played in honor of those who gathered on the land more than a century ago and in honor of their descendents who remain on the land to this day.

Attempts to Dissolve the Reservation

Unfortunately, attempts to isolate Indians on the reservation were matched by attempts by the larger society to appropriate pieces of reservation land. No sooner had the Coast Reservation been created than whites discovered the value of Yaquina Bay and the coast and began trespassing on the reservation.

Stories of the huge deer and elk in the forests were legend, and elders still talk today about the bounty of fish in the pristine rivers that were part of the local lore and lure. In pre-treaty times, the pursuit of beaver, otter, and other animal pelts and furs had been rapacious, but limited to a small number of European and American hunters and entrepreneurs. By treaty times and the decades that immediately followed, the dominant culture's popular strategies for quick economic gain focused first on gold and then on timber, fish, and land speculation.

In 1865, a thirty-mile-wide strip of land running east from Yaquina Bay was taken from the Coast Reservation, and almost immediately plans were made to eliminate the Alsea agency and the entire southern part of the reservation. Meanwhile, fifteen miles of land north of the Grand Ronde agency were being made available for eventual white use by removing the Indians who lived there and taking them to the Yamhill River headwaters. Congress later removed the southern section from the reservation and opened the lands north of Grand Ronde to settlement. By 1875 Siletz and Grand Ronde lands consisted of 298,000 acres out of the original Coast Reservation of 1,440,800 acres.

The Dawes Severalty Act of 1887 gave each Indian head of household title to 160 acres of arable land, with additional grazing land. Single people and orphans received less. Allotments were to be accompanied by full citizenship and the dissolution of tribes, while programs in education, forestry, health, and employment were to be instituted to help Indians become good citizens.

Any "surplus" lands could be purchased by the government and transferred to the public domain. By 1904 more than thirty-three thousand acres had been allotted, and twenty-six thousand "surplus" acres of prime timberland had been turned over to the government. The land was sold to private interests for about one dollar an acre. Much of the land was sold to timber interests. Minor children were to receive per capita payments for this land, but no payments were ever made.

Although the allotment program did not work smoothly, more plans for "civilizing" Indians and improving their conditions continued to appear. In 1934 the Indian Reorganization Act created major changes by authorizing Indian tribes to adopt constitutional forms of government and form business councils and corporations upon a vote of tribal members. At Grand Ronde the election took place in 1936, with most voters favoring the act.

After World War II, Congress adopted yet another policy: terminate entirely those reservations whose tribes were considered, by Congress, capable of managing their own affairs and ready to assimilate into mainstream American culture. Actually, there are good reasons to believe that the stronger motive for termination was in fact another grab for Indian land, water rights, and, in Oregon, for Indian timber: At the time, Oregon was one of the nation's leading timber producers, and the head of the Department of the Interior (which carries out federal Indian policy) was former Oregon governor Douglas McKay. The tribes terminated in Oregon were those west of the Cascades with considerable timber holdings, among them the coastal tribes and the Klamath Tribes. In 1954, when Congress terminated all western Oregon tribes, no provision was made for the loss of hunting and fishing rights. At that time, 597 acres were left in the Grand Ronde Reservation, and just before termination, eight hundred allotments were still held in trust.

These youngsters are the Grand Ronde Head Start graduates of 2006. Courtesy of Smoke Signals, *Confederated Tribes of Grand Ronde.*

The reservations were closed in 1956, and a trustee was appointed to dispose of the remaining land, most of which was sold by 1961. Tribal members received only a pittance, and many discrepancies in the financial records resulted, mainly related to the charges against the tribal account. The federal government chose to charge the Indians for every blanket or resource they had been given over the past 100 years, even though such things were thought to be taken care of in the treaty provisions. The question of land ownership was never fully resolved, and the tangled mass of federal, state, and local government jurisdictions thoroughly confused the question of Indian rights and status. Grand Ronde people received letters stating that they had to accept the sale of their allotments or they had a choice to buy back their lands from the government. Through all these changes, some Grand Ronde Indians still had no ratified treaties and had never been reimbursed for lands taken from them.

The failure of the termination policy was all too clear. Those few tribal members who had supported it had not foreseen its devastating impact. Many people did not realize the extent of the change in their status, and many others did not realize termination was occurring. In the late 1850s, the BIA received more than two thousand letters from Indian people applying for membership in a western Oregon tribe, only to be told they had already been terminated. Not only was land ownership in question, but services were also cut off, allotments were taxed, local jobs were scarce, and some people were forced to sell out and move away. Essentially, treaties signed in the 1850s in exchange for traditional tribal lands were not honored. Many Grand Ronde Indians moved to Portland, Salem, and elsewhere in search of work, but more than three hundred people remained on the former reservation. Those who moved returned when possible to visit friends and relatives and to tend family graves.

Concurrently with termination, the United States government instituted a series of programs to provide training and jobs at urban locations throughout the country for tribal members living on reservations. In Grand Ronde, the main employment opportunities were timber-related occupations like logging or working in lumber mills. The job training required moving to wherever the training was located. Elders today feel that relocating their people by luring them with training and jobs was yet another attempt to break apart the tribal community. In Grand Ronde, the main employment opportunities were timber-related occupations like logging or working in lumber mills. Most tribal members, however, accepted the new employment opportunities and moved their families, as they were aware even then that timber was a resource that could not be farmed forever.

Largely because of the relocation policy, the Confederated Tribes of Grand Ronde have members located in forty-five states and six different countries today.

Restoration

In the 1960s and '70s, Indians across the country who had never given up their tribal attachments worked to restore the reservations and tribes as federally recognized sovereign nations in an attempt to mitigate the effects of termination. At Grand Ronde, a tool shed on the remaining 2.5 acres of the tribal cemetery became the tribal headquarters, and a newsletter was issued regularly. The Grand Ronde Tribal Council soon reorganized under a state corporation charter and began receiving some federal and private assistance. Not everyone favored restoration, but a resolution in support was eventually passed.

After years of hard work by many people, the Confederated Tribes of the Grand Ronde Community of Oregon was restored ion November 22, 1983. At that time, Grand Ronde members had incomes averaging about one-third those of other Oregonians, 68 percent earned annual incomes below the poverty level, and unemployment was three times the state average. Restoration meant that treaty obligations were once again acknowledged, making health, education, housing, and other benefits available. On March 14, 1988, after several years of negotiating with local, state, and federal organizations and individuals, a reservation of 9,811 acres on Bureau of Land Management timberland in Yamhill County was established by act of Congress. Though the new reservation was a small portion of the former one, income from the timber was intended to provide the people of Grand Ronde with a subsistence base. To allay the fears of neighbors and local timber companies, the Grand Ronde tribe also negotiated a plan for hunting and fishing rights with the Oregon Department of Fish and Wildlife, and agreed not to export timber or compete in the local timber market for twenty years. The tribe also agreed to set aside 30 percent of timber receipts for economic development and adopt a twenty-year plan of payments to Yamhill, Tillamook, and Polk counties for revenues lost from the BLM land restored as the reservation.

When asked about the tribe's restoration, signed into law by President Ronald Reagan in November 1983, current elders repeatedly explain that the most important thing to know about restoration is to never forget termination. Every program offered to its membership represents an effort by the tribe to be self-sufficient—an effort to never again be in the position that the tribe was in when termination took effect in 1954.

Today Grand Ronde is concentrating on improving and expanding services for nearly five thousand members. The tribal logo shows Spirit Mountain, a sacred landmark, with five eagle feathers denoting five of the main tribes that make up the present-day confederation, symbolizing the secure and functioning community now being restored by people who have a sense of their past and an eye seven generations into the future.

Social and Economic Welfare of Members

While the Grand Ronde tribe relies heavily on its successful Spirit Mountain Casino for economic well-being, the tribe is also diversifying its economic portfolio and laying the social and educational foundation for its members to contribute as skilled people in a diversity of fields from business to technical professions—both for themselves and for the benefit of the tribe.

The tribe has demonstrated its commitment to education with its Grand Ronde Tribal Education campus, which opened in 2002 with more than thirty thousand square feet of space in four separate buildings, each with a distinct purpose—early childhood, youth, and adult education, and a gymnasium. The tribe not only helps with scholarships, internships, and mentoring programs for college students, but also with access to information and funds for vocational training, certification and licensing programs, testing fees, apprenticeships, and other services, including on-site classes. The tribe emphasizes educational opportunity for all members—from toddlers to elders. In 2003, a tribal library with many new books, other materials, and Internet access opened its doors in Grand Ronde.

As the twenty-first century began with a budget crisis in Oregon state education, the tribe stepped in with Spirit Mountain Community Fund grants in 2003, which amounted to $300,000 for the Willamina and Sheridan school districts. The tribe recognized not only that children who attend these schools are tribal members, but also that they are the children of casino and tribal government employees and the tribe's neighbors.

Services to tribal members go beyond education and include a Heath and Wellness Center completed in 1997, which provides medical, dental, and optometric services to its members. The tribe uses a self-funded health insurance plan, emphasizing prevention and reduction of illness through detection and education.

Elders and children receive additional benefits and are the focus of many tribal initiatives. Elders receive a small pension from the tribe and were the first to have rental housing built by the Tribal Housing Authority. Now the housing authority has an elder care facility under construction that is different than a typical nursing home: the new assisted-living facility is planned as a series of buildings, each with a large central room surrounded by six smaller rooms, five for individual elders and one for a caregiver. These buildings, a wellness center, and an elder activity facility located on 4.4 acres will be adjacent to the existing elder housing in Grand Ronde.

As of 2004, the Tribal Housing Authority, established in 1995 when the tribe owned no residential housing, has built seventy-four rental housing units for tribal elders and families, and thirty-six manufactured homes that are now occupied by individual homeowners. The housing authority also provides assistance with home repair, disability access, and down-payment grants. The Grand Ronde is the first tribe in the country to make project-sized use of federal Housing and Urban Development Section 184 loans, which enable first-time Indian homebuyers at Grand Ronde to purchase homes on thetribal lands.

The Social Services Department is responsible for the investigation and intake of child abuse and neglect, case management and foster care programs, emergency assistance, domestic violence, youth drug and alcohol prevention, and parenting education, among other programs.

Other member benefits include small per capita distributions from casino revenues and timber cuts, tax preparation assistance, and burial benefits.

In 1989, the tribal government established a Grand Ronde tribal court, which deals with child welfare and custody cases, marriages, divorces, enrollment cases, employment decisions, contracts involving the tribe, fish and wildlife licenses, and other mostly civil services. Today the tribe has a chief judge and, since 2001, a court of appeals with three judges. None of the carefully screened and chosen judges are Grand Ronde tribal members. The state and the tribe have joint criminal jurisdiction over the reservation. In 1995 the Grand Ronde entered into a policy agreement with the Polk County Sheriff's Office to provide law enforcement on both tribal and nontribal lands throughout the community of Grand Ronde. The community-based program, which has grown from one to six officers, is largely funded by the tribe's Spirit Mountain Community Fund.

Given the tribe's often-desperate historical circumstances since removal in the middle of the nineteenth century and then termination in the middle of the twentieth century, the tribe's needs are greater than the profits generated by its enterprises, including the casino. The tribe, like others in Oregon and around the nation, had to work creatively to combine federal, tribal, and nonprofit sources to meet the needs of the Grand Ronde's growing population. To serve members who live in Oregon's urban areas, the tribe partnered with the Administration for Native Americans in 2004 to open satellite offices in Portland and Eugene. In addition, the tribe has turned its attention to its ceded lands and is beginning to develop a continuous administrative presence from southern Washington and Cascade Locks on the Columbia River to the California Border, and from the Cascade Mountains to the Oregon Coast.

The tribe found multiple funding agencies and grants for the $3.2 million widening of Grand Ronde Road, for traffic management, pedestrian and bicycle safety, and a sewer main upgrade. The tribe anticipates that it will find the nearly $500,000 still needed before the project can begin.

Like other governments, the Grand Ronde tribal government and its three-hundred-person staff stretch to provide a full range of services, which include those already described as well as public works, legal services, information systems, planning and grants, public information, human resources, and others. The Natural Resource and Cultural Resource departments especially are the backbone of many of the developments of the tribe toward a restoration of economic, cultural, and spiritual significance.

The Grand Ronde Reservation sits in the Yamhill River watershed, which, as a tributary of the Willamette River, is part of the Columbia River Basin. However, the tribes' ceded lands, which encompass much of the area west of the Cascade Mountains, include lands in the coast range. While the Confederated Tribes of the Grand Ronde community has long-standing relationships with this larger territory, the scope and capacity of the Natural Resources Department is focused for now on the reservation and the adjacent areas in the Siuslaw National Forest and the lands of the Bureau of Land Management. The tribe has stewardship agreements with the two agencies, which enable the tribe to assess the health of streams and upland species, not on a jurisdictional and fragmented basis, but with a watershed approach. After several visits to the Willamette National Forest to view historic cultural sites, including the Obsidian Cliffs, a recent archaeological dig called the Yellowjacket cultural site, and a newly rediscovered camas meadow, the tribal council and forest officials are developing a relationship. The tribe would like to collaborate to build interpretive sites that integrate the story of the tribes' habitation on these lands.

Of the tribe's 12,281 acres, about 5,724 make up the timber base for the seventy-year harvest rotation under the Natural Resource Department's ten-year plan, which began in 2001. (The industry standard is a forty-year rotation.) While the state allows clear-cuts of a hundred and twenty acres, the tribe's cuts are limited to thirty to thirty-five acres and leave four to eight trees per acre for wildlife needs. Stream buffers will maintain trees up to three hundred feet along stream banks. In addition to stream buffers, the plan restricts harvesting in unstable areas, elk meadows, recreation areas, wetlands, and culturally significant areas. The department also works on fish and wildlife habitat improvement such as bridge and culvert replacements to improve access for migrating salmon, and it conducts surveys related to threatened and endangered species that inhabit the reservation, including the northern spotted owl, the marbled murrelet, native fish populations, and the Nelson's checkermallow (a plant species). The department assists the tribal council's fish and wildlife committee in managing reservation hunting seasons. Tribal members also continue to practice other subsistence traditions on their former homelands, including fishing and gathering berries and plants. Young people are educated about tribal land stewardship through the Grand Ronde's annual involvement, since 1991, with the Oregon Youth Conservation Corps.

Tribal Elder Pat Allen encounters Tomanowos, a fifteen-and-a-half-ton meteorite with spiritual significance to the Grand Ronde tribe. A tribal member delegation makes an annual journey to be reunited with Tomanowos, which is housed in the American Museum of Natural History in New York City. "Who knows how many generations before us have touched it in the same spots?" said Bobby Mercier, tribal member and the tribe's language specialist. The several-thousand-year-old Tomanowos once stood in the territory of the Clackamas people in what is now West Linn, Oregon. Courtesy of Smoke Signals, Confederated Tribes of Grand Ronde

Cultural Recovery

With the support of the Cultural Resource Department, cultural revival is part of the overall picture of Grand Ronde tribal renewal. The Cultural Resource Department's main duties are to manage the cultural collection, protect important cultural sites, teach Chinuk Wawa, and provide cultural education. Because of the number of tribes and bands in the confederation and the extensive nature of their original territories, there are thousands of sites, more than fifteen hundred of them already part of the department's database. The department anticipates that eventually the tribe will have a museum to serve as a comprehensive repository for all materials, including repatriated items that have historic importance to the Grand Ronde tribes.

A Chinuk Wawa dictionary and instructional methods have been and are continuing to be developed, and the language is currently being taught to young children and adults. The department recommends Chinuk Wawa classes for every grade through high school, although the tribal council has not made that commitment yet. The cost is estimated to be about $800,000 per year. For the first time, a tribal elder received high school credit for foreign language by working his senior year in the tribe's Chinuk Wawa immersion program, and two tribal members fulfilled their foreign language requirements for the bachelor's and master's degrees by studying and learning Chinuk Wawa.

A renewed interest in all traditional cultural activities including beading and in making baskets, drums, moccasins, canoes, plank houses, and adzes is occurring on the reservation, with members teaching each other informally and in classes sponsored by the Cultural Resource Department.

A traditional Indian naming ceremony was held at Grand Ronde in 2004 for the first time in memory. Wasco elders from the Warm Springs tribe helped the family conduct the name-giving ceremony.

The tribes recently contributed a Chinook-style canoe of Western red cedar to Fort Clatsop National Memorial in commemoration of Lewis and Clark's winter stay on the north Oregon coast. It took the carver, a member of the Cultural Resource Department staff, more than two years to find the appropriate tree and a year to make the canoe using hand tools. The oceangoing canoe will be used as well as displayed.

In 2003, tribal council members and cultural department staff visited the single most important collection of Grand Ronde culture—the Summers Collection—at the British Museum in London. The tribe is intent on having this collection returned. Episcopal priest Robert W. Summers purchased and documented hundreds of objects from Grand Ronde while in the McMinnville area from 1873 to 1881. Upon his death, the collection was sent by a friend to the British Museum. The three-hundred-piece collection has been in storage virtually since it arrived at the British Museum some 125 years ago; it is believed that the three pieces currently on display are the only ones ever to have been exhibited.

At the British Museum, the Grand Ronde delegation had to request to examine each piece individually. Museum staff brought the boxes out one at a time. In five days, cultural resource staff photographed and documented every piece. The delegation told museum officials, "We are here to repatriate our artifacts." The officials were sympathetic and did not deny that the collection belonged to the Grand Ronde people. But it will take an act of Parliament, apparently, to return the items in the museum, as British law considers everything in the museum to belong to the British people. While at the museum, the Grand Ronde team checked the museum's database and discovered other objects from Oregon.

The Clackamas tribal people, who are part of the Grand Ronde confederation, are also missing part of their patrimony. Tomanowos, the Willamette meteorite, fell to earth several thousand years ago and was deposited by the Missoula floods in the homeland of the Clackamas people and remained there until 1906, when it was acquired by the American Museum of Natural History in New York City. Weighing more than fifteen tons, Tomanowos is one of the largest sky people to come to our planet, and the largest meteorite ever discovered in the United States. Since 2001, Clackamas descendents and Grand Ronde representatives have made an annual trip to New York to be reunited with Tomanowos in a private blessing ceremony. The people of the sky live in their native legends, and, maybe one day, back in their homeland.

Community Relations

The Spirit Mountain Casino is the most profitable gaming enterprise in Oregon and the most generous. The Spirit Mountain Community Fund gives 6 percent of its profits to support education, arts and cultural organizations, health and environmental protection, historic preservation, problem gambling, and public safety. In recent years, as the economy has declined, the fund has awarded more of its grants to basic human services. Since 1997 it has given more than $26 million to more than 350 recipient organizations in the eleven-county area it serves. Funding decisions rest on some specific tribal values, including benevolence and compassion, the aspirations of youth, respecting and honoring elders, developing self-sufficiency, respecting and celebrating diversity, and sustaining and preserving the air, water, land, and their inhabitants.

The tribes and the community fund have also done well in promoting the tribe's public image with generous gifts to such worthy causes as Multnomah County Library's historic renovation, Portland Art Museum, the Anne Frank exhibit, A. C. Gilbert Discovery Village, Teatro Milagro/Miracle Theatre Group, Portland Taiko, Oregon Zoo, Oregon Coast Aquarium, Marion-Polk Food Share, Oregon Food Bank, Oregon Public Broadcasting, Salem Art Association, Artists Without Borders, Albina and Yamhill County Head Start programs, Oregon 4-H Foundation, Portland Classical Chinese Garden, Oregon Garden Foundation, Oregon Museum of Science and Industry, Henderson House Family Crisis Shelter, Safe and Sound, Sisters of the Road Café (serving the homeless), and many others. The Mid-Willamette Valley Council of Governments recognized the Spirit Mountain Community Fund for its giving, which began in 1997, with a 2004 Regional Cooperative Project Award.

No one claims that life today on what used to be the reservation is perfect. There are still families that have not found a way home into the new tribal housing project. Some families still live in poverty. Some choose not to work in the casino or the hotel or the new convenience store. Still, those jobs—more than fifteen hundred generated by these services—have become a major economic boon to the surrounding communities.

The tribes' current mission is to make sure that some aspects of the past do not repeat themselves by ensuring that the tribe can be self-sufficient no matter what happens to the country's government or economy. The tribe is successfully beginning to build endowments that will maintain health-care and education benefits for people in the future. Furthermore, the tribe is increasingly using the best tools and strategies of the business world while, at the same time, remaining grounded in its own culture and heritage.

Today a majority of the nearly five thousand members of the Grand Ronde tribes does not live in Oregon. Still, a core group of families remains, made up of the descendents of those who lived and died on the land that was once the Grand Ronde Indian Reservation. Despite forced relocation, termination, assimilation, racism, neglect, continual and wholly cruel misrepresentations, and the ravages of disease and social plagues unknown to native peoples before the dominant culture took hold, the tribal people have survived.

Current tribal elders tell their families about the days when they were young and their parents, especially their grandparents, would speak in Chinuk Wawa. They laughed and shared stories and gossiped in a language their grandchildren did not understand. The elders describe trying so hard to understand what was being said.

Today the elders take delight in knowing that when their grandchildren and great-grandchildren want to share something that they do not want their parents or grandparents to understand, they speak it in Chinuk Wawa. Indian children who live in the Grand Ronde area participate in a modern-day Chinuk language immersion class that teaches them the only surviving language of the peoples that make up the Confederated Tribes of Grand Ronde Community of Oregon.

A visit to the Grand Ronde community will make it clear that the people of the tribe feel they have the right to be who they are and continue to honor their heritage.

Chapter 7

The Klamath Tribes

Restoring Peoples, Restoring Ties to the Land

BY DOUGLAS DEUR

On several occasions, Klamath and Modoc elders recounted one of their most important oral traditions to researchers who passed through the tribe's homelands during the last century:

Long ago Gmukampc the Creator walked across the Earth. As he traveled, he made the lakes, the forests, the four-legged animals, the winged ones, and many other living things. In one place, in a cave, he made the first people, who emerged into the light and spread across the land. They settled in the richest places in the Klamath and Modoc world, places along the lakes, marshes, and rivers where they could find seasonal runs of salmon and mullet, and where waterfowl congregated in flocks so large that, once startled, they blackened the sky and drowned all other sound with their beating wings. There, lining the marshy lakeshores, they found tules to make baskets, mats, and many other items; they found wocas—the yellow pond lily—with its small and tasty seeds. The mountains encircling this watery world provided deer and berries as well as places of tremendous spiritual power.

During this time, some of the people lived and fished near Chiloquin where the river branches into two rivers. Standing atop a series of stone dams that routed the migrating salmon into narrow channels or chutes, men from the village there netted and speared the passing salmon each year. Their neighbors also harvested the salmon at fishing stations up- and downstream of the village. Over the years, the people at the forks began to forget the Creator's teachings; they became greedy. Building their dams higher and higher, they caught every fish traveling up the river. Fish no longer traveled to the villages and river reaches upstream—the fish that had spawned in

This page and opposite: Klamath life traditionally centered on the importance of families and elders as teachers and transmitters of culture. Federal educational programs that removed children from their homes disrupted this pattern. Photo courtesy of Oregon Historical Society, #OrHi23618 and the Smithsonian Institution, respectively.

these reaches died out, and the people of the upstream villages began to starve. Gmukampc, the Creator, saw this and called the animals into action. He sent loon under the water to poke holes in the dam, causing the water to rush through and topple the rock structures. As the people wailed in protest, their vast piles of fish were turned to stone. Then, aiming his wrath at the people of the village, the Creator turned to stone all the fishermen and all the people processing fish along the riverbanks.

While the Klamath people later reoccupied this fishing station—one of their most important and one they would depend on for sustenance over countless generations—these rocks always loomed large along the banks of this reach of the river, potent reminders of what had happened there. The moral and ethical teachings of the Creator, the rules about how to live in this world, could not easily be forgotten. Despite the railways, highways, and fences that crisscross the landscape today, many of these rocks still stand, reminding people how they should treat the Creator's works and how they should treat one another.

The landscape of the Klamath, Modoc, and Yahooskin world abounds with such places. There is Crater Lake, which erupted more than seven thousand years ago—an event that Klamath and Modoc oral traditions attribute to cosmological crises and describe with striking geological accuracy. There is Glass Mountain with its vast obsidian flows, a gift from the Creator to the people, who fashioned this stone into arrowheads and blades. Hundreds, perhaps thousands, of such places serve as vital landmarks within Klamath, Modoc, and Yahooskin oral traditions and, as such, are sources of guidance to people who have sought to navigate moral and ethical dilemmas, large and small. These places, each anchoring tribal oral traditions to the landscape, together constituted the guideposts of a ritual geography around which the three tribal peoples structured many other place-based ceremonial traditions. As many early anthropologists failed to appreciate, these cultural practices—even their most ritualized dimensions—are intimately and intricately tied to the land.

Today the Klamath Tribes consist of individuals of Klamath, Modoc, and Yahooskin (Northern Paiute or Shoshone) ancestry. These three tribal populations became politically integrated under an 1864 treaty that designated them as constituent members of the "Klamath Tribes." Prior to this time, the numerically superior Klamath and Modoc were closely related tribal populations, speaking very similar languages and together occupying the Upper Klamath basin. The Yahooskin are relative newcomers to the Klamath basin but have become so intermarried into the Klamath and Modoc population that today they are scarcely distinguishable as a group among younger tribal members. While discussions of pre-European practices in this chapter accentuate the Klamath and Modoc experience, much of what is said here applies to the Yahooskin community as well.

Even conservative scientific estimates suggest that the ancestors of the Klamath and Modoc have dwelt in their territories for much of the Holocene epoch. No part of the land was unknown, no part of the land unused. Their rich territories consisted of high-altitude deserts, densely forested mountains, fish-bearing rivers and streams, and the vast lakes and marshes that served as the centers of tribal settlement and subsistence. Year after year, the seasonal patterns of resource use followed similar paths. In spring, as the snow receded from the land, the Klamath and Modoc emerged from their winter villages to fish for mullet and salmon in runs that lasted for up to two months. As these fish runs tapered off in the late spring and early summer, women fanned out to root-digging grounds to gather ipos (*Carum oregonum*), desert parsley (*Lomatium canbyi*), camas (*Camassia quamash*), and many other edible and medicinal plants. Birds' eggs were also collected along the marshes.

July and August witnessed the harvest of wocas (*Nuphar polysepalum*). The ripe seedpods were gathered by families in canoes; on the shore, the seeds were parched, hulled, winnowed, and stored for later use. For Klamath and Modoc men, late summer was a time of mountain hunting for deer, elk, antelope, and bighorn sheep, while the women picked berries at vast berrying grounds containing huckleberries (especially *Vaccinium membranaceum*), wild plum and chokecherries (*Prunus* spp.), gooseberries (*Ribes* spp.), and numerous others. As families descended from the mountains, they set fires to clear away the competing brush, facilitating the regrowth of dense berry patches and the lush regrowth of meadows that would draw game animals in the year ahead.

The fall was a time to inventory one's provisions and remedy any deficiencies with supplementary hunting and fall salmon harvests. By October the Klamath and Modoc regrouped in their large winter villages, caching away food for wintertime and engaging in feasts, group rituals, and other large social gatherings. As the snows piled up during the winter, the Klamath and Modoc lived off stored provisions and retold stories of the many beings who had walked this land before, including Gmukampc, his spirit helpers, and the ancestors. Ice fishing supplemented stored foods, as did deer and antelope hunts carried out by men on snowshoes.

Lee Snipes, also known as Captain Sky, in 1920. Snipes is widely described as one of the last traditional Klamath shamans and the last spiritual leader to perform the First Chwaum Ceremony until the revival of this practice in the late-twentieth century. Photo courtesy of Oregon Historical Society, #OrHi014710.

All of the plants and animals the Klamath and Modoc depended on were recognized as living beings, the Creator's handiwork, and were typically said to possess a spirit. From the tribes' perspective, the consumption of these sentient and spirited beings created cosmological tensions and enduring debts. Just as with one's human neighbors, such as those living upstream of the stone dam at Chiloquin Forks, relationships with these plant and animal communities called for ethical and reciprocal relations. Ceremonial intervention that honored these species and their creator was viewed as a necessity if the staple food plants and animals were to return each year. Major resource harvests were initiated by first food ceremonies, including the First Mullet Ceremony, the First Wocas Ceremony, and the First Huckleberry Ceremony, each carried out annually at specific resource procurement sites throughout the tribes' territories. Such ceremonies acknowledged the enduring relationships between particular human communities and particular plant and animal communities over successive generations. Year after year, the plants and animals provided sustenance to humans, while the humans intervened both mechanically (for example, through the use of fire) and ritually to ensure the health and fecundity of their principal food species. These events consecrated and

solemnified the resource harvest. Resource harvest sites themselves
became sacred places.

This delicate set of relationships between the land, the plant
and animal communities, and the peoples of the Klamath basin, was
to be severely tested by the arrival of European American explorers
and settlers. Beginning in the mid-nineteenth century, Klamath and
Modoc control over their lands was contested by the expanding influence of non-Indian settlers and economic interests. The Applegate
Emigrant Trail passed through Modoc country, engendering frequent conflicts between settlers and tribal members, while horses,
guns, and other introduced goods upset traditional balances of power within and between the tribes of the area. Soon a smattering of
white settlements began to displace tribal members from certain key
ceremonial and subsistence sites. Displaced tribal members were increasingly compelled to become laborers, operating on the fringes of
the frontier economy, particularly in the agricultural operations of
the Willamette Valley. A handful of settlers agitated for Indian removal, which increasingly became part of the platform of development interests. These developers perceived the large Indian population and their competing claims on the lands and resources of the
Klamath basin as the primary obstacles to the emergence of an inland agricultural empire.

Seeking to define and defend the boundaries of their territory,
the Klamath and Modoc willingly participated in treaty negotiations with U.S. government representatives in 1864. During treaty
negotiations at Council Grove, near Fort Klamath, the Klamath requested much of their traditional territory, but were rebuffed by U.S.
treaty negotiators. The Klamath, in response, agreed to settle for a

reservation boundary encircling the heart of their territory in the northern Klamath basin and following a line defined by some of their most sacred peaks; they retained their rights to hunt, fish, and conduct other subsistence activities within their larger, original territorial boundaries. The Modocs, most believing that an earlier unratified treaty securing their claims to the southern Klamath basin was in effect, expressed few objections to these proceedings. Indeed, several Modoc headmen, along with representatives of the Yahooskins from the east, were compelled to sign the treaty as part of the Klamath Tribes, supporting the concept of a Klamath reservation centered on Klamath, and not Modoc or Paiute, lands.

This treaty, however, had a number of unintended consequences. The Treaty of 1864 provided non-Indian agricultural promoters with the legal leverage required to effectively remove the Indian presence, with its diffuse constellation of settlements, sacred places, and subsistence sites, from a sizeable and cultivable portion of the Klamath basin. Forcible Modoc removal to the Klamath reservation proceeded apace, the Modocs resisting removal from their homeland at every turn. Interethnic skirmishes soon escalated to organized episodes of retaliatory violence, resulting in the Modoc War of 1872–73. The final episode of this war represented a protracted standoff in the Lava Beds on the shores of Tule Lake, long a center of Modoc settlement, subsistence, and ceremonial activity. Modoc warriors held off the U.S. military, with its far superior numbers and armaments, as women, children, and the elderly were evacuated in the dark of night to find refuge with other tribes. With the aid of Indian scouts from distant tribes, the U.S. military ultimately routed the Modoc from the Lava Beds. Noncombatant Modocs were relegated to the Klamath reservation. Combatant leaders were hanged and beheaded by U.S. troops. Their supporters were shipped in railcars to Indian Territory in Oklahoma. The Modoc had been effectively extirpated from the Modoc homeland.

In the remaining decades of the nineteenth century, life on the Klamath reservation was severely controlled. In part due to the circumstances of the Modoc War, tribal members were not allowed to leave the reservation without a signed pass from the Indian agent. Visits to ceremonial and religious sites were all but forbidden. As was true among tribes throughout the country, federal policy encouraged the adoption of agricultural and religious practices that were not contingent upon the use of a sprawling hinterland but were geographically confined, eliminating competing claims to the land and its resources. Indian agents for the Klamath Tribes were instructed to pursue an accelerated program of cultural assimilation to bring about the acculturation of the Klamath and Modoc in a single generation. Indian agents sought to foster largely unprecedented concepts of private land ownership among tribal members as a prelude to subdivision, allotment, and the ultimate elimination of the Klamath reservation, as the history from the 1870s onward indicates.

Over the next several decades, the Klamath reservation was pared down through a number of resurveys and land deals that were brokered by the Bureau of Indian Affairs (BIA), often without the support or involvement of the tribes. The non-Indian logging and grazing of reservation land administered by the BIA brought waves of new settlement and transformed the economy and ecology of the reservation. A modest number of tribal members were able to maintain use of important fishery sites off the reservation, such as those at Link River and Olene Gap, but soon the emergence of non-Indian commercial fishing and generally hostile community sentiments resulted in the forcible removal of these seasonal fishing communities. In many portions of their traditional territory, the Klamath and Modoc became a minority on their own lands. Residential schools prohibited the transfer of knowledge between generations and the retention of local knowledge of the land, seasons, plants, or animals.

The lands and waters of the Klamath basin came under similar transformative pressures. In 1910 the California and Oregon Power Company built a large dam on the Klamath Canyon, where the Klamath River exited the territories of the Klamath and Modoc. The salmon could no longer ascend into the Upper Klamath basin. The events at Chiloquin Forks, as described in tribal oral tradition, had repeated themselves, yet this time the entire tribe was situated upstream. As part of the Klamath irrigation project, significant portions of the lakes and marshes in the Klamath and Modoc territories, including most of Lower Klamath Lake and much of Tule Lake, were drained and diked. Entire streams were diverted into irrigation ditches. Biologically rich marshes that fed human communities for millennia were drained to create marginally productive agricultural land. (Contemporary elders, identifying traditional salmon fishing sites, will sometimes point out such sites in the featureless dry expanse of a farmer's field.) Expanses of wocas and tules gave way to geometric plantings of potatoes and alfalfa. Even the lands of the Klamath National Wildlife Refuge were (and still are) used for intensive agriculture. The environmental transformations were so dramatic that Rachel Carson, who worked for a time in the Klamath National Wildlife Refuge, brought them to international attention in her classic work, *Silent Spring*.

In the 1950s, as part of a policy to integrate Indians into the

American mainstream, the Klamath Tribes were targeted for federal termination. In 1954, under severe pressures from the federal government and following contentious debate and divisions within the tribes, the Klamath Tribes ceased to exist. The former reservation was largely placed under the control of the Winema National Forest, while the reservation's prime agricultural lands were allotted or sold. While tribal members were nominally compensated for these lands, compensatory payments were not made for all lands. Payments that were made were not assessed at fair market values or distributed evenly among tribal members, creating legal headaches that are still being sorted out today. Perhaps for the first time in their history, a large number of tribal members participated in an exodus out of their homelands, seeking employment in the Rogue Valley, Willamette Valley, and Portland metropolitan area. The former reservation was logged, and subsistence resources, most critically fish and deer, declined significantly on these lands. Cultural sites fell out of tribal control; many of the most important ceremonial sites fell into the private hands of non-Indians. Even the rocks at Chiloquin Forks were placed off-limits and beyond tribal control.

Despite a century of efforts to assimilate the Klamath Tribes, however, traditional subsistence and ceremonial activities persisted, often quietly and clandestinely, throughout the former territories of the Klamath, Modoc, and Yahooskin peoples. Moreover, from almost immediately after termination, some tribal members participated in a solemn campaign to restore their tribal identity. This campaign took over three decades, but ultimately proved successful. The Klamath Tribes regained federal recognition in 1986. For the first time in a generation, the Klamath Tribes had the opportunity

Klamath marshlands covered with wocas. Wocas gathering—an ancient activity—is still being practiced and celebrated ceremonially. Wocas, the seeds of the yellow pond lily found on the edges of marshes and lakes, were once a staple of the Klamath diet. Today they are gathered in small quantities but are a culturally important delicacy. Photo by Edward S. Curtis, courtesy of Library of Congress, Prints and Photographs Division, LC-USZ62-136573.

to participate in tribal government, establish health and housing programs for their members, and have a voice in the management of cultural and natural resources within their traditional territories. The tribes have not, however, regained their former reservation. Efforts to restore the reservation, or simply provide the tribes with a land base of any kind, continue to be one of the primary goals of tribal government since restoration.

Buttons Shadley in traditional regalia with a ceremonial Eagle staff at the Klamath Tribes Veterans' Honoring and Flag Raising. Both traditional and modern ceremonies serve to mark the sacrifices of tribal veterans, a practice with roots in the Modoc War and the pre-contact battles that preceded it. Photo by Taylor David, courtesy of Klamath Tribes News Department.

Certainly, historical efforts to undermine the culture of the Klamath, Modoc, and Yahooskin peoples involved bold efforts to extinguish both tribal ties to and controls over the lands and resources of their traditional territories. Today an inverse process is occurring, as the perpetuation and restoration of the tribes' cultural practices are accompanied by growing Klamath, Modoc, and Yahooskin efforts to restore and reassert their ties to the land. As many imposed limitations on tribal cultural expression have evaporated, the Klamath Tribes are now experiencing a renaissance of traditional cultural knowledge and practices that are tied to specific places. This return to the land and the cultural practices associated with the land is being carried out by individuals, entire families, and increasingly by informal or formal tribal organizations.

Tribal members continue a number of traditional subsistence activities, and many tribal members seek to maintain or reestablish respectful relationships with the land and its inhabitants through ritual means. Hunting is still an important rite of passage for young men. Hunting rituals, intended to show respect for deer or other game species, are observed by many tribal members, particularly the tribal elders, who demonstrate a knowledge of and concern for the health and size of individual herds that would rival that of any professional wildlife manager. Wocas is still gathered in modest quantities, and a growing number of young people now learn methods of wocas procurement and preparation.

The First Mullet Ceremony continues to play an important role within the lives of many tribal members. Carried out annually at a fishing site not far from the Chiloquin Forks, this ceremony provides a venue for cultural continuity and transmission as well as a means for tribal members to provide remedial intervention in an ecological crisis over which they can exert only limited political control. Likewise, a small number of tribal members continue to ritually honor the salmon and seek to foster the return of salmon through both legal and ceremonial means. Despite roughly ninety years without salmon in the traditional territories of the Klamath and Modoc, salmon fishing sites still retain a high degree of cultural and historical significance to some tribal members, and some sites are still visited today for specific ceremonial purposes, especially to pray for the salmon to return. As ritual displays of respect traditionally ensured the annual return of the salmon and mullet, the disappearance of these fish is interpreted by many tribal members as a result of the disrespect shown to these fish by the non-Indians who have reshaped the Klamath and Modoc world. The loss of these fish, as well as the myriad organisms on which the Klamath, Modoc, and Yahooskin people depended, is widely perceived to be the result of forces that are as much cosmological as they are biological.

A growing number of large, organized gatherings of tribal members take place at sites of enduring cultural significance, in addition to the First Mullet Ceremony mentioned above. Such gatherings now bring together Klamath tribal members at places that continue to be of personal and group importance today, including the Lava Beds and other specific traditional ceremonial sites, berry-picking grounds, root-digging grounds, and historical hunting and fishing camps. These are typically annual gatherings, often timed to coincide with the traditional seasonal activities associated with each place. Centering on social and ceremonial activities, these gatherings sometimes last for days at a time. Importantly, children are part of these gatherings where they have an opportunity to learn about traditional cultural activities on the land. Traditional plant and ani-

Members of the Klamath Tribes protesting the continued loss of salmon on the Klamath River, alongside Shasta, Karok, Hoopa, and Yurok tribal members, at the California state capitol in Sacramento. The construction of dams on the middle Klamath, beginning in 1910, blocked all salmon passage into the upper Klamath Basin while degrading salmon stocks downriver. In recent years, following a dramatic salmon die-off and chronically small salmon runs, tribes from the full length of the Klamath River have been united in their call for the removal of these dams and judicious reductions of water diversions from the river for agricultural, residential, and industrial uses. Photo by Taylor David, courtesy of Klamath Tribes News Department.

mal foods are a cornerstone of some of these events, and young tribal members receive training in traditional methods of food procurement and preparation as well as some of the ceremonial traditions that serve to honor these plant and animal species.

Since tribal restoration, the Klamath Culture and Heritage Department has played an important role in reconnecting with the land. Through the work of this department, the children of the Klamath Tribes may now participate in "Culture Camp." For two weeks each summer, these children are given the opportunity to learn in a group setting about the language, history, and traditional practices of their ancestors. In this venue, children visit many places of enduring importance to the tribes' culture. Children learn about the uses of plants and visit wocas-gathering sites. They are also given the opportunity to work obsidian from Glass Mountain and fashion tules from the shores of Upper Klamath Lake into floating duck decoys. Throughout the year, a skilled team of language specialists has worked with the remaining fluent speakers of Klamath and Modoc to record the language and create teaching materials for the next generation of tribal members. Language program staff has often taken elders on field trips to places of traditional significance to record site-specific oral history, place-names, and a lexicon that is intimately tied to the natural world.

On public lands in particular, tribal members have been able to maintain or regain a degree of influence over land management decisions. The Klamath tribal efforts to regain a say in the management of their former lands, particularly sites of cultural significance, have been aided by a number of federal laws developed in recent decades, including but not limited to the American Indian Religious Freedom Act, the National Historic Preservation Act, the National Environmental Policy Act, the Native American Graves Protection and Repatriation Act, as well as Executive Orders 13007 (Indian Sacred Sites) and 12898 (Environmental Justice). These laws have provided the impetus for the documentation of traditional cultural activities and have provided the Klamath Tribes with many opportunities to support research on places of enduring cultural significance. National Park Service Historic Preservation grants to tribes have supported documentation efforts and the identification of traditional cultural properties in many locations within the traditional territories of the Klamath, Modoc, and Yahooskin peoples.

Certainly, there are many tremendous challenges ahead. The entire Klamath basin has become a center of environmental controversy, overtaxed by antiquated irrigation systems, plagued by droughts, and manipulated by groups bearing larger political agendas on all sides of the debate. Many of the fish on which the Klamath, Modoc, and Yahooskin people depended are now gone or are still endangered. Of the several distinct mullet species once recognized by tribal elders, only a few species remain, and these populations are imperiled. Even below the Klamath River dams, problems of water quality and quantity have killed off salmon in awesome numbers. Many culturally important places have been eliminated from the landscape or dramatically transformed by the events of the last century, and ongoing development within the Klamath basin continues to consume places of cultural significance. In the view of most tribal members, today's widely publicized conflicts over land, water, fish, and wildlife in the Klamath basin are just the most recent expression of a century-and-a-half-long struggle. For better or worse, they recognize that people are still making history in the Klamath basin.

Today is, however, a time of great optimism. The restoration of the historic Klamath reservation, in part or in whole, now seems as likely as ever. All levels of the Klamath tribal government now participate in focused planning efforts, seeking to acquire these lands and prepare for their sensitive management in the event that the reservation is restored. Natural resource and cultural resource specialists within the tribe, recognizing and respecting the fundamental interrelationships of cultural activities, plants, animals, and the land, increasingly seek ways to integrate their efforts. The restoration of fish populations and habitats, marshes of culturally preferred plant and animal species, and healthy forests in the Klamath basin is a high priority for the tribe. The Klamath Tribes seek to learn from the history of the Klamath basin and the history of Indian tribes throughout the West. The Klamath Tribes seek to establish management plans and protocols that will allow the Klamath, Modoc, and Yahooskin people to survive and to thrive alongside the plant and animal communities on which they have long depended. In time, with diligence and patience, the Klamath Tribes may once again be able to live, as their ancestors did, in respectful proximity to the land.

Siletz Or Oct 24

For Your Indian Corner

Chapter 8

The Confederated Tribes of Siletz Indians

Diverse Peoples Brought Together on the Siletz Reservation

BY ROBERT KENTTA

Prior to treaties being signed by leaders of the ancestral tribes of the Confederated Tribes of Siletz Indians and the tribes' removal to the Siletz Reservation beginning in 1856, these tribes and bands maintained approximately twenty million acres in combined aboriginal territories. These lands include all of Oregon west of the summit of the Cascades to the Upper Klamath, Shasta, and Smith rivers in northern California. Some Wasco- and Sahaptin-speaking Klickitat people, whose homelands are in south-central Washington, also came to live at Siletz. Each of the tribes removed to Siletz brought its own language, arts, and traditions. The Siletz tribes represent many separate and diverse language families: Salishan, Penutian, Hokan, Sahaptin, and Athabaskan. Traditional lifeways and subsistence practices varied significantly from the coast to the inland valleys and western Cascades and even from northwestern Oregon to southwestern Oregon.

Depending on the location of the tribe's territory, different primary foods were the focus of seasonal subsistence activities. In some places, wapato and camas were plentiful; in others, lamprey eels were abundant. Where annual crops were dependable, acorns were an important staple food source. All berries, including huckleberries, were collected in great volume. Ocean fishes, shellfish, and sea mammals were common meals along the coast. In most areas of the Siletz ancestral homelands, salmon, elk, and deer were also a large part of the diet. No matter where the people lived, they had a healthy and varied menu to choose from, including meats, fishes, nuts, berries, roots, bulbs, and other plant parts.

The land has always been the peoples' garden. For thousands of years, the beautiful bounty of nature was encouraged into peak production by practices such as the periodic burning of meadows and forest understory and traditional harvesting seasons and methods. The Siletz peoples' traditional beliefs revolve around appreciation for the Creator's many blessings. Ceremonies or ritual prayers for each food at the beginning of a new gathering season have always been central to ensuring the continuance of these good gifts.

By the late 1700s, large sailing ships were visiting our coast and trading for sea otter furs and other goods on a regular basis. Early visits brought devastating, catastrophic epidemics and eventually led to the social and economic ruin of our people. When Lewis and Clark visited in 1805–06, our people were still fairly strong in numbers along the lower Columbia River, yet even the expedition's diarists felt compelled to comment on the obvious recent declines in populations and the smallpox scars carried by survivors. Later, especially through the 1820s, '30s, and '40s, epidemics ravaged the tribes of the lower Columbia, the northern Oregon coast, and the Willamette Valley.

Shortly after Lewis and Clark's visit, land-based trade with American and British traders began at Astoria, Fort Vancouver, Fort Umpqua, and other places. Originally trading with our people for furs and other goods, the traders soon became trappers themselves as they got to know the lay of our lands and waters. The taking of tribal resources without permission or compensation was rightly considered to be theft of tribal property, and conflict was sometimes the result.

The British Hudson's Bay Company reacted violently to any local resistance to their intrusions, sometimes attacking and killing the innocent to send a clear message that resistance would be met with brute force and result in large numbers of dead.

The Northwest Ordinance of 1787 had promised good treat-

Overleaf: Five generations of a Siletz family, circa 1909. From the left: Mary Yanna, her daughter Molly Carmichael, baby Stanley Strong, his mother Mamie Strong, and her mother Mary Catfish (Mary C. being the daughter of Molly C.). Stanley was a member of the Siletz Tribal Council in the 1970s and '80s. This family represents Southwest Oregon Athapascan ancestry from Smith River, California to the Sixes River. Photo courtesy of Confederated Tribes of Siletz Indians.

ment of our people by the United States and its citizens under U.S. law, but Congress broke its own rules and policies of peaceful settlement when it passed the Oregon Donation Land Act in 1850. This, the most generous land-granting law ever enacted in the United States, followed the establishment of the Oregon Territory in 1848. The Oregon Donation Land Act promised married couples one square mile (640 acres) of our lands if they settled there as U.S. citizens. This act went into effect before our tribes had signed any land-ceding treaties relinquishing aboriginal title to lands for lawful settlement by U.S. citizens. Immediately, large blocks of our territory were fenced, plowed, and removed from our inventory of places where we harvested the necessities of life, conducted ceremonies, recreated, and lived. Claims were generally filed first on open prairies—lands our people maintained by the use of frequent fires for the production and harvest of camas, tarweed, acorns, and other essential foods. Within its five years of existence, the act resulted in donation land claims being filed on nearly 2.5 million acres of the most productive Indian lands in western Oregon.

George Harney (Takelma) and his first wife Klamath Maggie (Shasta) and their baby. This tintype photo was taken during a trip to Washington DC in the early 1870s. Superintendent of Indian Affairs for Oregon A.B. Meacham arranged for the delegation of Oregon tribal leaders to make the trip to express their peoples' needs to the President. Once in Washington, Meacham ran out of funds, and the Siletz agent had to wire money to various stops along the way for the Harneys to return to Siletz. Harney was the nephew of Tyee George, a famous Upper Rogue tribal leader during the Rogue River Wars. The Confederated Tribes of Siletz Indians made George Harney their first elected chief. Photo courtesy of Confederated Tribes of Siletz Indians.

While our people were being pushed aside by permanent settlers, gold was discovered in 1851–52 in our ancestral lands along the Rogue, Klamath, and Umpqua rivers, their tributaries, and the adjacent coast. Overnight, formerly isolated places became mining camps populated with drunken, greedy, lawless, and violent men. As conflicts arose or were anticipated (often over the abduction or abuse of Indian women by miners), the miners would create a state of emergency, meet to elect officers, and attack our villages, later submitting invoices to the government for their "work" fighting Indians.

In 1851 Anson Dart, U.S. Superintendent of Indian Affairs for Oregon, signed treaties with several western Oregon tribes in an attempt to gain title to tribal lands for the United States and provide for the protection of tribal peoples' rights and safety. His efforts failed, however, when territorial delegates Joseph Lane and Samuel Thurston successfully lobbied to prevent Senate consideration of the treaties. Instead of lawful and orderly settlement, our lands became occupied by people who were averse to our use of traditional resource areas and who saw us as dangerous obstacles to their efforts. Consequently, the crisis erupted in war. In 1853 Joel Palmer replaced Dart as superintendent. In August and early September of 1853, the Rogue Valley was consumed by open hostilities. Hundreds of our people were killed between 1851 and 1856, when formal hostilities ceased.

A cease-fire and a peace meeting were agreed to, and September 10, 1853, was set as the date for formal treaty negotiations. The

This photograph, circa 1900, shows a Siletz baby wrapped in a traditional cradle basket. Shell money (dentalia and shell disk) surrounds this baby, whose blanket is decorated with shells and beads and fringe that is wrapped with bear grass and maidenhair fern in a pattern. Photo courtesy of Confederated Tribes of Siletz Indians.

treaty discussions continued, despite miners' efforts to disrupt the treaty process by hunting down and murdering tribal family groups hiding in the hills. On that date, our tribal people of the Rogue Valley (Takelma, Shasta, and Applegate River people) confederated under the 1853 Rogue River (or Table Rock) Treaty and agreed to cede the Rogue Valley to the United States while reserving the right to a temporary reservation at Table Rock until a permanent reservation was selected by the president of the United States.

Several days later, our Takelma people living to the north on Cow Creek signed a similar treaty. These treaties were sent to Washington, DC, and were ratified by the Senate, becoming the first treaties signed by any tribe in Oregon Territory (present-day Oregon, Washington, Idaho, western Montana, and Wyoming) to be ratified and proclaimed law. These treaties would stand as the template for all other western Oregon treaties, which would be signed and ratified over the next several years, all of which promised a permanent reservation to be selected and established by action of the president or that of the superintendent of Indian affairs.

Conflict raged on in southern Oregon and along the Klamath River through the summer of 1856, but Palmer's plan for establishing a permanent reservation for all the western Oregon tribes had already been approved on November 9, 1855, by President Franklin Pierce. The 1855 Executive Order stated that the Siletz Reservation was being established for the Coast, Willamette, and Umpqua tribes. Three days after the presidential order was signed, it became federal policy to discontinue the Table Rock Temporary Reservation and remove the Rogue Valley tribes confederated there to the Siletz Reservation.

Removal to the reservation began in the winter months of early 1856. Because the Siletz Valley was isolated and no preparations had been made for it to serve as an Indian agency, a temporary camp on the south fork of the Yamhill River was selected and briefly considered as an addition to the Siletz Reservation. In May 1857, the majority of the Rogue Rivers (Takelma), all of the Shasta, and other associated tribes of the middle and upper Rogue country (Applegates, Galice Creeks, etc.) were brought to the Siletz Agency, including two-thirds of the Cow Creeks. In June 1857, the temporary camp, instead of being added to the Siletz Reservation, became established as the Grand Ronde Reservation.

The early days on the Siletz Reservation were very difficult. Supplies that had been promised under treaty agreement often failed to arrive. All able-bodied tribal people were forced to labor in agricultural fields that were frequently a complete failure; then they would have to scramble in order to catch enough fish or gather enough of the other traditional foods to get them through the winter. The absence of adequate food and shelter in the cold, damp climate weakened the health of the people, and many died from diseases in the first few years at Siletz.

Intertribal conflict also occurred among various tribes at Siletz over joint resource use and competition, and because of the general tension resulting from so many different tribes being uprooted from everything familiar and placed in close proximity to each other. Another contributing factor was the stress and suffering resulting from nonfulfillment of treaty promises and unequal treatment of the tribes living side by side at Siletz. Eventually, these sorts of conflicts eased.

In 1865, just as conditions were improving on the Siletz Reservation, Oregon representatives in Congress talked the Secretary of the Interior and President Andrew Johnson into an executive order that, in violation of the ratified treaties, opened two hundred thousand acres in and around Yaquina Bay to settlement by whites. The order severed the Siletz Reservation into two distinct parcels: the Siletz Agency (north of the Yaquina tract) and the Alsea (or Yachats) Sub-Agency to the south. The order was signed in late December, and speculators immediately entered the Yaquina tract and evicted tribal families from the homes and farms they had previ-

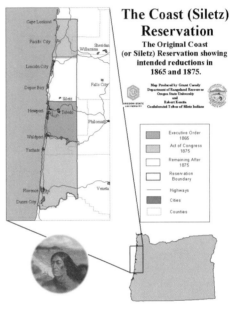

A map showing the original Coast (Siletz) Reservation as intended in 1865 and 1875. Courtesy of Confederated Tribes of Siletz Indians.

This photograph of the Siletz Agency from about 1910 shows, from the left, the Siletz Agency Hospital, BIA Agent's Office, the boarding school and dormitories (with a row of shops and offices extending behind the agent's office). The field area in the foreground was a small portion of the school and the agency farm. After the boarding school was closed, the BIA sold the school area and agency farm as government lots, which were eventually incorporated as the town of Siletz. Photo courtesy of Confederated Tribes of Siletz Indians.

ously been encouraged to make there.

In 1875, Oregon Senator John Mitchell succeeded in getting legislation passed under which another seven hundred thousand acres of the Siletz Reservation opened to white settlement, including the entire Alsea Sub-Agency and the land from Cascade Head to Cape Lookout. The Congressional act (which, ironically, was a rider on the annual appropriations bill meant to fulfill U.S. treaty obligations) was carried into effect despite the fact that it violated both the U.S. treaty obligations to maintain those areas of the reservation for the use of the tribes confederated on the Siletz Reservation and a provision within the act requiring tribal consent for such an alteration of the reservation. After the 1875 act, the Siletz Reservation was recognized as consisting of the remaining 225,000 acres of the original Siletz Reservation.

Further reductions to the Siletz Reservation continued through the era of the General Allotment Act. The Allotment Act (also known as the Dawes Act), passed in 1887, took effect at Siletz in 1892. Many tribal families had been driven to living and working in the white settlements outside of the existing reservation because of the loss of reservation land and its deplorable conditions. Allotments were issued to the 551 tribal members present. Those who did not return in time were denied allotments. Some were forced to homestead land or take off-reservation allotments. The Indian agent told Siletz children who were born off-reservation that they did not have rights to allotments. Before confirmation of the Siletz allotments, the Secretary of the Interior declared the unallotted lands surplus and forced the Siletz people to give up 192,000 acres for 74¢ an acre. Promises of additional allotments to future generations and other assurances that were accepted in good faith went unfulfilled.

At first, the Siletz people saw allotment and paper titles to lands as the only way to escape the constant threat of being entirely dispossessed of their lands. The General Allotment Act, however, turned out to be one of the most devastating policies directed at Indian people. Additional related laws and policies, such as the Siletz Indian Inherited Lands Act passed by Congress in 1901, encouraged the sale of allotment lands by the Siletz Agency. By 1912, more than half of the Siletz Allotments were owned by non-Indians. A steady decline in tribal land and resource ownership spurred the BIA to discontinue providing many of the programs and services available on most reservations.

In the early 1900s, the Grand Ronde Agency was closed and its affairs administered by the Siletz agent. The Siletz Agency, which then included Grand Ronde, was eventually moved in the mid-1920s and administered out of an office at Chemawa Indian School near Salem.

While the Indian Reorganization Act of 1934 did end the allotment of Indian lands, it was also meant to usher in a period of recognition of and respect for tribal sovereignty. The Siletz people were afraid of the act, partly because an early draft called not only for the abolishment of the allotment system, but also the transfer of previously made allotments back to tribal control. It was difficult to trust the legislation's positive intentions after so many devastating laws had been passed against tribal people. Votes taken to incorporate under the Indian Reorganization Act failed at Siletz. It is impossible to say how much things would have changed had the Siletz people accepted the act, but it is likely that the reservation was already so close to being abolished thanks to the massive reductions in its land and resource base that little would have changed.

Siletz feather dancers in Newport for Fourth of July festivities in the early 1900s. In this dance line there are people representing every Southwest coastal band of the Siletz confederation from northern California to the Alsea River. From left: Baldwin Fairchild, Annie Fairchild, Martha Johnson, Coquelle Nellie Lane, Ella Spencer, Jim Watts, Simpson Billy, Ed Bensell, Mary Rooney, Billy Metcalf, Hank Johnson, Sadie Cook. Photo courtesy of Confederated Tribes of Siletz Indians.

As the nation entered the post–World War II period, when some tribes had or were beginning to build commercial lumber mills and other resource-based businesses on their reservations, the Siletz tribes were struggling to get by. Although some Siletz people were relatively well-off, the majority were not. Siletz men often worked as loggers, hired to work for non-Indians on what still should have been Siletz reservation lands, or they netted salmon to sell to the canneries established at the mouth of the Siletz River by non-Indians (though earlier proposals by Siletz agents to open tribally operated canneries to provide tribal employment were rejected). Siletz women held many families together, often making an income by selling or bartering their traditional basketry for clothing, produce, or other family needs.

Although obviously a stiff and posed picture, this married couple, Colusa Williams (Shasta and Applegate River Athapascan) and Johnny Williams (Molalla, Wasco, Kalapuya), were both active in keeping traditional dances going at Siletz. Colusa was the daughter of Shasta chief Percy Wash and Johnny, the son of Molalla Kate Chintelle, daughter of Molalla Chief Yelcus. Photo courtesy of Confederated Tribes of Siletz Indians.

In 1954 Congress passed the Western Oregon Termination Act, intending to end and forever eliminate the federal government's trust responsibility and all other government-to-government relations between western Oregon tribes and the federal government. By late 1956, the Bureau of Indian Affairs had ended the U.S. government's formal recognition of the Confederated Tribes of Siletz Indians, selling or deeding the last remaining parcels of Siletz reservation lands.

Siletz families, however, refused to disappear. Even if the federal government no longer recognized a tribal government at Siletz, traditional gatherings, subsistence activities, ceremonial dances, arts such as basketry, and other manifestations of tribal community continued. In the 1970s, Siletz families began holding meetings to discuss ways to reverse the devastating effects of termination. After Congress restored the Menominee Tribe of Wisconsin in 1973, the Siletz people began several years of intense lobbying for similar legislation.

The Siletz Restoration Act was passed and signed into law on November 18, 1977, making the Confederated Tribes of Siletz Indians the first terminated tribe in Oregon to regain federally recognized tribal status and the second tribe in the nation to have its termination reversed by federal legislation.

In 1980 the Siletz Reservation Act was passed, which reestablished a small, scattered land base for the Siletz tribes, consisting of about thirty-six hundred acres of Bureau of Land Management–administered lands in the Siletz area and most of the old Siletz Agency parcel, which the tribe had turned over to the city of Siletz at termination in 1956.

Since 1980 the Confederated Tribes of Siletz Indians have made great strides in accomplishing tribal goals and objectives to provide a future for the Siletz people and maintain the unique history and cultural identity of the Siletz tribes. Tribal administrative offices are now located in Siletz, Portland, Salem, and Eugene, offering services to tribal members in an eleven-county service area within western Oregon. More than one hundred homes and multiple-unit dwellings have been built on several tribal properties in the Siletz area, and the Siletz Tribal Housing Authority continues to strive toward meeting tribal members' needs for safe, affordable housing.

Louisa Smith (Siuslaw, Lower Umpqua) and husband William Smith (Alsea) were both active informants to anthropologists in the early 1900s and contributed greatly to the recorded knowledge of their peoples' languages. Photo courtesy of Confederated Tribes of Siletz Indians.

In 1992 the Siletz tribes dedicated a new Siletz Community Health Clinic. More recent additions to tribal services include the Tenas Illahee Child Care Center. The Siletz tribes have devoted funds, staff support, and other resources to the Siletz Valley School, a Siletz community charter school started in 2003.

In 1995 the Siletz Tribal Administration Building was dedicated and now houses the Siletz tribal government and tribal programs, including tribal council, tribal court, tribal police, employment services, tribal planning, elders programs, accounting, contract health services, education programs, youth center activities, *Siletz News* and public information, enrollment office, Indian Child Welfare program, other social services, information systems, facilities and fleet, and a natural resources department with responsibilities for forest, water, fish, wildlife, and environmental management. Other facilities within the Siletz community provide space for drug and alcohol counseling and prevention programs, cultural programs, public works, and the Siletz Tribal Housing Department.

In addition, in 1995 a gaming compact was signed, paving the way for the tribe's most ambitious economic development project, the Chinook Winds Casino in Lincoln City. That same year, the casino was built on ancestral lands that were within the original Siletz Reservation as established in 1855. The parcel later became part of an individual Siletz tribal member's allotment in 1892. It was held by that family through the termination of the Confederated Tribes of Siletz Indians in 1956, then eventually lost to private ownership. The Siletz tribes reacquired the parcel in the 1990s, and it was returned to Siletz Reservation status.

Since then the tribe has continued to expand its operations and scope to include monthly headline entertainment, a 35,000-square-foot convention center, and most recently, a 240-room oceanfront hotel. The newly renamed Chinook Winds Casino Resort is the largest employer in Lincoln County, with more than nine hundred employees. The casino's involvement in the community is far-reaching. Many groups, schools, charities, and events benefit from the charitable donations given by Chinook Winds. In 2004, adjacent to the Chinook Winds Casino Resort, the Siletz tribes opened the state-of-the-art Logan Road RV Park with many modern amenities. In Siletz the tribe also owns and operates the Siletz Gas and Mini-Mart.

In 1996 the Siletz Dance House was built and dedicated at Siletz, the first traditional ceremonial house since the local Indian agent ordered them all to be burned in the 1870s. Having the ceremonial house in the community has fostered even more interest in maintaining Siletz tribal ceremonies, languages, arts, and all aspects of culture. Public events such as the Nesika Illahee Powwow (held the second weekend in August) welcome all to share in Siletz culture and help the Siletz tribes celebrate their continued existence.

Coquelle Nellie Lane, of Coquille River ancestry, was the wife of Moses Lane, a Siletz tribal policeman who was the son of Shasta Chief Tyee Joe Lane. Nellie sits in her living room in the early 1900s weaving a basket, probably with spruce roots and hazel sticks. She is surrounded by similar examples of Siletz weaving. Many Siletz household incomes were very dependent on the sale of these baskets. Photo courtesy of Confederated Tribes of Siletz Indians.

Honoring its tradition of sharing with the community, the Siletz tribes have distributed more than $3.5 million through the Siletz Tribal Charitable Contribution Fund and other tribal resources. Since 1995, Chinook Winds has donated more than $550,000 in cash and fundraising items. The casino also donates convention space for various fundraisers, as well as technical support, advertising, and personnel for many events.

The Siletz tribes have suffered many hardships through the course of history, particularly after treaties were signed and the people were removed to the Siletz Reservation. Eventually that large reservation was whittled away to nothing in spite of treaty obligations to maintain it. The tribe was terminated one hundred years after being removed to the reservation, but it survived even that devastation. Having restored federal recognition, the

Siletz Featherdance on the beach near Newport. From left: unknown, Molly Carmichael, Sissy Johnson, Ellie Spencer, Coquelle Nellie, Martha Johnson, Jakey Johnson, Stewart Rooney, Ed Bensell, Jim Watts, Billy Metcalf, Simpson Billy, Hank Johnson. Photo courtesy of Confederated of Siletz Indians.

Siletz tribes have built a solid foundation of programs, services, and other resources for its membership. The Siletz people are now moving toward cultural, economic, and social restoration so that our community can again live secure in the blessings our Creator provided countless generations ago.

Chapter 9

Confederated Tribes of the Umatilla Indian Reservation

Modern Indian Peoples Sustained by the Land and Rivers of Their Ancestors

BY WIL PHINNEY AND JENNIFER KARSON

Thomas Morning Owl, who was taught the Umatilla language by his mother, carefully chooses words to define what it means to be Indian: "To be native is to be true to the teaching given from our elders and our past. It is more than just being counted in a minority," he says. "Our life was given to us with a purpose and a responsibility to understand who we are as a people. It is important that we accept who we are, that we are of this land.

"We were not created by a pen stroke in 1855 on a piece of paper. We were not created to be an anomaly to the rest of the world. This was our land, which identified who we were and who we are, and the day we allow ourselves to be identified otherwise will be the day we are truly defeated."

The Confederated Tribes of the Umatilla Indian Reservation have accomplished more—economically and politically—in the last thirty years than in any other time since the U.S. government and the Cayuse, Umatilla, and Walla Walla Indians signed the 1855 treaty.

The three tribes were autonomous territorial peoples who mastered survival within distinct and permanent areas through cultural lifeways brought into being by the patterns and preservation of available foods. Each tribal village was self-governing, largely independent, and self-sufficient for thousands of years before explorers and settlers arrived in their homelands.

Today, the Confederated Tribes—with a population of about 2,600 enrolled members—have established in rural Eastern Oregon a thriving and expanding economy and, because of some charismatic leaders in elected office, a powerful political presence with local, regional, and national influence.

While the Confederated Tribes' economy currently relies heavily on gaming, the tribes are building upon previous success by strengthening existing assets and carefully planning economic diversification. Wildhorse Casino, which opened in 1994, was expanded by seventeen thousand square feet in 2007 to a total of nearly sixty thousand square feet with two new restaurants, a cabaret and lounge. The casino boasts more than eight hundred slot machines, plus a variety of table games that draw residents from within a hundred-mile radius, including Tri-Cities and Walla Walla in southeastern Washington. The casino employs more than five hundred people and turns a profit of about $1 million each month.

According to the original Confederated Tribes' Gaming Revenue Allocation Plan, 15 percent of gaming profits is distributed to individual tribal members. In 1996, 15 percent amounted to $500 a year for each tribal member; in 2002, each tribal member received just over $900. In 2006, it amounted to about $1,400 for each tribal member.

The remaining gaming profits are used to operate the tribal government and provide essential governmental services, invest in funds that will enhance tribal assets, provide scholarships to students, assist with burial expenses for tribal members, provide financial assistance to elders, fund economic development projects, and provide charitable contributions throughout the region.

The casino is the primary economic engine within Wildhorse Resort, which also includes a one-hundred-room hotel, an RV park, and an eighteen-hole championship golf course. Also situated on the resort grounds is Tamástslikt Cultural Institute, a tribally owned and operated museum and educational facility that tells the story of the

The frames of three forms of early historical lodgings are part of the tribes' Living Culture Village. The building is the tribe's Tamástslikt Cultural Institute, completed in 1998. Photo courtesy of Jennifer Karson, Tamástslikt Cultural Institute.

three tribes and the U.S. westward expansion from a tribal perspective. Opened in 1998, it has become a renowned cultural beacon of the reservation and surrounding area. As tribal elder and treasurer Les Minthorn says, "Tamástslikt is a source of strength and a repository for all tribal members." Recent projects include a tribally authored history book, the Homeland Heritage Corridor driving tour CD, and a reprint of Robert Ruby and John Brown's *The Cayuse Indians: Imperial Tribesmen of Old Oregon*. These and other ongoing projects fulfill Tamástslikt's mission to present accurate history for educating tribal members as well as the general public.

In 2007, the Confederated Tribes, in a partnership with Accenture, a global management consulting, technology services, and outsourcing company, began construction on Cayuse Technologies, an outsourcing business that is expected to employ as many as 200 to 250 people over its first two years. In a forty thousand square foot building, Cayuse Technologies, the first company to be located in the Confederated Tribes' Coyote Business Park, will provide technology services to governmental and commercial clients, offering digital document processing, software development, and a call center. The Confederated Tribes also own and operate Arrowhead Travel Plaza, which caters to truckers and other motorists driving east and west along nearby Interstate 84; Mission Market, a convenience store located close to tribal housing projects; and a grain elevator leased by Pendleton Flour Mills. The Confederated Tribes have also forged partnerships to construct a natural gas-fired power plant to produce electricity on tribal land near the Columbia River. The Tribes have also partnered on a wind-power project near Arlington, Oregon. In 2004, Nixyaawii Community School, a charter school in the Pendleton school district, opened on the Umatilla Indian Reservation. The enrollment had climbed to seventy-five students as the third year came to a close in 2007.

The Confederated Tribes' government employs more than five hundred people and occupies a campus of mostly modular office units—testimony to its fast-paced expansion over the last two decades. Engineering and architectural work has begun on a planned ninety thousand square foot Capital Building. Departments and programs within the government include administration, health and human services, natural resources, economic and community development, education, fire protection, police and a court system, plus a public information program that produces a monthly newspaper, an Internet website, and a low-power nonprofit FM radio station. Additionally, many tribal members own land that they either farm or ranch themselves or lease to other agricultural and livestock producers. A handful of tribal members rely on salmon fishing, while many more supplement their incomes by fishing during the spring and fall fishing seasons on the Columbia River.

With more than a thousand employees, the Confederated Tribes of the Umatilla Indian Reservation rank second only to the State of Oregon as the top employer in Umatilla County, which is the largest county in Eastern Oregon, with a population of more than seventy thousand. In 2004, the tribes generated a $31 million payroll.

As of July 2004, the people employed by the Confederated Tribes included 383 enrolled members and 156 other Indians. Most of them live in homes built with federal Housing and Urban Development (HUD) funds and managed by the Umatilla Reservation Housing Authority, which was honored in 2006 by Harvard University's Honoring Nations Program for its financial literacy program that teaches long-term asset building through self-sufficiency to help tribal members learn about savings, budgeting, credit reports, interest rates, and predatory lending.

Early documented historical records for the three tribes is sparse. Handed down from generation to generation, however, are oral stories from as early as about 1750. These stories contend that Indian people were placed on the earth by the Creator perhaps as long as fifty thousand years ago. Archaeological excavations—such as the East Wenatchee Clovis site in Central Washington, which included stone tools fashioned from colorful agates and chalcedony, and the 1996 discovery of the Ancient One, a nearly complete skeleton of a man referred to by mainstream media as Kennewick Man, are conclusive evidence of humans living on the Columbia Plateau at least as early as 10,000 to 12,500 years ago. The Ancient One was

In June 2006 Vince Sohappy (foreground), Joe Ball (middle), and Law Enick (far left) gaff for salmon in the Umatilla River. Thanks to fish restoration projects initiated by the tribes, fishing is again open to tribal and non-tribal members. Photo courtesy of Confederated Umatilla Journal.

discovered on the banks of the Columbia River within the ancestral territory of the Umatilla Tribes in 1996. A coalition of five tribes— the Umatilla, Nez Perce, Yakama, Colville, and Wanapum Band— filed a claim for repatriation under the 1990 Native American Graves Protection and Repatriation Act (NAGPRA). After eight years of litigation, the district court and Ninth Circuit Court of Appeals determined that the Ancient One did not meet the definition of Native American as defined in NAGPRA and, therefore, was not subject to repatriation. Despite this, the native claim to these ancestral remains became a landmark case, creating a national awareness of NAGPRA and the Archaeological Resources Protection Act, and illuminating the tribes' unified purpose—to maintain authority over the graves and remains of their ancestors.

For millennia, petroglyphs and pictographs were the earliest forms of communication to record life and events on the Columbia Plateau. The first known written accounts are those of the Lewis and Clark journals in 1805 and 1806. The remarkable Cayuse-Nez Perce Sketchbook is considered one of the earliest surviving native pen-to-paper references of the Indians living in what is now Eastern Oregon and Idaho. Its thirty-two drawings, which illustrate the art and history of the tribes, refer to the mid-eighteenth century, when horses were acquired from the Shoshones, an event that dramatically changed the tribes' way of life. The sketchbook was discovered when an abandoned house was being demolished. The house, near St. Andrews Mission, had once belonged to Cap'n Sumkin. Sumkin, a Cayuse-Nez Perce, was the son and namesake of Cayuse Chief Telokaikt, who was hanged in 1850 for the slaying of Marcus Whitman. The artist of the sketchbook remains unknown. In 1963, Louise Longhair gifted the sketchbook to ten-year-old Hilda

Halfmoon. Her father shared it with Professor Theodore Stern and it now resides in the Special Collections of the University of Oregon Knight Library.

Long before they were horse people, the Cayuse, Umatilla, and Walla Walla moved seasonally to semipermanent camps, dependent on the cycles of salmon, wild game, roots, and berries. Salmon remain at the heart of tribal member subsistence as well as cultural and religious well-being. As previously mentioned, Columbia River fishing still provides a livelihood for a small but resolute number of tribal members who now rely on a few short fishing seasons—authorized by agreements between tribes and the states of Oregon and Washington—to catch and sell salmon, steelhead, sturgeon, and other fish.

Perhaps the Confederated Tribes' most meaningful accomplishment is the restoration of salmon in the Umatilla Basin. Salmon had become extinct around 1914, when the federal government built a dam to channel water to irrigate crops near the river's mouth. In 2002, the Umatilla Tribes' success at bringing salmon back to the watershed earned the Confederated Tribes high honors from Harvard University's Honoring Nations Program. Now, the Walla Walla Basin is being restored through the efforts of the Tribes' Department of Natural Resources, along with programs to protect and reintroduce other traditional river organisms, such as lamprey eels and freshwater mussels.

The tribes have carefully guarded their sovereign right to fish, hunt, and gather roots and berries. In the 1855 treaty, the tribes reserved these and other rights, including the right to graze livestock, within the 6.4-million-acre homeland they ceded in that agreement. (Fishing rights extend to "all usual and accustomed sites," even if

Fermore Craig riding in the tribal entry at the Pendleton Round-Up, which the tribes have participated in since 1910. Photo courtesy of Confederated Umatilla Journal.

those locations are outside tribal ceded territory.) Under the U.S. Constitution, treaties are the supreme law of the land. To this day, tribal members exercise treaty rights on and off reservation under codified legal guidelines established and enforced by the government of the Confederated Tribes.

Water was and is the baseline of tribal existence. The terrain of the ancestral homeland of the three tribes was within the major watersheds of the Umatilla, Grand Ronde, Imnaha, John Day, Tucannon, and Walla Walla rivers—all tributaries of the Snake or Columbia rivers.

The three tribes' traditional cultural, spiritual, and economic life revolved around the permanent orb of water, land, fish, wildlife, and plants in wetland, upland, range, and forest habitats. Fishing, hunting, gathering, and storing were the principal sinews of the culture. Fish and wildlife provided tools, clothing, shelter, and ornamentation. Fish and wildlife were both a source of economic subsistence as well as a means of barter and trade.

Many would argue that the Cayuse (a name of unknown origin, but perhaps from the French word *cailloux*, or "stones") were the most aggressive tribe among the three. Their Nez Perce name, *Weyíiletpuu*, means "the people of the undulating grass." A word they used for themselves in the now-extinct Cayuse language was recorded as *Liksiyu*, whose meaning is unknown. Their homeland stretched from the headwaters of the Walla Walla, Umatilla, and Grand Ronde rivers and from the Blue Mountains west to the Deschutes and John Day rivers. However, once they had horses, the Cayuse were known to ride into the Great Plains for months at a time, hunting buffalo and returning with foodstuffs, furs, and the survival technology of Plains tribes.

The Umatillas and Walla Wallas were considered more peaceful Indians. The Umatillas—named for the ancient village located at what is now called Umatilla (*Ímatalam* in their own Columbia River dialect)—lived on the lower reaches of the Umatilla River and on the north and south banks of the Columbia River upstream to the mouth of the Walla Walla River. The Walla Wallas, or *Wallulapum*—"People of the Little River(s)"—lived on the lower Walla Walla River and along the east bank of the Columbia from the Snake River to the Umatilla River in present-day Washington and Oregon.

Today's tribal names usually refer to areas where people lived, but these names are not direct, written translations of Sahaptian language. Rather, they are derivations of Indian place-names that have evolved over time through contact. *Cayuse*, for example, is perhaps not a place-name at all, and *Umatilla*, now popularly translated as "water rippling over sands," is neither a precise translation nor is it a Sahaptian word.

Louis Dick has lived on the Umatilla Indian Reservation all of his seventy years except for the four he served in the U.S. Marines. He is a full-blooded Indian with the blood of six different tribes traced through five generations.

Today, the indigenous people of this region have been placed by each other and non-Indians in three categories. The local native people were *natítayt*—before anything else, Dick says, with one language, one food, one religion, and one belief. "When we were 'discovered' by the white man, he called us Indians. We dropped many of our ways and were introduced to other things that led to the loss of our original identity," he says.

Today, the term "Native American," in Dick's estimation, refers to an Indian who has "completely lost his culture, his speech and religion, and has been assimilated" into the non-Indian society, fluent only in English and relying on modern-day conveniences.

"The nearest I can be is 'Indian,' combining the two cultures, live as a *natítayt* as best I can in a white man's world," Dick says.

Although the Umatillas and Walla Wallas have been aptly referred to as "salmon people," the Cayuse were also known as "buffalo people," since they were well known as horsemen. During treaty negotiations, which took place in the Walla Walla Valley over many days in the late spring of 1855, buffalo were mentioned more than a dozen times. Yet buffalo hunting only occupied two limited periods of the tribes' very long history. The relatively short periods of their history as buffalo people occurred when buffalo were briefly present on the eastern Columbia Plateau before horses, and after they acquired the horses and were able to travel east to hunt buffalo on the Plains. The majority of Cayuse history was spent travelling overland on foot and as canoe people.

Territorial Governor and U.S. Army General Isaac I. Stevens, speaking at the Walla Walla treaty council, told the three tribes, as well as the Yakama and Nez Perce: "We want you if you wish to mount your horses and go to the buffalo plains." And in 1916, Fish Hawk, a Cayuse, told Cayuse headman Gilbert Minthorn a story that included a reference to buffalo: "Long ago, when they used to go to buffalo country, many Nez Perce and Cayuse people were living there in the East, and there a man dreamed that he saw a Sioux fallen asleep, and he said to the young men, 'Now I'm going on the warpath day after tomorrow, and I shall travel.'"

It is a commonly accepted fact that the three tribes depended on fish and lamprey, as well as roots, and that hereditary property rights were attached to ancient fishing stations on the rivers for both spear fishing and dip net fishing. Those same rules still apply today to fishing sites and platforms on the Columbia River.

For the most part, the Cayuse, Umatilla, and Walla Walla people lived in longhouses covered in tule mats and in pit houses. They made the seasonal rounds—the spring migration to root grounds and rivers and streams for salmon, in summer to the high country for game, and late summer for huckleberries. The people relied on deer, elk, pronghorn, bison, bighorn sheep, mountain goats, and small animals. Men hunted deer, elk, and fowl with clubs and bows and arrows. They used concealed pits and bait to hunt bear, cougar, wolf, fox, mink, and otter. The women processed and preserved the fish and meat and were also in charge of digging, gathering, processing, and preserving the numerous roots, berries, and other plant crops. In fact, roots such as camas and those from the *Lomatium* genus may have accounted for more calories in the traditional diet than salmon.

Beyond subsistence needs, there was an abundance to trade with Indians from the east across the Rocky Mountains, from the west across the Cascades, and from far south of the Columbia River. Trade centers grew around major fishing and camas-gathering sites. Exchange and barter became the lifeblood of the regional indigenous economy. Other activities at trade centers included ceremonies, political councils, athletic competitions, and horse racing. Distinct trade languages developed, which allowed tribes from neighboring regions to communicate with each other and which were also later used by English-speaking traders as well.

One tribal elder called the horse "the high point of our Indian culture." Another recalled that people sometimes rode great distances to hunt, fish, and gather roots. Pictured here is Luke Minthorn. Photo by Major Lee Moorhouse. Courtesy of Knight Library, University of Oregon.

A variety of materials, including weapons and horses, were traded along a system of trails connecting the Plains to the Northwest Coast through the Columbia Plateau. Also traded were native foods—including salmon, nuts, and berries—furs, tanned skins, artwork, baskets, clothing, ornament shells, oil, roots, feathers, cosmetics, and buffalo robes. At fishing sites, nets, floats, and weights were exchanged.

Annual trade fairs were also held at the confluence of the Snake and Columbia rivers, a "favorite rendezvous where Umatilla, Nez

Perce, Walla Walla, and other Sahaptian-speaking tribes gathered by the thousands at particular times," wrote historian Gillett Griswold, whose 1954 master's thesis at the University of Montana was titled, "Aboriginal Patterns of Trade between the Columbia Basin and the Northern Plains."

For many millennia, historians agree, tribes gathered in the Columbia River's Celilo Falls vicinity—about seventy-five miles west of today's Umatilla Indian Reservation ceded boundary—for subsistence and trade. Early explorers of the 1800s took careful note of the abundance of the Indian fishery, estimated at the time to yield some eighteen million pounds a year. Fur trader Alexander Ross called Celilo "the great emporium or mart of the Columbia."

Jeremy Wolf with son, Aiden Wolf, ride in the 1855 Treaty Sesquicentennial Commemoration in Walla Walla, Washington, in 2005. The event was evidence of a strong people who have not only survived but are thriving. Photo courtesy of Confederated Umatilla Journal.

The village at Celilo Falls was an intertribal city consisting of lodges, tents, and longhouses where separate tribal fishing societies gathered seasonally. There, trade was conducted in sign language and Chinook Jargon, languages shared by the Northwest tribes and others. Celilo also had a permanent intertribal community, ready with canoes, dip nets, smokehouses, and arbors for drying fish. Many tribal families continue to mark the annual spring arrival of salmon at Celilo with sacred ceremonies of thanksgiving.

In 1805, Lewis and Clark's of the Corps of Discovery served as President Thomas Jefferson's "advance agents of an expanding United States, emissaries for a government headed by politicians who saw the American West as a place to enter and occupy," wrote William G. Robbins, a professor of history at Oregon State University and the author of nine books about the American West. The journals of Lewis and Clark referred to brief, hospitable relations Walla Walla leader Yellept and the ancestors of today's Cayuse and Umatilla on the way west and again on the Corps' return trip.

Within a decade, fur and commercial traders arrived, opening Fort Nez Perce in Walla Walla country in 1818 and Fort Lee at The Dalles in 1820. The first cattle arrived from California in 1836—the same year Presbyterian missionaries Marcus and Narcissa Whitman left New York with another missionary couple, Henry Harmon and Eliza Spalding. The Whitmans reached the Walla Walla River on September 1, 1836, and founded a mission among Cayuse at

Waiilatpu in the Walla Walla Valley. The Spaldings traveled northeast to present-day Idaho, where they founded a mission among the Nez Perce at Lapwai.

Meanwhile, Bristish trading houses and introduced new food to tribal people, cloth replaced skins and furs, and new cooking implements and seeds triggered the beginning of crop irrigation among Indians, particularly the Walla Wallas. Many families of all three tribes began cultivating gardens and raising cattle.

It did not take long before it was clear that the Whitmans' proselytizing efforts were bearing little fruit, particularly among the Cayuse, who were largely unresponsive to the missionaries' Christian sermonizing. The Whitmans made little effort to accommodate the Cayuse, refusing to offer their messages in terms familiar to them. Narcissa Whitman wrote about the "heathen savage" behavior of the Indians that needed to be changed. The Cayuse found the missionaries "haughty." Their distaste for each other only grew.

As emigrants began passing along the Oregon Trail, the Whitmans were spending more time assisting American settlers than ministering to the Cayuse. The swelling numbers of European Americans coming into Oregon brought with them numerous diseases that ravaged the Cayuse, and others, and the Whitmans' aid to the wagon trains made the Cayuse especially suspicious of them. Even Narcissa observed this, noting in July 1847, "the poor Indians are amazed at the overwhelming numbers of Americans coming into the country. … They seem not to know what to make of it."

That same year, Roman Catholics established St. Andrew's Mission on land made available by Umatilla Chief Taawitoy. In contrast to the Whitmans, one of the church's first priests, Father Brouillet, learned to speak Cayuse.

Late in 1847, an epidemic of measles struck nearby whites and Cayuse alike. Although the Whitmans doctored both, most European American children lived while about half of the Cayuse, including nearly all of their children, died.

On November 29, 1847, several Cayuse, under the leadership of the Chief Tiloukaikt, took revenge for what they perceived as treachery. They killed fourteen European Americans, including the Whitmans, and burned down the mission buildings. Tensions between the Whitmans and local Cayuse leaders had escalated before the epidemic, feuled by competition with the British as both fought to claim the Pacific Northwest. In December, as a result of the Whitman incident, a mounted regiment of five hundred volunteer riflemen was organized to fight Indians. One of many battles, Sand Hollow (southwest of the Umatilla River in present-day Morrow

County), resulted in the deaths of both soldiers and Indians, including the Cayuse Chief Great Eagle.

After Congress passed the Organic Act of 1848, creating the Oregon Territory, there was no stopping settlement by American immigrants. They heard the clarion call of Manifest Destiny and the promise of land and opportunity. Although the United States was obliged to make treaties with the indigenous peoples, the transformation of Indian life was now certain.

Two years after the Whitman attack and non-Indian counterattacks in the spring of 1850, Tiloukaikt and several others voluntarily surrendered in an effort to avoid the destruction of the Cayuse tribe. On May 21, 1850, they were indicted, tried, and convicted. Defiant to the end, Tiloukaikt announced on the gallows on June 3, 1850, "Did not your missionaries teach us that Christ died to save his people? So we die to save our people."

Perhaps as much as the disease that triggered the Whitman incident, the hanging of five warriors caused irreparable damage to the Cayuse people and culture. A linguistic isolate unrelated to the Sahaptian family of languages, Cayuse merged with Nez Perce, the predominant tongue of the tribe's neighbors and allies, even before the remaining few elders who spoke Cayuse passed away in the first half of the twentieth century. Today tribal languages are recognized as natural resources, indelibly tying culture and history to place. Language preservation and renewal is now being undertaken in earnest through language and technology projects and a tribal language program.

"In my time," Cayuse Chief Jesse Jones said, "I learned to speak Indian at the table at home. My grandmother, Rebecca Jones, hardly talked English. My father and mother talked Indian. I was real smart and didn't listen like I should have, and there's a lot I don't remember." For Chief Jones, language, together with traditional craftsmanship, such as buckskin tanning and beadwork, are ways to keep the culture alive.

When the treaty negotiations began in May 1855, the officials representing the United States were Isaac Stevens, governor and superintendent of Indian Affairs for Washington Territory, and Joel Palmer, superintendent for Oregon Territory. Head Chief Weyatenatemany ("Young Chief") led the Cayuse, Head Chief Peo-peo-mox-mox led the Walla Wallas, and Head Chief Wenap-Snoot, the Umatillas.

Stevens and Palmer tried for days to convince the Indians it was in their best interest to cede land to the United States. White settlers, Palmer said, would soon be coming to the region "like grasshoppers on the plains." Palmer promised that entering into a treaty

Tribal elder Dan Motanic salutes at the CTUIR veterans' memorial. Many continue the warrior tradition, serving in the armed forces today. Photo courtesy of Confederated Umatilla Journal.

would allow the Indians to choose their lands.

Stevens and Palmer promised schools, mills, shops, and farms. Stevens, in transcripts of the minutes from the 1855 treaty negotiations, said: "[W]e want your people to learn to read and write; your men and boys to be farmers or millwrights or mechanics, or to be of some profession as a lawyer or a doctor. We want your wives and daughters to learn to spin and to weave and to make clothes and all the labor of the house." The government promised plows, hoes and shovels, plates and cups, brass and tin kettles, "frying pans to cook your meat and bake ovens to bake your bread, like white people."

Stevens outlined a plan for two reservations—one in Yakama Country and the other in Idaho for the Nez Perce, the Spokane, the Cayuse, Walla Walla, and Umatilla. Tribal leaders for the Cayuse, Umatilla, and Walla Walla did not acquiesce to the government's offer. Said Young Chief: "I wonder if this ground has anything to say. I wonder if the ground is listening to what is said. I wonder if the ground would come to life and what is on it. Though I hear what this earth says, the earth says, 'God has placed me here.' The earth says that God tells me to take care of the Indians on this earth."

Palmer and Stevens, according to transcripts of the negotiations, belittled tribal leaders for not recognizing the bargain they offered. "How long will these people remain blind?" Palmer asked. "We came to try to open their eyes; they refuse the light. … We don't come to steal your lands, we pay you more than it is worth. … Why do we offer so much? It is because our Chief has told us to take care of his red people."

On June 8, Young Chief spoke again: "[I] think the land where my forefathers are buried should be mine; that is the place that I am speaking for. We will talk about it, we shall then know, my brothers, that is what I have to show to you, that I love the place we get our roots to live upon. The salmon comes up the stream. That is all." Young Chief's words prompted Palmer to make another proposition, designating a reservation in Eastern Oregon for the Cayuse, Umatilla, and Walla Walla tribes.

This "peace treaty" negotiation resulted in cession of 2,151,680 acres in Oregon Territory and 1,861,120 acres in Washington Territory, and in the reservation of about 512,000 acres of the traditional homeland, which, through a series of federal legislation and policies, has been reduced to about 172,000 acres today.

After the treaty was signed, Palmer and Stevens, in a June 13, 1855, letter to Indian Commissioner George Manypenny, concluded: "Thus has ended a most difficult and protracted negotiation. The Council ground was in the Cayuse country near the place consecrated by the blood of the missionary Dr. Whitman and his family who were killed in 1847 by the Indians of the Cayuse tribe. Its effect on the peace of the country hardly admits of exaggeration. Had no treaty been effected there would probably have been blood shed and open war the present year."

Only months later, in October 1855, a war did break out. The Yakima War was precipitated by the influx of gold prospectors and settlers trespassing on Indian lands, allowed by Stevens and others before the treaties could be ratified and reservations established. Congress reacted by delaying until 1859 ratification of many Oregon treaties, setting in motion a series of legislative events over the next several decades that would further reduce the size of reservations, providing more Indian land for white settlement and fostering continued discontent between the people who gave up their homeland and the intruders who claimed it as their own. The Yakima War

Tribal leaders on horseback head the parade at the 1855 Treaty Sesquicentennial Commemoration in Walla Walla, Washington, in 2005. From left: Fred Hill Sr., Antone Minthorn, Douglas Minthorn, Gary Burke, and John Barkley. Photo courtesy of Confederated Umatilla Journal.

One of the most successful farmers on the reservation was Parson Motanic, seen in this photograph driving his new Hudson and wearing a ceremonial headdress. A member of the Cayuse tribe, Motanic was renowned for his strength. Photo by Major Lee Moorhouse. Courtesy of Knight Library, University of Oregon.

festered with intermittent fighting for three years, ending with the military slaying of about a thousand Indian horses at the Battle of Spokane Plains in August of 1858. The U.S. Army conducted hangings of war chiefs and tribal leaders for many months.

In 1859, Oregon became a state, and a month later the U.S. Senate ratified the Umatilla treaty. People from the three tribes were constrained within new, shrunken borders, leaving their ancient areas, traditional fishing stations, subsistence grounds, and burial sites, and moving their household goods, horses, and livestock to the south. The Cayuse people moved more than five thousand horses and eight hundred cattle.

The aim of the federal government was to create an intertribal agricultural society. "Treaty farmer" employees were retained, and horses, oxen, mule teams, steel plows, and leather harnesses were obtained. Land inside the reservation borders was cleared with Indian labor. Sowing of grains and vegetables required the first reservation water diversions. Blacksmith, wagon, and carpentry shops, outhouses, and corrals were put up by using green cottonwood poles and daubing them with mud.

A year later, in 1861, some 470 acres on the reservation were under cultivation. In 1865 Indian farmers won top ribbons for their produce at the Oregon State Agricultural Society's annual state fair. Forty-one years later, in 1906, an estimated seventy thousand acres on the reservation were in cropland.

By 1877 the population of the Umatilla Indian Reservation was counted at 1,023 people and the livestock count was 22,315 head. Over the next few years, a police force was created and a boarding school opened with seventy-two students—thirty-four boys and thirty-eight girls.

In 1885, the Slater Act provided 160 acres to married heads of household, eighty acres to single heads of household, and forty acres to each child. The following year, the Slater Act resulted in 120,000 "surplus" acres offered for sale to settlers. The surplus included precious mountain watersheds. A century later, inheritence of highly fractionalized interests would require the Confederated Tribes to set policies to protect tribal lands once again.

In subsequent years, the Umatilla Agency officially deposed traditional chiefs, used tribal police to enforce a policy of compulsory education, and established census records to verify bloodlines for land ownership.

Yet, contrary to suggestions made by an agent twelve years before, Agent George W. Harper believed Indian traditions were strong and that the agricultural society was not coming into full flower. "The majority of the Indians live along the water courses in teepees, constructed after the pattern adopted by the forefathers, and dress also 'in the good old fashion,' as in the days of yore. I mention this simply to show how slow the Indian is to change his habits."

At the turn of the century, the Umatilla Indian Reservation included a new jail, a new agency office, an industrial school, an engine house and storehouse, a new wood-sawing machine, and a new boy's dormitory. Water and sewer systems were planned.

In 1906, Agent O. C. Edwards reported twelve hundred residents on the Umatilla Indian Reservation, of which about one-fourth were "of mixt blood, principally of Canadian-French descent."

"I'm either a full-blood half-breed or a half-breed full-blood," Thomas Morning Owl says. "My father is a Blood Indian in Canada and my mother is Umatilla-Warm Springs. The laws of the United States consider me a half-breed because my father lives in Canada."

Tribes welcome home Oregon National Guard troops. National Guardsman David Williams, officer with Umatilla Tribal Police, leads the riderless horse during a parade November 15, 2005, as the 116th Cavalry is welcomed home to the Umatilla Indian Reservation. The tribe and George St. Denis American Legion Post 140 adopted the Scouts and Mortars in summer of 2004 before they were deployed to Iraq, then welcomed them home as warrior heroes. Others pictured include, from left, Deric Gavin, Iraq veteran; Lindsey X. Watchman, Persian Gulf War veteran; and right of Williams is J.C. Penney, World War II veteran. Photo courtesy of Confederated Umatilla Journal.

Because of her mixed heritage, Caroline Motanic Davis says that, as a youngster, she "suffered persecution from both sides, Indians and non-Indians, but I also shared the best of both worlds." Her father's ancestry was Umatilla, Walla Walla, Nez Perce, and Modoc. Her mother is a mixture of Indian, French, Welsh, Scotch, and Irish. In school, the other students "didn't accept me as I was, and I wasn't about to change," she says. When she told her father about the predicament, he suggested she find new friends, and she did.

On November 4, 1949, voters on the reservation took a giant step into the modern world when they adopted a constitution and bylaws, which established the Confederated Tribes' Board of Trustees as the day-to-day governing and policy-making unit, and set annual meetings of the general council. The tribal government operates today under that 1949 constitution.

Dam construction, perhaps the largest obstacle for migrating fish, began early in the twentieth century and continued for some thirty years. Construction of The Dalles Dam was completed in 1957, and the reservoir behind the dam covered Celilo Falls. Richard LaCourse, in *Days of Nicht-Yow-Way: A Political History*, wrote about the flooding of Celilo Falls: "Thousands of tribal people came to witness the event, and it became a symbol of destruction and irretrievable loss to all whom remembered the bountiful falls and the centrality of the location in the history and culture of the inland fishing tribes. The loss of the historic falls was the darkest day in the common psychological history of the tribes in the twentieth century."

Congress appropriated $4.1 million for the Confederated Tribes—$3,800 for each tribal member—for the loss of treaty fishing rights at Celilo Falls.

In the early twentieth century, several Supreme Court cases, including *U.S. v. Winans* in 1905, reaffirmed tribal rights with regards to off-reservation fishing. Then, in the 1960s, another batch of court judgments again confirmed treaty fishing and hunting rights, leading in the 1970s to decisions that required the tribes and Oregon and Washington to work out a comprehensive plan for preservation and conservation of fish resources. Tribes were assured 50 percent of the harvestable fish (those not needed to perpetuate future fish runs) that passed their usual and accustomed fishing places.

In 1973, the Nicht-Yow-Way Community Center and Yellowhawk Clinic were completed, ushering in an era of economic and community development and the expansion of government programs that continues today.

The father of three children, Thomas Morning Owl might not be as confident about the future as is Louis Dick. "Children today don't understand who they are," Morning Owl says. "They begin to accept and follow other ways, they shrug their shoulders when they are told what it means to be native, a person of the land. To be Indian is to be a person who is independent, who is worthy, who is disciplined in life and respectful of things around you—elders, home life, education. Too many of us fit the stereotype that fails and blames everybody else for our own actions."

Dick says he worries about the children but must remain optimistic. "When there is a funeral," Dick explained, "the procession walks by the grave and each person gives earth three times, representing the past, present, and future generations. That's what we are.

"My grandkids aren't learning the language, and the language is what motivates an Indian to preserve his cultural values," he says. "But I have to follow the Creator's law. That's what keeps past values linked to the people living today."

These feelings reflect a continuity that moves from the past to the present and into the future on this reservation. In 1855, the treaty signers would never have imagined that the fish would stop running, that Celilo Falls would disappear, that the homeland would experience such encroachment, that species and water would be threatened, that languages would cease to be heard and spoken. Yet defining events in recent history have repaired much—the return of the salmon, the return of economic viability, the national leadership in Native American issues, and the intergovernmental goodwill with neighbors that has been a tribal practice since time immemorial. And after many shifts and changes in the tribes' history, a cultural continuity remains that will guide the principles and actions of the *natitayt* for another ten to fifty thousand years.

Chapter 10

The Confederated Tribes of the Warm Springs Reservation of Oregon

The Relationship between Peoples, Good Government, and Sovereignty

BY ELIZABETH WOODY

"E-Wah'-Cha'-Nye"—that is the way it has always been. That is the way it is today and always will be. This is the then, now, and tomorrow of the Confederated Tribes of the Warm Springs Reservation of Oregon. Tribal people have governed themselves since time immemorial, managing and using resources within a cultural and spiritual framework given to us from the time of Creation. The governments of indigenous peoples are the original governments of the land and all precede the United States and the State of Oregon.

This senior government exists today for the 4,260 members of the Confederated Tribes of the Warm Springs Reservation of Oregon because of the values, participation, and wisdom carried forward by past generations. Tribal members are beneficiaries of "good government" from those who planned for our generation as if we were actually present. The commingling of the past and future into one voice built the foundation for the self-sufficiency, determination, and sovereignty the Warm Springs tribe enjoys today.

Overleaf: Some of the artifacts that form the core collection of the Museum at Warm Springs surround the late Liz Cross, curator for the Middle Oregon Indian Historical Society. A special feature of the museum is interpretation of the Indian culture from a tribal perspective. Photo courtesy of Tony Neidek, Northwest Regional Educational Laboratory.

As the tribe's Declaration of Sovereignty reads, "Our people have exercised inherent sovereignty, as nations, on the Columbia Plateau for thousands of years, since time immemorial. Our Sovereignty is permeated by the spiritual and the sacred, which are, and always have been, inseparable parts of our lives, for the Creator leads us in all aspects of our existence." This document was adopted on behalf of tribal members on June 25, 1992, after district-wide community hearings. It primarily describes the nature of the tribe's innate sovereignty and states that our traditional tribal governments were preeminent and possessed inherent rights for thousands of years.

In 1937, nearly a half century before the Declaration of Sovereignty was adopted, tribal members approved a constitution and bylaws for the Warm Springs tribe after many months of community discussions. My grandmother recalls people visiting from all points—on the reservation and from other tribes—to talk and listen late into the night about tribal government. Some of those who had led the discussion and drafting of the documents were elected the following year to represent the three tribes as part of our first modern tribal council. Prompted by the Indian Reorganization Act of 1934 (also known as the Wheeler-Howard Act), which encouraged the tribe to revive and revise tribal governing structures, tribes throughout Oregon remember this as an active time when members engaged one another in important and sometimes heated dialogue about their form of government and their future. At Warm Springs, in particular, members participated in collaborative and consensual discussions that resulted in the adoption of the constitution and bylaws, which remain in effect today, and the election of a tribal council whose record still stands as a most exemplary one. This inclusion of many streams of thought, I believe, is why the Warm Springs tribe is considered a leader in retaining its traditions, self-preservation, self-determination, and innovation in economic development. The thoughtfully formed government we have today represents the best of three distinct tribal groups: those who speak Ichiskiin (Sahaptin), those who speak Kiksht (Chinookan), and those who speak Numu (Paiute).

One of the tribal council's first actions was to draft and approve a corporate charter to give the tribe a framework for economic development. The corporation makes each enrolled member of the Warm Springs tribe a shareholder. This progressive trend, as some have called it, started in 1942, just as the country was emerging from the Depression. It began with a twenty-year contract for the selective harvest of five hundred million board feet of reservation lumber, and, eventually, the purchase of a plywood plant and sawmill in 1967. The tribe also negotiated agreements for tribal lands to be used for the Pelton and Round Butte hydroelectric dams, beginning in 1955 and 1961, respectively. The renewable leases provided a revenue stream for tribal activities and projects, such as land acquisition and additional development.

Our leaders took the task of self-governance and planning seriously. They thought beyond small increments of time, considering several generations, both past and future. Creating a solid management plan—a people's plan—and codifying our laws into documents of common use for tribal life required the effort and consent of the membership as well. The Warm Springs tribe provides stability and infrastructure to their members as well as to the region. In 1992, the tribal government and enterprise payroll exceeded $20 million. In 2002, the payroll was $35 million. Approximately 60 percent of the revenue is spent outside the reservation. The tribal government is the fifth major employer in Central Oregon. In this and other respects, the tribe is a good neighbor to have.

Most tribal members live on the reservation; its population is over thirty-six hundred people. Nearly half of all

Decades after they were confined to the Warm Springs Reservation, some tribal members visited traditional sites on the Columbia River each year. This photo was taken near Celilo Falls in the early twentieth century. By mid-century the Celilo fishing grounds were destroyed to make way for The Dalles Dam. Now Indian fishers use both motorized boats and dipnets and scaffolds to harvest salmon from the Columbia River. Photo by Edward S. Curtis, courtesy of Oregon Historical Society, #OrHi81497.

Today tribal members still fish from platforms such as these at Sherars Falls on the Deschutes River. Photo courtesy of Warm Springs Museum archives

tribal members are younger than twenty years old. Indian students attend public elementary schools on the reservation and secondary schools in Madras, the closest non-reservation community. A portion of dam revenues and federal aid for schools with significant Indian populations, however, helps support local school districts. In 2003, for example, those revenues amounted to $3.8 million for the Madras-area schools alone.

I cannot fully represent my people with simple facts and figures in a standard scholarly montage. Just as a life or a person cannot be segmented and expected to function as a living being, living history cannot be fragmented into facts and chronologies without losing the sense of the organic whole. Every single tribal member receives and bestows a legacy. Each person possesses rights and responsibilities for the sake of life's continuance. Every single soul holds forth a purpose. Cultural heritage is made up of the peoples' hope and adherence to the tradition lived, and is handed down generation to generation over millennia. Nonetheless, we are united and equally invested in determining our future through tribal governmental operations and corporate entities and ventures.

While the written history of the three Warm Springs tribes generally starts at contact with European Americans, our traditional stories, oral histories, and those of us living our cultural heritage provide a deep memory of the land. The United Nations recognizes the legitimacy of oral history and tradition in the treatment of indigenous peoples all over the world; this is the history the three tribes understood when they confronted treaty-making.

The treaty of 1855, also known as the Treaty of the Middle Oregon Tribes, outlines the ceding of more than ten million acres of land to the United States for non-Indian settlement. The treaty also delineates some of what we kept in reserve for the benefit and sustenance of our people. The land base we retained (the reservation) is approximately 66,000 acres of high desert timberlands, mostly in the Deschutes River basin, and includes our sacred Mount Jefferson in the Cascade Range. The tribes reserved rights to fish and hunt and to gather roots and berries at the "usual and accustomed places" in our original territory. It is important to know the tribes were not "given" land, rights, and responsibilities. As a confederation, the tribes retained their national sovereignty, while the United States took on new obligations, or as stated in the tribe's 1992 Declaration of Sovereignty, "assumed trust duties, a high obligation to protect the reservation, and all off-reservation rights from outside forces." The U.S. Constitution considers treaties as "the supreme law of the land."

The tribes believe that the Creator and the land itself vest ultimate sovereign authority in the people. The land we joined with is imbued with the vibrancy of a beloved homeland, and we are fully accountable for our conduct upon it. The Warm Springs peoples have delegated only limited authority to the tribal council and have reserved for themselves the remainder of our national sovereignty. Conversely, official federal policy denied religious freedom and the right to speak our native languages until the American Indian Religious Freedom Act of 1979 and the Native American Languages Act of 1990, which comes as a shock to many Americans. For nearly a century, the primary means of separating Indian children from their ceremonial life and their languages was the strict and repressive boarding school policy, initiated by Congress in 1879. Not considered U.S. citizens until 1924, indigenous people had only a minor voice in legislative chambers. Yet by patient perseverance, we maintained our primary responsibilities—to care for the land, to maintain our sovereignty, and to carry on the teachings and beliefs given by the Creator—through hard times and good times alike.

For a culture whose wealth lay in familial relationships and in salmon, "our little relatives," access to traditional fishing grounds was vital. Many sites were handed down, and fishing chiefs knew best management of the resource. This 1909 photograph is of an Indian man fishing the swift waters of the Columbia River in the age-old manner using a dipnet and wooden scaffold. Photo by Edward S. Curtis, courtesy of Library of Congress, Prints and Photographs Divisions, LC-USZ62-47007.

The three tribes that comprise the confederation have endured and emerged from hardship and separation from vast homelands and traditional livelihoods. From deep in myth, or story, the tribes have reclaimed practical and eternal elements for our rules of conduct. We acknowledge natural systems and creatures from lessons of the earth's shaping and its law. Singing our thanks for those lives we take for our sustenance demonstrates how the tribes who speak Ichiskiin provide ceremonial respect for every being we come in contact with. Some call this a "subsistence lifestyle," while others recognize it as the practice of traditional ecological knowledge.

This approach is best illustrated by the seasons' first foods and first fish ceremonies, which acknowledge that the way we treat our land and the partners who live on it determines future abundance. In these ceremonies, both travails and successes are appreciated as teachings. One of the major goals of the Confederated Tribes of Warm Springs is the promotion of self-sufficiency based on the development of sustainable resources on tribal land, a goal based in the belief that we can be self-reliant while still caring for the land as a cohesive community.

The Warm Springs bands called themselves Wana-thlama, the river people. A few of the better known bands are the Tenino and John Day bands; Upper Deschutes, known as the Tygh; Lower Deschutes; and the Wyam. These peoples moved between seasonal villages and depended on game, salmon, roots, and berries. Many crossed territories because of the ties and privileges afforded by intertribal marriage. Enough food could be caught, gathered, dried, and prepared for personal stores and trade. While the tribal people were great traders, they also were considered very spiritual in their daily conduct of family life. The sacred foods are still recognized and respected as the little relatives. Like their relatives in the greater Columbia Plateau, the Warm Springs bands handed down oral traditions and songs, revered Coyote's prominence in the creation and development of the world we know today, and bestowed a high value on individual vision and talents. This primary belief system continues to be practiced in Washat Sunday services and winter dances.

The best example of our tenancy in the Columbia River Basin is Celilo Falls and village. The village site has been continuously inhabited for more than twelve thousand years. Leaders practiced a system of fish management that looked after the resources and saw that no law was broken or disrespect shown to the salmon. The women prepared and processed the salmon, kept the stores, and traded the excess. But Lewis and Clark's arrival in what would become Oregon Territory set a wave of colonial tumult into motion, sometimes resulting in the alliance of multiple nations.

Originally considered the most eastern inhabitants of the Chinookan river network, the Wasco peoples (Dalles, Ki-gal-twa-la, and Dog River) coexisted in a trading system founded on fishing, hunting, and gathering. The distinct and cohesive Chinookan culture boasted many permanent villages from the mid-Columbia River to its mouth. Today, the Wasco, Wishram, Chilluckittequaw, Multnomah, Watlalla, Clackamas, and Cathlamet villages are prime real estate. During treaty times, the Chinookan-speaking peoples were separated; for example, the Wishram, who lived on the Big River's north shore, were largely assigned to the Yakama Reservation, while the Wasco, who lived directly across the river on the south shore, were assigned to the Warm Springs Reservation. Some, like the Cascades, or Watlalla, were declared extinct, as people perished from pernicious foreign diseases, and the remnant survivors joined upriver relatives. Considered extremely passionate as far as trade and commerce are concerned, the Chinookan nation was one of wealth, great productivity, and prestige. The Chinookan people valued the individual's vision and held dances of ceremony and gift exchanges, much like the Warm Springs bands did.

Lewis and Clark bemoaned the business acumen of the traders along the Columbia or "Big River," as it was called in translation. They could not afford but a bit of these peoples' wealth. The cedar plank houses and the finely woven and distinctively crafted objects of the Chinookan peoples have no equivalent in the world of art today. Their canoes and other items are lost to us because of the frailty of wood. The stone markers, basketry, and burial objects are so rare that it is nearly impossible to find these objects in the marketplace. Since they lived between major centers of trade, the Wasco peoples prospered in the flowing barter system that stretched across North and South America and reached into Asia. Legends of these peoples are stored and remain unspoken in academic institutions. What remains of this ancient culture are the people who recall the network of family ties, the rich quality of life, and the ability to adopt changes and build a new commonwealth. Collections of written materials await the Chinookan descendent and aficionado of classic world literature who can read and speak one or more of the Chinookan dialects. Perhaps one of the most unusual activities was raising condors to offset the chance of lightning. These were unique people.

The lifestyle and language of the thirty-eight Northern Paiutes who arrived from Yakama in 1879 were radically different from the Wasco and Warm Springs bands already established on the Warm Springs Reservation. Until that year, the reservation had bordered all tribal territories and mutual gathering grounds. Theirs was a culture spread across a large territory in the Great Basin—a geographic range including Oregon, Idaho, northwestern California, Nevada, and Utah.

The U.S. Army removed Northern Paiutes to the Yakama Reservation after they joined the Bannock Indians in an 1874 attempt to oust the Americans by attacking United States military forces in the region. The first Paiutes walked away from the Yakama Reservation in 1879 and journeyed on foot to the Warm Springs Reservation; other Northern Paiutes followed them over the next four and five years and also settled in the southern part of the Warm Springs Reservation. After settling on the reservation, the Paiutes received allotments of reservation land and became members of the confederated tribes. Sovereign Paiute laws and religious mores continued to be established by custom and administered by headmen and a principal chief.

Because their traditional cultural practices and subsistence require a large geography, what seemed nomadic to European Americans was really a large arc of movement that the Paiute people needed to make life possible on a landscape of open horizons and minimal rains. The Paiute belong to the Shoshonean language family, one of the largest in the aboriginal western United States, unrelated to the other languages spoken on the Warm Springs Reservation. However, like the other Warm Springs people, being in the right place at the right time mattered. Villages spread across the seasonal land base. Homes were what one could physically carry or cache long-term and what one could metaphorically carry in the map of mind and heart.

The Warm Springs, Wasco, and Paiute peoples are represented distinct from one another on the tribal council—the basic form of government—by the inclusion of each of the tribe's three hereditary chiefs. The Warm Springs constitution also requires eight elected council members from districts that roughly correspond to the regions where the Warm Springs, Wasco, and Paiute peoples reside.

According to the Warm Springs constitution and bylaws, the tribal government consists of the voting membership, tribal council, and all subordinate boards, committees, officials, employees, and organizations charted or appointed by the tribal council. A vision for the tribal government began early in the twentieth century with the first council made up of Frank Winishut, Isaac McKinley, Joe McCorkle, Chief Frank Queahpama Sr., James Johnson, George Meacham, Moses Hellon, William McCorkle, Sam Wewa, Fred Wagner, Oliver Kalama, Chair Jerry Brunoe, and Secretary-Treasurer Louie Pitt, Sr., a nontribal member enrolled with the Yakama

Nation. (Louie Pitt, Sr., is my grandfather. His parents, being of both Warm Springs and Yakama heritage, enrolled half of their children in each tribe.) As the first secretary-treasurer of the tribal council, Pitt set the precedent for allowing a nonmember to hold this position, if qualified. Secretary-treasurers are not elected.

This priceless act of preserving our sovereignty also formalized a means of governing independently of the United States' wardship of our precious peoples and valuable resources. A democratic government document, which on the surface looks like the U.S. Constitution, the tribal constitution and bylaws carry forth the participatory practices of the indigenous village governments and the pre-1855 alliances of the Big River into modernity. The traditional forms of governance and alliance followed a familial pattern and can still be witnessed in the formal and informal proceedings of civil life on the reservation today.

Traditionally, a village headman was designated through acclamation. If one disagreed with the leadership or his or her actions, an individual or family simply moved to another village where one probably had relatives. As with councils held in the past, meetings of importance might continue for days. Each person had a blanket resting over his or her shoulders, and after expressing one's view, each person closed the blanket around one's self. When all blankets were closed, from elders to children, the discussion ended. Family leaders often spoke for their relatives and would meet to discuss options. When a proposed course of action came from this "subcommittee" meeting, decisions were announced to the people. If you or your family did not agree, you were not forced into the matter but abstained from the action and left the circle.

The current council is structured much like this, with representatives from each district who meet regularly. Information is presented in a thorough manner. If the decision is not acceptable to someone, that individual or family may petition for a resolution to the tribal council and, if approved, a general vote of eligible members is held. While these processes are consistent with democratic traditions, what is different is that the Warm Springs constitution, I am proud to say, states that women possess equal rights to men—a departure from the U.S. Constitution.

Warm Springs Chief Delvis Heath explained:

> As a leader, I must listen to what the people say. As a
> tribe, we are no different or better than another tribe. We
> must follow the ways as our people did in the past. Other
> people may make the comparisons, focus on materialism

or money, but we are taught that our time is limited on earth. When money is gone the land will be there. The [natural] law comes from the land and it will not perish or disappear. We must make everything—all our little relatives, the wildlife, and neighbors—comfortable. We are all equal. We must keep planning beyond today for a spiritual life. We also must not be put into one basket, as "Indians," since each of us is different for a reason. Also, the tribes have innate sovereignty. We never gave it up or lost it. It goes back to Creation. For us, education and tribal ways are equal. The women are the stronghold of family, the stone hearth."

By comparison, Article III of the Northwest Ordinance, July 13, 1787, a seminal document on policy regarding indigenous peoples, focuses on a similar framework, though little of it was actually practiced in the treatment of "foreign nations," as the tribes were called:

Religion, morality, and knowledge, being necessary to good government and the happiness of mankind, schools and the means of education shall forever be encouraged. The utmost good faith shall always be observed towards the Indians; their lands and property shall never be taken from them without their consent; and, in their property, rights, and liberty, they shall never be invaded or disturbed, unless in just and lawful wars authorized by Congress; but laws founded in justice and humanity, shall from time to time be made for preventing wrongs being done to them, and for preserving peace and friendship with them.

Friendship is honorable, but leadership moves beyond external, impermanent perceptions of indigenous peoples and addresses long-range concerns. With our cultural mores and experiences, the tribes have put forth a realistic plan of action to make our way in the United States. This type of old leadership is timeless and, above all, essential in preserving place-based knowledge. The practicing root digger and the fisherman, for example, pass on to the next generation part of the intimate knowledge of our homelands.

Even in the darkest days of loss, when the Celilo Falls and Wasco villages went under the backwaters of the Bonneville Dam and The Dalles Dams, the tribe took action and did not spend much time in despair. The tribe succeeded because our leaders did not generalize, or cry out in rage, but took a hard look at the needs of a growing people and the resources available to them. They opted to plan and to lead.

In 1957, the tribes used a small portion of a $4 million settlement for the loss of fishing sites at Celilo Falls to contract with Oregon State College (now Oregon State University) for a study of the reservation's resources and potential for economic development. This was meant to offset the economic disaster caused by the transformation of a free-flowing river into a power network of twenty-plus hydroelectric dams.

Today the results of that investment in an economic study can be seen in the tribe's decision to invest in hydroelectric power, forest products, and tourism. Water development projects on the Deschutes River (which borders the reservation) required extensive studies and negotiations. Pelton and the Round Butte dams generated income from annual leases that added to the tribe's investment portfolio. What followed included the repurchase of Kah-Nee-Ta, the hot springs lost during the allotment years, which is now an upscale resort with swimming pools, a beautifully designed lodge, golf course, teepee campgrounds, horseback riding, and more.

Tribal members benefit from the economic successes of tribal enterprises. In 1942 the tribes approved the first dispensation of dividends to each member from the proceeds from the first cut of reservation timber. This formed the basis for the tribal payments to individual members (per capita payments, as they are called) and the establishment of trust funds for minor tribal members. The federal government also supports some services on the Warm Springs Reservation just as the federal government does for cities and counties. All tribal employees, whether they are tribal members or non-Indians, pay federal taxes on their earnings. (Tribal members did not pay state taxes as a result of tribal sovereignty and are thus not generally subject to state tax laws). Thirty percent of the workforce is non-Indian, which means that the State of Oregon receives taxes from these employees. Although the impact of the Warm Springs Reservation on the regional economy has never been precisely calculated, it is significant.

Despite the changes that Warm Springs Indians have had to undergo, their timeless ceremonies and traditions have endured. These dancers were photographed in 1956 at the ceremonies marking a farewell to Celilo. Photo courtesy of Oregon Historical Society, #OrHi007244.

As contemporary citizens and as leaders of permanent and responsible land occupancy, we are obligated to continue in the vein of collaborative success and to continue to inspire humanity with the tenacious practice of our culture, which is our rich ancestral legacy. This is especially significant when today's frenzied and mobile society can make one feel like a drone in the hive of a faceless transnational corporation.

Besides, the three tribes knew a different sort of economy existed for centuries in the Americas, one with allowances for a generous give and take between all peoples and species. A gifting economy requires gratitude and adherence to the Creator's Law. These tribes also knew of sovereignty as an inherent responsibility of the people to participate in governance and diplomatic relations with other peoples, and to generally manage our common affairs. As Wasco elder Walter Spedis said about how circumstances have changed and not changed: "Congressional plenary powers do not preempt the natural law of the Creator."

The Declaration of Sovereignty describes tribal understanding of nationhood, tribal histories, and the spiritual aspects of tribal existence and governance. Our traditional tribal governments were preeminent and possessed inherent rights for thousands of years. Our peoples' lives were held together by religious practice, as a responsibility of the individual and the leadership that is delegated to lead the village. As explained in the declaration, "Warm Springs people followed an elaborate structure of sovereign tribal responsibilities embodied in the Sahaptin phrase, 'tee-cha-meengsh-mee sin-wit na-me- ah-wa-ta-man-wit,' which means, 'at the time of creation the Creator placed us in this land and He gave us the voice of this land and that is our law.'"

However, the time of contact with European Americans created tension and conflict. After 1805, with the Corps of Discovery

These students from Chemawa were trained for work in the Portland shipyards during World War II. Many young Warm Springs women worked here. Photo courtesy of Oregon Historical Society, #OrHi013610.

breaking the way, all trails came west. American trade and religions began settling in. According to Nat Shaw, writing for the Warm Springs tribe and Oregon State University Extension:

> In 1843, one thousand immigrants passed through the Dalles; in 1847 there were four thousand. By 1852, up to twelve thousand settlers were crossing Wasco and Warm Springs territories each year. Most of these people moved on, but some chose to stay. Although they had always welcomed newcomers in the past, the Indians along the Columbia River began to realize they could no longer control what was happening on their lands.

Yet, as Indian people, we have tenure and cannot relinquish our connection and responsibility to protect the land we occupied and took care of for so many thousands of years. Our tribal identity is a living and thriving cooperation between the people, our leadership, and the places that have always been home. As my tribe operates in today's political climate, it often falls back on the leadership of the last century for inspiration and guidance.

In contrast, futurists project that a modern person in a global society will wander and traverse boundaries freely with information as the common currency, hence, connections to a particular base of knowledge and a cohesive community will not be necessary. I disagree with this vision and see "being of" and "in place" a necessity and even an advantage in a transnational economy. In such an economy—and the United States is not immune to this economic phenomenon—those who remain grounded in local realities and needs will be assets in protecting local places and communities. I predict that the tribal leadership at Warm Springs, which can be generally characterized as exemplary, strategic, and wielding a tenacious goodwill, will allow our participation in global events and commerce. To know one's history and to have the ability to adapt swiftly is an advantage. If collective tactical intelligence enabled our ancestors' survival against tremendous odds, we too can persevere.

An example of our successful participation in global commerce comes from the tribe's forest products industry, which recently won certification by the Forest Stewardship Council, an independent, not-for-profit organization based in Bonn, Germany. Certification means the tribe met environmentally appropriate, socially beneficial, and economically viable management standards in its harvest and manufacture of forest products. This tribal enterprise follows the old means of accumulating information (in person) and utilizes the best of the present science, management, and marketing knowledge.

In its introduction, *Uncommon Controversy*, a book about the Northwest fishing rights struggles of the 1960s and '70s, characterized the dominant society as suffering from too much fragmentation and not enough community feeling. Instead it called for deeper recognition of the way indigenous peoples integrate their work, education, play, religion, and their relationships with their environment into a whole way of life.

My good fortune is to have connections to multiple generations of influence through my family. They used metaphor and story to convey dearly held concepts. The transmission of knowledge did not preclude present problems and unknown futures, but brought the past into the present as lessons. While this way of knowing is intensely personal in nature, it is applicable to the process of community discovery and validates the need for multicultural education in today's Oregon. The simultaneous process of personal and community discovery, I feel, is something people crave at an elemental level.

Tribal traditions—tolerance, individual participation, providing knowledge by example, a historical perspective, the integration of spirituality into all of life, and responsibility for and understanding of the land and water, among many others—comprise a means for the empowerment of the child or the apprentice. In the company of the master fisher, one learns that the natural embodiment of knowledge is within the river system and oneself and is supported by many generations. One's story is a segment of a millennial existence: an apprentice weaver meets her ancestress when examining a basket; a master weaver learns the technology behind what mainstream society considers a "fiber art." Through generations these collapsible containers preserved our stores and our stories. The design and

Started by Warm Springs artist Apollonia Santos, Journeys in Creativity brings native youth to the Oregon College of Art & Craft to introduce them to contemporary techniques in printmaking, ceramics, and painting. The popular program quickly expanded to include young people from other Indian communities. In the foreground, Titus Kalama (Warm Springs), and from left: Melissa Tverberg (Ojibway); Tony Stevens (Warm Springs); Peter Nichols, the college's printmaking studio manager; and Jeremy Anderson (Warm Springs). Photo courtesy of Shirod Younker.

competency of various skills demonstrated our ingenuity. We also convey our knowledge through technological communications and the organization of the printed word. Building on our traditional strengths, our ancestors and leaders have yielded to the responsibility of a single purpose—providing for the common good, which also expresses the common values of humanity. This is a heritage of building potential, if need be, one person at a time.

Chapter 11

Federal-Indian Relations

BY STEPHEN DOW BECKHAM

The history of the United States' relationship with Oregon Indians is one shaped by fear, greed, cultural differences, exploitation, and racism. The original federal intent appeared noble. It was summed up in the assurance of "utmost good faith" in the Northwest Ordinance (1787), a philosophy of dealing with Indians that was later extended across the Trans-Mississippi West: "The utmost good faith shall always be observed toward the Indians; their lands and property shall never be taken from them without their consent; and in their property, rights, and liberty, they never shall be invaded or disturbed unless in just and lawful wars."

Unfortunately, later lawmakers, government officials, and citizens did not live up to these assurances. The hunger for Indian land and resources proved too alluring. The presumption of European American cultural superiority shaped too many attitudes toward Indians. Consequently, the pattern of exploitation and dislocation of the colonial period continued across the continent in the wake of pioneer settlement.

Early Federal Laws

The source of federal authority in Indian affairs stemmed from the "Commerce Clause" of the Constitution (1789). In five simple words—"and with the Indian tribes"—Congress presumed to have complete authority to deal with American Indians and did so. These words were considered to give Congress "plenary authority" to ratify and abrogate treaties, create and disband reservations, recognize and terminate tribes, and take other actions. The Constitution did not lay out this authority, but over time, Indian affairs were carried out in this manner.

In 1823, the U.S. Supreme Court ruled in *Johnson's and Graham's Lessee v. McIntosh* that the "doctrine of discovery" gave the new Americans the right to dispossess Indian tribes. The court arrived at this decision in part by accepting the erroneous idea that Indians were nomads and therefore had a "mere occupancy right" to the soil. According to the Court's logic, the Indians' right was less than that of the European Americans who had "discovered" the lands in question.

Later, in the 1831 *Cherokee Nation v. Georgia* decision, the Court softened its attitude by ruling that tribes were "domestic dependent nations" and, as such, possessed some sovereignty or power but were subordinate to the United States. The Court also found that the federal government had a "trust responsibility" for Indians, observing that the tribes stood as a "ward to his guardian" and that as guardian, the government had certain obligations in dealing with the native peoples. In 1832's *Worcester v. Georgia* decision, the Supreme Court decided that in "Indian Country," tribal, not state, law prevailed—a concept Indians had always assumed, but one that proved disturbing to trespassing pioneers and other European Americans.

These Supreme Court decisions eventually had bearing on the Indians of Oregon. So, too, did the Indian Trade and Intercourse Act of 1834, a trade law later extended to Oregon that further defined all Indian lands not covered by a ratified treaty as "Indian

Country." While these turning-point decisions and laws thus set the stage for the loss of Indian lands and reduced tribal sovereignty, they also helped support modern realities for tribes. Today the "trust" responsibility of the federal government for Indian lands and welfare, as well as the limited authority of the state on reservations, can be traced to these early federal laws.

The First Federal Policies in "The Oregon Country," 1846–50

The beginnings of federal dealings with Oregon Indians took place in an atmosphere of rapidly changing lifeways, population dislocation, fear, and confusion, as several thousand emigrants poured into Oregon between 1843 and 1845, setting the stage for competition for resources and a scramble for Indian land. The Indians—weakened by new illnesses brought by the settlers and forced to cope with a swift flood of cultural changes—needed special care and consideration.

These were the challenges that confronted the federal government in 1846, but Congress did nothing. It took no steps to set up a territorial government or deal with the Indians. However, a bloody attack by several Cayuse Indians on a mission operated by Marcus and Narcissa Whitman near present-day Walla Walla, Washington, provoked specific action by Congress: on August 14, 1848, it passed the Organic Act, a law that created the Oregon Territory and laid out new federal policies for dealing with those who lived there.

Section 1 of the Organic Act acknowledged Indian land title:

> Nothing in this act contained shall be construed to
> impair the rights of person or property pertaining to the
> Indians in said territory, so long as such rights shall
> remain unextinguished by treaty between the United
> States and such Indians.

Section 13 of the Act appropriated $10,000 for presents to the Indians to preserve the "peace and quietude" of the country, and Section 14 applied the Northwest Ordinance of 1787 to Oregon Territory, extending the ordinance's "utmost good faith clause." The Organic Act thus established a four-part philosophy for dealing with the Indians in the Pacific Northwest:

1. The federal government recognized Indian title to all of Oregon Territory.

2. Indian affairs were to be administered in the field by a superintendent and such staff as he might need.

3. Indians were to be treated with the "utmost good faith"; protected in their lands, rights, and privileges; and not invaded unless in just and lawful wars.

4. Congress from time to time would appropriate money to assist the Indians and to further peace and friendship.

However, within the next two years, more than ten thousand European Americans were living in western Oregon. Thousands of these people had staked lands and filed provisional land claims, anticipating that Congress would soon pass a law to make those claims their legal property. In July 1849, the Oregon territorial legislature endorsed a memorial that would make Congress aware of the settlers' problem. In the memorial, the legislature pointed to what it considered the immediate need to extinguish Indian land title and provide for the Indians "early removal from those portions of the Territory needed for settlement, and their location in some district or country where their wretched and unhappy condition may be ameliorated." Many Oregon residents favored moving all Indians to the more arid lands on the Columbia Plateau or into the northern Great Basin.

On June 5, 1850, Congress somewhat belatedly responded by appropriating $20,000 to fund a treaty commission to negotiate with the Indians west of the Cascades and by passing a law that did the following:

- Called for the Indians to cede their lands and move east of the mountains,
- Created the post of Superintendent of Indian Affairs separate from the office of governor,
- Provided for three agents, and
- Extended to Oregon the Indian Trade and Intercourse Act of 1834—a measure that defined "Indian Country" as that region not ceded to the United States and under tribal law and custom.

In other words, federal law in 1850 declared all of the Pacific Northwest to be "Indian Country" and stipulated that the Indians must sign treaties agreeing to abandon their homelands before the settlers could have title to their provisional land claims. However, before the treaty commission set out for Oregon, Congress acted again—and in contradictory fashion—to encourage Indians to cede their lands. On September 27, 1850, it passed what was popularly

called the Oregon Donation Land Act—a law that authorized the
government to give away hundreds of thousands of acres of Indian
land to settlers. This act stipulated that white men and women,
"American half-breed Indians included," and immigrants who had
filed for naturalization were entitled to free lands. Before the law
expired in 1855, a total of 7,437 settlers had filed for more than 2.8
million acres in Oregon—doing so before any of the treaties had
been ratified. In light of the way Congress so easily disposed of
Indian lands, which for centuries had sustained the first Oregonians,
the promises of "utmost good faith" seemed hollow.

The Ill-Fated Treaty Program,
1851–65

What followed the passage of the Donation Land Act was tragic.
First, the Oregon Treaty Commission left for Oregon. Next, on
February 27, 1851, before the Oregon Treaty Commission even began its work in western Oregon, Congress revoked the commission's
powers. However, in April and May, the commissioners (who did not
know their powers had been taken away) assembled hundreds of survivors of the Kalapuya bands from the Willamette Valley in treaty
councils at Champoeg on French Prairie. Over a period of days and
repeated ar-
guments—

*In exchange for the loss of their
land, the U.S. government
offered blankets, tents, and
clothing to poverty stricken
tribes. Here, agent Heinlein
issues goods to Paiutes. Photo
courtesy of Oregon Historical
Society, #OrHi44161.*

while serving food and talking about the "Great White Father in Washington"—the commissioners attempted to persuade the Indians to give up their lands and move.

In almost every case, the Indian leaders refused to relocate, asserting that they had always lived in the valley, that they were at peace with the settlers, and that their ancestors were buried in these lands. The commissioners, feasting on oysters, canned strawberries, and champagne, easily expended the $20,000 appropriated for the treaty program but obtained only six treaties. In none of these documents did the Indians agree to leave the valley.

These treaties failed to gain Senate ratification because the commission no longer had treaty powers and, above all, none of its treaties required the removal of the Indians to the east of the mountains. The Indians had agreed in good faith to these treaties, which provided supplies, services, and promises of peace, but months and then years passed while more settlers moved in and shoved them off their lands. The promises of the treaty commission remained unfulfilled.

During the summer of 1851, troubles erupted between gold miners headed to and from California and the Indians of the Rogue River Valley. When bloodshed occurred, Governor John Gaines rushed south to quell the fighting. Ultimately, he negotiated a treaty with the Takelma in the Rogue Valley, but because he had no authority to do so, Congress ignored it.

Joel Palmer was doggedly determined to terminate Indian land title. Between 1853 and 1855 he secured a number of agreements in which tribes ceded much of western Oregon and part of the Columbia Plateau. Illustrtation courtesy of Oregon Historical Society, #OrHi86876.

In 1851 Anson Dart became Oregon's first full-time Superintendent of Indian Affairs. That summer he launched his own ambitious treaty program with tribes near the mouth of the Columbia River in Oregon and Washington, holding councils at Tansy Point in Clatsop County and Port Orford on the southwestern coast.

Dart's Tansy Point treaties provided for a variety of "reserved rights," including catching fish, taking whales from the beach, grazing livestock, and cutting firewood. Unfortunately, none of Dart's treaties gained ratification either. As with the treaty commission's work, none of the agreements provided for Indian removal to land east of the Cascades. Thus, more promises were made, but while the Indians waited patiently, only more settlement and dislocation occurred.

While Dart lobbied unsuccessfully in Washington, DC, for action on his treaties, the superintendency passed to Joel Palmer, who, in September 1853, initiated a new treaty program in the mining region of southwestern Oregon, where a gold discovery had led miners to drive the Indians from their nearby villages. Competition for land and food resources, unprincipled miners who murdered Indians, and disruption of the ecological balance were all factors that led Palmer to the potentially explosive region of southwestern Oregon. To some extent, Palmer was successful. On September 10, 1853, he secured a treaty with the Takelma (referred to in documents as the "Rogue River Tribe") and on September 19 with the Takelman-speaking Cow Creek Band of Umpqua. These agreements ceded hundreds of square miles to the United States for approximately 2.3 cents per acre. Palmer did not have treaty-making authority and, before the Senate would act, had to return to obtain amendments to these treaties, again signed by tribal leaders. These two treaties, ratified in 1854 and proclaimed in 1855, were the first approved with Indians in the Pacific Northwest.

Doggedly determined to terminate Indian land title in Oregon, Palmer mounted a program that led to a number of agreements. Joel Palmer's treaty philosophy differed dramatically from that of Anson Dart or of Governor Isaac I. Stevens in Washington Territory. Palmer initially provided no reserved rights in his treaties. After he participated with Stevens in the Walla Walla Treaty Council of 1855, Palmer acknowledged, however, that the Columbia Plateau tribes in Oregon needed protection of traditional fishing, hunting, and gathering rights. Thus treaties with the Umatilla, Nez Perce, and Warm Springs tribes included those guarantees, while other Palmer-negotiated treaties in Oregon did not.

Joel Palmer's Treaties, 1853–55

Date	Tribe or Band
September 10, 1853/ November 11, 1854	Rogue River Tribe
September 19, 1853	Cow Creek Band of Umpqua
November 15, 1854	Rogue River Tribe
November 18, 1854	Chasta, Scoton, Grave Creek Band of Umpqua
November 29, 1854	Umpqua and Calapooia
January 22, 1855	Confederated Bands of Kalapuya
June 9, 1855	Walla Walla, Cayuse, and Umatilla
June 11, 1855	Nez Perce
June 25, 1855	Tribes of Middle Oregon
December 21, 1855	Mol-lal-la-las or Molel Tribe

Arrival of the Nez Perce Indians at Walla Walla Treaty [...]

These treaties all gained ratification and ceded much of western Oregon and parts of the Columbia Plateau south of the Columbia River. Palmer's treaty with the Tualatin Band of Calapooia (March 25, 1854) and with the tribes and bands along the entire Oregon Coast (August 11–September 8, 1855) remained unratified. In spite of the Senate's failure to act, the government presumed that those Indian lands had passed into the public domain.

The treaty program with Oregon Indians was terminated with Palmer's administration and remained on hold until June 9, 1863, when the government persuaded some Nez Perce to sign a treaty ceding millions of acres, including the lands of Joseph's band in northeastern Oregon. That treaty became a critical issue in the subsequent Nez Perce War of 1877. On October 10, 1863, the controversial treaty of "peace and friendship" with the Western Shoshone at Ruby Valley, Nevada, appeared to confirm Indian title in southeast Oregon. However, the government subsequently claimed it ceded Shoshone lands.

J. W. Perit Huntington negotiated the treaty of October 14, 1864, with the Klamath, Modok, and Yahooskin Band of Snakes (Northern Paiutes), ceding much of south-central Oregon but reserving the Klamath Reservation. On August 12, 1865, the Wollpah-pe Band of Snakes (Northern Paiute) agreed to cede lands in the Harney Basin. On November 15, 1865, the tribes of the Warm Springs Reservation signed a treaty ceding their off-reservation fishery. Almost immediately they denounced the ratified agreement as fraudulent and continued to exercise their reserved, off-reservation fishing rights.

In 1871 Congress suspended the formal treaty program, though for many years thereafter, the House and Senate jointly approved "agreements" with Indian tribes that had treaty status. The Oregon treaties ceded millions of acres for paltry sums. Only the Columbia Plateau treaties contained provisions of "reserved rights." The treaty era drove Indians from their old homes and left them almost landless.

Warfare and Destruction of Tribal Life, 1851–78

Pioneer settlement, the faltering steps of the treaty program, the gold rush, and the actions of unprincipled persons plunged Oregon Indians into warfare in the 1850s. The most bitter and prolonged troubles erupted in southwestern Oregon in the drainages of the Rogue and Umpqua rivers and along the nearby coast. Between 1852 and 1856, the region was beset with conflicts, many fomented by self-styled Volunteers who attacked the Indians. These men, operating without legal standing, acted as vigilantes to avenge alleged wrongs. A petty theft might provoke them to hang Indian men and—on occasion—even children.

Warm Springs scouts served in the Modoc War of 1873. The conflict between Captain Jack's band and the U.S. Army was the consequence of trespass, settler attacks, and repeated efforts to force the Modocs to live on the Klamath Reservation. At the war's conclusion, a military tribunal tried and executed four Modoc leaders; 153 prisoners were removed to the Quapaw Agency in Oklahoma. Photo courtesy of the Smithsonian Institution Negative #2899A.

For example, in August 1853, Martin Angel rode into the gold rush town of Jacksonville screaming, "Nits breed lice. We have been killing Indians in the valley all day. Exterminate the whole race!" Within minutes, the rabble, a mob estimated at eight hundred men, had hanged a seven-year-old Indian boy. Such events, multiplied many times, fostered in some Indians a determination to fight to the finish. Others gave up all hope and gathered on the Table Rock Reservation on the north side of the Rogue River Valley. Even there they were not safe. In October 1855, a mob attacked and massacred eight men and fifteen women and children. This incident provoked the final Rogue Indian war, which lasted until June 1856.

In a series of engagements during the spring and early summer of 1856, the combined efforts of several companies of the U.S. Army and the Oregon Volunteers defeated the Indians. The survivors fled deep into the canyon of the Rogue River, where in June they finally surrendered at the Big Bend.

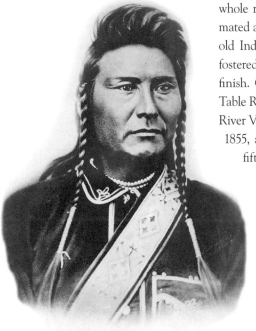

Chief Joseph. Photo courtesy of Oregon Historical Society, #OrHi5172.

As early as January and February of 1856, the Bureau of Indian Affairs (BIA) began removing the refugees over a long "trail of tears." The scattered remnants of the Indian bands of southwestern Oregon were marched nearly two hundred miles through the snows of winter to the Grand Ronde Reservation on the Yamhill River. The army took others, either by steamboat from Port Orford or by trail along the coast, to the new Siletz Reservation.

During the 1860s, conflicts between the Northern Paiutes and the U.S. Army erupted several times in central and southeastern Oregon. During this period the army moved into the region and established military posts, including Fort Harney, Camp Warner, and Fort Klamath. For many years, Indian leaders eluded the troops and sustained an Indian presence that deterred cattlemen and settlers.

In 1873 the Modoc War broke out along the Oregon-California border. While the Modocs attacked emigrant parties on the Applegate Trail in the early 1850s, the retribution of settlers from Yreka, California, was barbaric. They massacred Modocs and mutilated the bodies, collecting fingers and ears. A bitter legacy of these events was lingering distrust. The government's unwise efforts to compel the Modocs to move to the Klamath Reservation only renewed the potential for conflict.

Overall, the Modoc War proved costly and brutal. The Modocs attacked the Peace Commission and killed General E. R. S. Canby, the only American general to die in an Indian war. After the Modocs surrendered in June 1873, the government hanged Captain Jack and other leaders and sentenced two to life imprisonment at Alcatraz Island. That fall the government shipped 153 Modoc prisoners to the Quapaw Agency in Oklahoma. In 1903 a few returned to the Klamath Reservation.

Another tribe, the Nez Perce, occupied the lower Snake River drainage, including the beautiful Clearwater country along the western flanks of the Bitterroot Mountains in Idaho. Their 1855 treaty confirmed a reservation of 7.6 million acres, but the discovery of gold in their territory led to widespread invasion of their reservation and pressures to disinherit them. An unratified treaty in 1861 opened part of the reservation to trespass. On June 9, 1863, some tribal leaders agreed to a treaty reducing the reservation to a mere 1.1 million acres.

The lands of Joseph's band of Nez Perce who resided in the Wallowa Valley of northeastern Oregon were swept into the public domain with the 1867 ratification of the treaty, though in 1873 the band temporarily obtained a reservation in the Wallowas. In frustration, Old Joseph tore up his New Testament. By 1877 his son and others, embittered by what they saw as a sellout by the Protestant-Presbyterian Nez Perce who accepted the 1867 treaty, were drawn into war. In a vain effort to escape into Canada, Joseph, Looking Glass, and White Bird led their people on a eighteen-hundred-mile journey across the Rocky Mountains. Some survivors were imprisoned at Fort Leavenworth, then exiled to Oklahoma. After eight years, Joseph's band was removed to Nespelem on the Colville Reservation. Although some were allowed to join the Nez Perce in Idaho, they were denied settlement in the Wallowas.

Reservations

By treaties in 1853, the BIA created reservations at Table Rock in the Rogue River Valley and on Council Creek in the South Umpqua Valley. It constructed houses for chiefs, held out the prospect of allotments of land to individual Indians, began programs of instruction in agriculture, and garrisoned troops at Fort Lane to help confine the Indians to the reservations. In 1854 it also created the Umpqua and Calapooia Reservation in the Umpqua Valley, and in 1855 the treaties of the Walla Walla Council reserved lands for the

Oregon Reservations, 1853–1990

Name	Date Created	Location
Table Rock	September 10, 1853	Rogue River Valley
Cow Creek	September 19, 1853	Council Creek
Umpqua and Calapooia	November 19, 1854	Umpqua Valley
Umatilla	June 9, 1855	Eastern Columbia Plateau
Nez Perce	June 11, 1855/ June 16, 1873	Northeast Oregon
Warm Springs	June 25, 1855	Western Columbia Plateau
Siletz (or Coast)	November 9, 1855	Central Coast
Grand Ronde	June 30, 1857	South Yamhill Valley
Klamath	October 14, 1864	Klamath Basin
Malheur	March 14, 1871/ September 12, 1872	Harney Basin
Coos	February 11, 1941/ October 14, 1984	Coos Bay
Siuslaw	June 1, 1948	Florence
Burns Paiute Indian Colony	1935/October 13, 1972	Lincoln County
Siletz	September 4, 1980	Lincoln County
Cow Creek	September 15, 1986	Canyonville
Grand Ronde	September 8, 1988	Yamhill County

Umatilla and Warm Springs reservations on the Columbia Plateau. The Nez Perce retained much of northeastern Oregon in that council. Then, by executive order of June 16, 1873, they secured designation of the Wallowa Valley as a reservation.

The 1856 Rogue River Indian War persuaded the BIA to remove all Indians from southwestern Oregon and the Willamette Valley. The bureau therefore abandoned the reservations at Table Rock, Council Creek, and the Umpqua Valley and began colonizing Indians on the Siletz and Grand Ronde reservations. In the 1870s pressures from ranchers who desired the lush meadowlands of the Harney Basin persuaded the President to revoke the orders creating the Malheur Reservation. In these matters the federal government presumed to exercise supreme authority, and on a number of occasions it did so—hardly ever considering the needs, wishes, and rights of the Oregon Indians.

In the nineteenth century the reservation system was premised on removal and residency. Indians were compelled to give up their seasonal round, abandon traditional villages, and surrender to the control of the BIA. Colonized on the reservations, they were subjected to many constraints. The army established Fort Umpqua, Fort Hoskins, and Fort Yamhill to surround the Siletz and Grand Ronde reservations. It garrisoned troops at Fort Dalles to monitor the Warm Springs Reservation and at Fort Walla Walla to watch the Indians at Umatilla. During the Civil War, it established Fort Klamath to play a similar role at the Klamath Reservation and sent troops to Fort Harney.

The BIA segregated Indians from the surrounding European American communities. Sometimes, when starvation threatened, the Indians could obtain work permits to leave the reservation. The goal, however, was to isolate them from evil influences and prevent them from returning to their old homes.

On the Columbia Plateau those efforts ultimately led to the much-disputed treaty of November 15, 1865, with the Confederated Tribes of Warm Springs. By this ratified agreement, the tribes were compelled to relinquish their off-reservation fishing rights at their "usual and accustomed stations" on the Columbia River. The Indians subsequently claimed deception and fraud, and bitterly contested their confinement. Finally, in 1888, Commissioner of Indian Affairs J. D. C. Atkins observed, "I think it highly improbable that the Warm Springs Indians would have relinquished their rights in these valuable fisheries for the mere asking."

Over several decades the reservations were subjected to abolition by executive order, sale because of termination by Congress, opening to public entry by statute, and allotment with sale of "sur-

Fort Klamath, established in 1864, was one of several military posts guarding Oregon reservations. Other facilities included Fort Lane, Fort Yamhill, Fort Hoskins, Fort Umpqua, and Siletz Blockhouse in western Oregon and Fort Dalles and Fort Harney east of the Cascades. Photo courtesy of Oregon Historical Society, #OrHi1677.

OLD FORT KLAMATH

plus" lands. Reservations were created by executive order, act of Congress, or treaty, or subsequently by the BIA taking land into "trust" for tribes. In this last instance the lands might be deeded to the U.S. for the tribe, purchased by the BIA, or purchased by the tribe itself.

"Civilization" Programs

The Bureau of Indian Affairs planned to transform Oregon Indians into sedentary, agricultural, English-speaking Christians. From 1855 to 1956, it promoted these goals, first, by designing the reservation as an isolated place where cultural and linguistic change could be fostered, then by advocating farming as the highest "calling" and telling Indians they would benefit if they mastered the techniques of crop production and livestock management.

Some tribes, such as the Umatilla and Cayuse, which possessed large herds of horses and had acquired gardening skills from their contact with the Whitman Mission, received high marks in agent reports for their march toward a "civilized" state. By contrast, the Northern Paiutes, dedicated to their traditional lifeway and determined to maintain their seasonal round and usual foods, were bitterly denounced in BIA reports as savages and barbarians. Most Indians, however, had mixed press in the BIA annual reports. Usually the new agent in his first year spoke of wretched conditions on the reservations: crop failures, hunger, poor housing, lack of understanding about sanitation, broken tools, and inadequate sawmills, grist mills, or numbers of livestock. Within a year or so, however—in order to look "good"—the agent wrote glowingly of the progress of his charges. Then, because of the constant turnover of agents, the cycle was repeated again with each agent seeming to fault his predecessor.

Oregon Indians were the victims in this brutal system. Thousands died needlessly as a result of problems from overcrowding, while many others perished of malnutrition because of crop failures. A number of tribes received no annuities because of the Senate's failure to ratify their treaties, and other Indians suffered because of the agents' malfeasance or corruption. Finally, in the 1870s, the administration of President Ulysses S. Grant attempted to reform Indian affairs nationally with its "Peace Policy."

This policy parceled out the reservations among the Christian denominations, allowing various sects a monopoly for staffing and operating missions on reservations. The Methodists gained Siletz, the Presbyterians Grand Ronde and Klamath, and so it went. The assumption was that people of high principles would deal fairly and humanely with the Indians.

At Siletz, however, agent Edmund Swan, a lifelong Methodist, found otherwise. In 1881 he lamented to the Secretary of the Interior how the Oregon Methodist Conference dictated whom he should employ and from whom he was to buy supplies. Writing of the agency employees, he observed,

Cultural assimilation at boarding schools included teaching young Indian women European American gender roles and personal appearance. Both photos were taken at Chemawa, above in 1923 and left in 1949. Photos courtesy of Oregon Historical Society, #OrHi36845 and #OrHi007202 respectively.

Top: The Indian Training School moved in 1882 from Forest Grove to Chemawa near Salem. Today it is the nation's oldest Indian boarding school. In 1915 the male students wore military uniforms. Photo courtesy of Oregon Historical Society, #OrHi36112. Bottom: The Bureau of Indian Affairs taught cooking, sewing, and homemaking skills to girls and young women at Chemawa, 1915. Photo by Major Lee Moorhouse, courtesy of Knight Library, University of Oregon, negative #5473.

"I have found it necessary to remind them that Reservations were not formed for the benefit of them, as a class, but rather for other and higher purposes."

While a number of selfless missionaries like Adrien Croquet (who ministered from 1859 to 1898 on the Grand Ronde Reservation) devoted their lives to the Indians, many BIA employees proved to be corrupt and bigoted. With the Indians under the control of denominations, the prospect of forcing attendance at church was enhanced. Parents were informed that children who did not attend the Sabbath School would not receive clothing. Others found their interest in messianic religions, such as the Ghost Dance, Earth Lodge Cult, or Dreamer Religion, challenged by BIA officials on religious grounds. The potential for coercion was increased by this policy until the 1890s, when the federal government abandoned it and put the BIA under the civil service.

On many reservations the civilization programs were driven by a desire to transform the children. While most reservations had day schools, some—either by treaty or special appropriation—secured funds for boarding schools, which were of highest priority to the government because of the complete isolation of the child from the parents and grandparents. The schools enforced a strict English-only policy and punished children for speaking in their native languages. This requirement went far beyond the classroom and included conversation in the dormitories and at meals. The curriculum was heavily oriented toward manual labor: carpentry, blacksmithing, shoemaking, and farming for boys, and needlework, sewing, beadwork, housecleaning, washing, ironing, and cooking for girls. At best, the BIA saw Oregon Indians as becoming cheerful, thrifty, hardworking common laborers and did little to prepare them for leadership roles or for higher education.

The brightest and best students of the reservation schools were tapped to attend Chemawa Indian School. Founded by the U.S. Army in 1881 in Forest Grove, this regional boarding school elicited bitter complaints from the local residents about the presence of Indian children in town. In 1885 the bureau selected a rural, agricultural site five miles from Salem and there the students helped build Chemawa School. The boys mastered brickmaking and carpentry and helped construct the campus, while the girls cleaned the buildings, cooked, and did the laundry. Both boys and girls worked in the surrounding fields to produce food for the facility.

Occasionally, graduates of Chemawa went on for more education, attending Haskell Institute in Kansas or even Carlisle Indian School in Pennsylvania. This system of education segregated the most able students and removed them farther and farther from family and tribal life. The BIA worked on the mistaken assumption that this system would produce a new generation of tribal leaders. Instead, it often so transformed the students that many left tribal life and moved into the non-Indian community, never returning to the reservations, where they no longer knew the language or even recognized family members.

Boys and young men gained instruction in shoemaking at the Indian schools in Forest Grove and Salem. Manual labor skills dominated the curriculum. Photo courtesy of Oregon Historical Society, #OrHi36845.

The Bureau of Indian Affairs disrupted the traditional seasonal subsistence round and tribal residency patterns by forcing Indians onto reservations. To enforce its control over the reservation, agents hired Indian men to wear uniforms and badges to work as the Indian Police Force authorized by Congress in 1878. These seven men served as police at Grande Ronde in 1890. Photo courtesy of Oregon Historical Society, #OrHi86917.

To be sure, some returned to the reservations, but each generation had less knowledge of traditional lifeways, and by 1900 the number of speakers of western Oregon languages was dropping rapidly. By the 1920s some languages were entirely extinct, and in the 1930s linguists scrambled to record the vocabularies and voices of the "last" speakers of the Galice Creek dialect, Takelma, Hanis and Miluk Coos, Tillamook, and Kalapuyan.

The impacts of the civilization programs were evident. The Bureau of Indian Affairs had largely succeeded in destroying many elements of Indian identity. The reservation system and the schools had partly achieved their goals.

Allotment, 1887–1934

As early as the Rogue River Treaty of 1853, the federal government raised the prospect of dividing up reservations among the Indians. With the passage of the General Allotment Act of 1887, this idea gained national endorsement. Also known as the Dawes Act, the allotment program sought to destroy tribes by dividing their communal land base. Individual Indians—men, women, and children—would receive acreage held in trust. When they had proven their "competency" or had waited for twenty-five years, the BIA would issue a deed or "fee-patent" for the land. To accelerate the process, Congress passed the Burke Act in 1906, eliminating the twenty-five-year waiting period and permitting local agents to determine "competency."

For most reservations the allotment program proved to be a nightmare. First, the Indians had to hold a conference, a meeting staged by the BIA, to agree to accept the law. Once this was done, the process began with the selection of lands. Some people received valuable acreage; others got tracts that were nearly worthless. Some lands were inaccessible, isolated, densely forested, or lacked water. While the agents generally tried to help the Indians make good selections, the competition for prime pieces sometimes pitted families against one another. Powerful individuals obtained cleared, fenced, or otherwise improved lands; children, the aged, and others had to be content with lesser lands.

The allotment process was sometimes surrounded by an almost circuslike atmosphere. Such was the case at Siletz, where in 1892 the Indians agreed to the program. Although reduced by executive order in 1865 and act of Congress in 1875, the Siletz Reservation still contained nearly a quarter of a million acres, most of it virgin timber or rapidly replenishing coniferous forest. Not surprisingly, eager speculators in timberlands hovered nearby. Indeed, some even volunteered to assist in the surveys to speed up the process. Their interest was rewarded by a compliant Congress, which threw open to entry 191,798 "surplus" or unallotted acres. The allotment program allocated 44,000 acres to individuals, reserved 3,000 acres for the tribes, and turned over more than 75 percent of the lands to non-Indians.

The scramble for Indian lands, some of them highly valuable even at the turn of the twentieth century, became part of the widespread land frauds of the era. After his conviction as "King of the Oregon Land Fraud Ring," S. A. D. Puter wrote *Looters of the Public Domain* from his jail cell in 1908. An important chapter in Puter's account focused on the "The Story of Siletz" and "How the Indians Were Robbed of Their Homes for the Benefit of Pale-faced Looters, Under the Guise of Treaty Rights."

The allotment program consumed some reservations. By 1904 all of Grand Ronde was allotted except for the tribal cemetery and the lots where the Catholic Church and the agency headquarters stood. Future generations had no prospect of securing land, nor did the confederated tribes have a land base for economic development. At Warm Springs, prime properties passed from the tribes to individuals and often—and almost as quickly—to non-Indians. Fee patenting bestowed citizenship on Indians, but also the obligation of

In 1887, Congress passed the General Allotment Act to break up reservations and destroy tribalism by creating individually owned tracts of land. The "Story of Siletz" so phrased by S. A. D. Puter in Looters of the Public Domain *(1908), occured with the wild and dishonest scramble for the alleged "surplus" lands opened in the 1890s for homesteading and sale by Congress. Photo courtesy of Oregon Historical Society, #OrHi10691-b.*

paying taxes. Within four years, many lost their allotments when the counties foreclosed for nonpayment of taxes. Thus, the Umatilla Reservation took on the appearance of a gigantic checkerboard made up of tribal lands, individual trust lands, and alienated lands in non-Indian ownership.

While allotment may have facilitated citizenship, it also accelerated the destruction of tribalism and horribly complicated reservation administration. Where allotments remained in trust, there developed complicated heirships of several, sometimes dozens, of owners. Decisions on rights-of-way, reforestation, and land-use planning became almost impossible to make. Non-Indians acquired key properties, such as the hot springs on the Warm Springs Reservation. The status of some allotments remained ambiguous when the BIA lost contact with heirs who had moved away. Neither the tribe nor individuals could acquire the land without a lengthy, often confusing process of tracking down heirs or waiting for the BIA to probate Indian estates.

Some Indians, however, liked the allotment program. They gained land, secured citizenship, and gradually left tribal life. For them, the allotment provided a way to move into the majority culture that had surrounded the tribes in the nineteenth century. Off-reservation Oregon Indians found the allotment era even more appealing because amendments to the General Allotment Act and the Indian Homestead Act (1875) permitted them, for the first time, to secure land. When granted under these laws, the land was in trust and therefore exempt from taxation.

After 1887 several thousand Indians in Oregon obtained public domain allotments. These included 11,014 acres to Northern Paiutes in the Harney Basin and more than 10,000 acres to members of the Coquille, Coos, Lower Umpqua, and Siuslaw tribes along the southern Oregon coast. Some Indians obtained allotments in the western Cascades of Douglas County and others along the south bank of the Columbia River near their age-old fishing sites at Five Mile Rapids and Celilo Falls.

Too often, however, non-Indians manipulated the Indians and plundered their lands. In the 1950s, in fact, employees of the Portland-area office of the BIA were charged, tried, convicted, and sentenced to jail for stealing hundreds of thousands of dollars in timber monies from allotments on the lower Rogue River. The disabilities of the allotment era were so evident that Congress abolished the program in 1934 and extended "trust" indefinitely on all individual and tribal lands.

Eddie Ned, a Coquille, was one of dozens of Oregon Indian men and women who served World War I. Many more served in subsequent wars. Belatedly, Congress passed the Indian Citizenship Act (1924) to acknowledge that all Native Americans, including those who had served in the military, were American citizens. Photo courtesy of Bandon Historical Society.

Indian Reorganization, 1934–46

A growing sense of reform hit America in the 1930s. John Collier, named Commissioner of Indian Affairs in 1933, had voiced strong criticism of the BIA and federal Indian policy for nearly a decade. Occupying a key position in the New Deal government of President Franklin D. Roosevelt, Collier attempted to change directions in policy. As a reformer, he believed Indian civilization had intrinsic values. He championed Indian art and music and forbade BIA schools to subvert traditional Indian religions. He also viewed the allotment program as a disaster that destroyed tribes and foreclosed their future.

Collier played a pivotal role in helping secure the Indian Reorganization Act (IRA) in 1934. This law ended allotments, extended trust, and encouraged tribes to form modern governments with written constitutions. It set up a revolving loan fund, permitted tribes to form business corporations, and called for sound conservation of land, water, and mineral resources on reservations. Acceptance of IRA was mixed. Some tribes saw it as an opportunity to build for the present and future, while other tribal leaders denounced it as another trick from Washington, another program that would come and go. These conflicting voices greeted the proponents of IRA when they assembled Oregon tribal leaders at Chemawa School in 1935 to discuss the new law.

Some Oregon tribes ignored IRA and did not vote on it. The Klamath and Confederated Tribes of Siletz rejected it. The Grand Ronde Indian Community adopted IRA and organized a corporation under the law, as did the Confederated Tribes of Warm Springs. Whether tribes accepted or rejected IRA, only a few found much change in Indian policy. The Great Depression and then World War II created economic circumstances that precluded the adequate funding of revolving loans or the land acquisition programs. The Confederated Tribes of Coos, Lower Umpqua, and Siuslaw, however, while not voting on IRA, benefited from the changed atmosphere of the 1930s. In 1941 the Bureau of Indian Affairs accepted into trust a 6.1-acre reservation for these Indians, erected a fine tribal hall on the land at Coos Bay, and for the first time provided modest medical care—a once-a-month clinic—through the Indian Health Service.

After years of litigation, the Klamath at last won $5.3 million in 1938 for taking of their lands for the Oregon Central Military Wagon Road and Crater Lake National Park. Tribal members gathered to discuss with their attorneys and government officials how to distribute the money per capita among the members. Photo courtesy of Oregon Historical Society, #OrHi57659.

Lawsuits and Claims, 1899–1984

In 1869 Congress invoked sovereign immunity to protect the United States from a lawsuit by Indian tribes. After that date, any tribe with a grievance had to mount a campaign that would convince a congressman to introduce and secure passage of a jurisdictional act permitting the tribe to sue the United States. For most tribes, this process was complicated, costly, and almost impossible. In spite of its challenges, however, Oregon Indians displayed great tenacity and tried to use this system.

In 1899 the Clatsop, Kathlamet, and Tillamook bands—signatories to treaties negotiated in 1851 by Anson Dart—joined Chinookans from the Washington shore of the lower Columbia River to sue in the Court of Claims. Silas Smith, whose mother was the daughter of Clatsop chief Coboway, served as legal counsel for these Indians. Although Smith did not live to see the suit settled in 1912, the tribes won a judgment and in 1913 received modest compensation for their lands. They were the first Oregon tribes to use this system.

In 1920 the Klamath, Modoc, and Yahuskins gained permission to sue for the loss of 86,418 acres from their reservation in a wagon-road grant. They lost the case in 1935, but a subsequent act permitted another lawsuit that led to a claims award of $5.3 million, which the Supreme Court confirmed in 1938.

In 1929 the Confederated Tribes of Coos, Lower Umpqua, and Siuslaw obtained an act to permit suit over the appropriation of all of their homelands in southwestern Oregon without ratified treaty or compensation. Sadly, after the tribes labored for twelve years to get into court, the claims court rejected all oral testimony and their unratified 1855 coastal treaty as proof of ownership, concluding in 1938 that the tribes had no "right, claim, or title to any part of the coast of Oregon whatsoever." The Supreme Court denied an appeal.

Other tribes lobbied Congress and secured favorable action on their bills, and then—as in the case of the Cow Creek Band of Umpqua in 1932—saw their measures vetoed by the President. To "clear the nation's conscience" and—many believed—end once and for all these lawsuits and petitions for jurisdictional acts, Congress created the Indian Claims Commission. Established in 1946, this special court was to receive complaints for five years, act informally to settle the claims, and go out of business in 1956. Thirty years later, its work still unfinished and virtually all the original plaintiffs dead, Congress abolished the commission and passed its still pending cases to the claims court.

Between 1946 and 1951, almost all Oregon tribes responded and filed complaints with the Indian Claims Commission, some securing what at the time were perceived to be substantial judgments. (The Nez Perce Tribe, for example, was awarded $9.2 million.) Other tribes, however, obtained only token sums, and some found their complaints dismissed. All worked under a terrible burden to use this "window of opportunity" to file suit. The rules were, except in highly unusual circumstances, that the tribes could obtain no interest, the settlement would be only financial (no tribe could settle its claim with land), and the price of the tribal land was to be fixed at the "date of taking"—the year when the Indians lost it through warfare, removal, treaty, or other factors—rather than at the land's current value.

In spite of these rules and the tacit acknowledgment that by participating in the process they were abrogating aboriginal title, tribes from across the country stepped forward. Many had fought vainly for their day in court and saw the work of the claims commission as their only opportunity. Unfortunately, when the cases reached the claims commission, they dragged on and on. Tragically, some of the judgments were then consumed in offsets—deductions that included attorney fees and "benefits" the BIA had paid out to the tribes over the preceding century through reservation programs. When the Indians protested that they had been unwilling beneficiaries of such programs, their pleas were unheeded. The process moved inexorably but slowly forward.

In 1981 the Cow Creek Band of Umpqua Indians obtained a jurisdictional act and brought its land claims case to the claims court. The case resulted in a 1984 negotiated settlement of $1.5 million. Having observed the impact of per-capita payments to other Oregon tribes, the Cow Creeks voted to invest their judgment fund in an endowment. The BIA, however, rejected the tribal plan and demanded payments to individuals—in spite of the Indian Judgment Fund Act, which had rejected that unwise and discredited program. Congress then intervened and mandated the tribal plan. The Cow Creeks thus preserved their legacy from the past and banked it. Today their endowment provides annual interest for education, housing, and economic development.

Termination, 1956–89

The sentiment to reverse the policies of John Collier mounted steadily in the 1940s. Following World War II, some in Congress decided to get the federal government out of Indian affairs. They argued that economy and efficiency dictated cutting back, perhaps even eliminating, the Bureau of Indian Affairs. Indians, they observed, should move into the mainstream. They should be "set free" from the disabilities of second-class citizenship and life on isolated reservations. These views accorded with those held by a number of President Dwight Eisenhower's cabinet members, among them Douglas McKay, secretary of the interior and former governor of Oregon. Presiding over the BIA, McKay concluded that Oregon should be a showcase for the new era of Indian policy. McKay saw the termination of "government-to-government relationships" with Oregon tribes as being "in line with the established policy of our state." He argued that Termination would bring Oregon Indians "full and equal citizenship."

Several members of Congress introduced bills to speed the transition of Indians into mainstream American life. In February 1954, joint house and senate committees heard debate on the "Termination of Federal Supervision over Certain Tribes of Indians." McKay's assistant, Orme Lewis, led off by stating:

> It is our belief that the Indians subject to the proposed bill no longer require special assistance from the Federal Government, and that they have sufficient skill and ability to manage their own affairs. Through long association and intermarriage with their white neighbors, education in public schools, employment in gainful occupations in order to obtain a livelihood, and dependence on public institutions for public services, the Indians have largely been integrated into the white society where they are accepted without discrimination.

Even in 1954, however, Oregon law continued to prohibit the marriage of an Indian and a non-Indian with the punishment of fines and imprisonment for the officiating minister or public official and the couple. At that time, none of the Oregon tribes met the standards of readiness for immediate termination of federal services laid down by William Zimmerman, former acting commissioner of Indian affairs. Clearly other factors were at work.

One was the desire by timber companies to gain access to the vast resources of the Klamath Reservation in south-central Oregon, where thousands of acres of virgin timber stood. If the Klamath were "terminated," some argued, their timber could be logged and they could find gainful employment in the timber industry.

Coercion became another factor. Although the Klamath had been awarded a judgment of $2.6 million against the United States, Senator Arthur Watkins, one of the primary proponents of Termination, held up approval of the appropriation until the Klamath agreed to terminate. The bill he rushed to pass was ill-conceived and made little assessment of social or economic consequences for the Klamath people or for the Oregon timber industry. "The committee members' only desire," wrote Vine Deloria, "was to get the termination of the tribe over with as quickly as possible. If it meant cutting every tree in Oregon, they would have so authorized, simply to get on to another tribe."

In 1956 Congress, in its exercise of plenary power, terminated every tribe and band west of the Cascades and the Klamath in south-central Oregon. As quickly as possible, the Bureau of Indian Affairs issued deeds to allotments, sold off tribal lands, ended health benefits, and declined to admit Indian children from the affected tribes to BIA schools. For some tribes, the bureau prepared Termination Rolls, in part to have a list for disbursing the modest assets resulting from the sale of communal holdings. In some instances, the BIA turned over tribal land and buildings to non-Indian trustees. When tribes objected, demanded an accounting, and charged fraud, they were ignored.

The impact of Termination was disastrous. For tribes like the Klamath, it meant substantial, one-time-only cash payments on a per-capita basis. Many Oregon Indians had never had so much money at one time before and few were prepared to manage the windfall of claims payments or the checks received for the sale of tribal lands. A number lost everything in weeks or months, to the delight of car dealers and others. For families in which a dozen or more heirs suddenly owned an allotment outright, the requirement was to pool resources and pay the taxes. The land had never before been taxed and many were unable to persuade their cousins, brothers, and sisters to contribute. By 1960 Oregon counties began foreclosure. Several hundred Klamath put their assets in a trust managed by a Portland bank, which permitted their assets to grow under careful management. Eventually they disbanded the trust and all but one, Edison Chiloquin, took substantial per-capita distributions. For the western Oregon tribes the assets were modest—a few hundred dollars, or sometimes a check for a few cents.

For twenty years Congress ignored Oregon's terminated Indians, as did the Bureau of Indian Affairs. These people may have looked like Indians, affirmed their Indian identities, maintained their tribal governments, or even retained their languages, but they were no longer Indians in the eyes of the federal government. Finally, in 1976, the Joint Congressional Commission on the American Indian held hearings in Salem, Oregon. Among those who testified were the Klamath, Grand Ronde, Coquille, Cow Creek Band of Umpqua (Upper Umpqua), Lower Umpqua, and Willow River Benevolent Association (Coos, Lower Umpqua, and Siuslaw). At the hearings, tales of deprivation, poor treatment, and discrimination poured out from witnesses, many challenging the BIA's handling of assets at Termination. Merle Holmes of Grand Ronde, for example, described the fate of the tribe's handsome community building:

> That hall at termination time, Bureau of Indian Affairs
> had a value of $6,689 for this building and almost ten
> acres of land. And now this land, under the stipulation
> with the trustee—he was not to even lease that building
> to anyone else without tribal consent—now he then, in
> turn, sold it. But now the price he got for it, as per this
> trustee, he sold that land and the building for $800, and
> he no more than sold it for the $800 and he turned right
> around and the white man bought it, turned right around
> and sold it for $8,000 plus land equity, and Mr. Fuller yet
> today says the land was worthless over there. But only
> when we had it, it was worthless. As soon as the white
> man got it, it was valuable.

Termination hung like a cloud over other Oregon tribes, as well as those in other parts of the country. When tribes became assertive, congressmen or BIA employees raised the specter of more Termination legislation. The Termination era only made Indian problems invisible; it did not ameliorate them. Low income, poor health, early death, and limited educational opportunity did not go away with Termination. By 1976, the record proved that the situation for the terminated tribes had only worsened.

Restoration and Self-Determination, 1977–90

In the 1970s Indians increasingly asserted their rights and federal responsibilities. A new generation of Indian leaders, many of them college-educated and supported by able legal assistance, called for redressing the problems of Termination. These currents in Indian affairs, which included the Red Power Movement and the American Indian Movement, were felt in Oregon. In 1977 Congress responded to a carefully developed campaign by the Confederated Tribes of Siletz by passing a bill restoring the tribes to "recognized" status. Other bills followed, on a case-by-case basis, for the Cow Creek Band of Umpqua; the Confederated Tribes of Coos, Lower Umpqua, and Siuslaw; the Confederated Tribes of Grand Ronde; the Klamath Tribes; and the Coquille Tribe.

At the annual Pendleton Round-Up, an Indian rider bears the American flag. Photo courtesy of Oregon Historical Society, #OrHi010516.

Not only had these tribes, through tremendous effort, secured the restoration of their federal relationships, other Oregon tribes had successfully staved off the efforts of the states of Oregon and Washington to abrogate their treaty-reserved fishing rights on the Columbia Plateau. The Confederated Tribes of Warm Springs, the Umatilla, and the Nez Perce waged a spirited battle in federal court to uphold the guarantees of the treaties of 1855, which assured their right to fish "at usual and accustomed grounds and stations."

The states raised many objections to the Indian fishing rights. They argued that the Indians were not conserving the resource. Some argued that the treaties were negotiated "a long time ago" and presumed that because they were old, they were no longer binding. The Indians pointed out that they had not built the dams that spanned the Columbia and transformed it from a free-flowing river into a series of great reservoirs. They noted that they had not poured sewage into the rivers, nor had they logged the hillsides and altered the habitat that diminished the runs of anadromous fish such as salmon. In fact, they pointed to their reluctant acceptance in the 1950s of the federal government's buying out their great fishery at Celilo Falls and Five Mile Rapids. They and the River tribes, those Indians who had steadfastly refused to be moved to the reservations, kept pointing to the assurances of the treaties or the hollow promises of the law creating the Bonneville Dam project, which called for the identification of "in lieu" fishing sites.

The "fish wars" of the 1960s and 1970s ultimately led to adjudicated settlements before judges Robert Belloni in Portland and George Boldt in Seattle. The decisions of these judges affirmed the tribes' treaty rights. Boldt's landmark decision was affirmed in 1975 by the Ninth Circuit Court and in 1979 by the U.S. Supreme Court. Judge Belloni, a peacemaker, compelled the state and federal fisheries interests and agencies to sit down with the tribes to negotiate fishing periods and determine the size of the catch, fishing days, and standards for gear. The tribes approached the matter through their Columbia River Inter-Tribal Fish Commission, an organization representing four Columbia River treaty tribes on the Plateau.

Increasingly, Oregon Indians found reasons to work together throughout the 1970s. As tribes they participated in the Affiliated Tribes of Northwest Indians and the National Congress of American Indians. On the state level they sat down several times each year in meetings of the Oregon Commission on Indian Services, whose membership included two members of the Oregon legislature, to discuss issues of common concern and have a voice in the state capitol. Through Indian education programs, usually financed with federal monies, they coordinated curriculum development, teacher training, culture camps, tutoring, and related activities. Dozens of Indian parents served on advisory committees to assist their local school districts in multicultural education.

In the 1970s and 1980s, some tribes obtained special funding through the Comprehensive Employment Training Act, the Indian Education Act, Housing and Urban Development, and development grants from the BIA or from the Administration for Native Americans. These resources, tribal monies, and able leaders encouraged a number of Oregon Indian tribes to launch economic development programs. The Confederated Tribes of Warm Springs became a national model for this work.

The Native American Graves Protection and Repatriation Act and its implementing regulations address the rights of lineal descendants, Indian tribes, and Native Hawaiian organizations (collectively referred to as "parties with standing") with regards to Native American human remains, funerary objects, sacred objects, and ob-

Tribal members roasted this Columbia River salmon for a public event. The ability of modern tribes to provide large quantities of fish for the public is a one sign that litigation and restoration efforts have made a difference. Photo courtesy of Elizabeth Woody.

jects of cultural patrimony (collectively referred to as "cultural items"). It requires agencies and museums that receive federal funds to provide information about Native American cultural items to parties with standing and, upon presentation of a valid request, dispose of or repatriate these objects to them.

Economic Development, 1990–2000

The Indian Gaming Regulatory Act (IGRA), enacted in 1988, establishes the jurisdictional framework that presently governs Indian gaming.

The purposes of IGRA were several: promote tribal self-sufficiency, ensure that Indians were the primary beneficiaries of gaming, establish fair and honest gaming, prevent organized crime and corruption by careful regulation, and establish standards for a National Indian Gaming Commission.

Gaming has long been integral to the Native American experience. Indians bet on the shake of marked beaver teeth, the outcome of foot races, the fortunes of shinny players driving a hockey puck over a level surface, and the outcome of javelin tosses or shooting of arrows at targets. Games of chance were an important part of their entertainment and leisure activities.

In the 1980s, the Cabazon Band of Mission Indians concluded that if the Catholic Church could operate bingo, a game regulated but not prohibited under California law, it could do the same with its own regulatory authority. As a tribe possessing certain powers of self-governance, however, the Cabazons did not accept the $1 million limit imposed by the state on its games of chance. The state of

Indian Gaming Casinos

Chinook Winds Casino
Confederated Tribes of Siletz Indians
1777 NW 44th Street
Lincoln City, Oregon 97367

Kah-Nee-Ta High Desert Resort & Casino
Confederated Tribes of the Warm Springs
Reservation of Oregon
6823 Highway 8
Warm Springs, Oregon 97761

Kla-Mo-Ya Casino
The Klamath Tribes
34333 Highway 97 N
Chiloquin, Oregon 97624

The Mill Casino & Hotel
Coquille Indian Tribe
3201 Tremont Avenue
North Bend, Oregon 97459

The Old Camp Casino
Burns Paiute Tribe
2205 W Monroe
Burns, Oregon 97720

Seven Feathers Hotel & Casino Resort
Cow Creek Band of Umpqua Tribe of Indians
146 Chief Miwaleta Lane
Canyonville, Oregon 97417-9700

Spirit Mountain Casino
Confederated Tribes of the Grand Ronde
27100 SW Salmon River Highway
Grand Ronde, Oregon 97347

Three Rivers Casino
Confederated Tribes of the Coos, Lower
Umpqua, and Siuslaw Indians
1845 U.S. Highway 126
Florence, Oregon 97439

Wildhorse Resort & Casino
Confederated Tribes of the Umatilla Indian
Reservation
72777 Hwy 331
Pendleton, Oregon 97801

California disagreed and tried to close down the Cabazon bingo hall. The ensuing litigation, *California v. Cabazon Band of Mission Indians*, went to the Supreme Court. In 1987 that court affirmed the right of the Cabazon Band to engage in gaming, a regulated, but not prohibited, activity. Congress then enacted IGRA to provide a framework for the anticipated proliferation of Indian gaming development.

The act establishes three classes of games with a different regulatory scheme for each. Class I gaming is defined as traditional Indian gaming and social gaming for minimal prizes. Regulatory authority over class I gaming is vested exclusively in tribal governments.

Class II gaming is defined as the game of chance commonly known as bingo (whether or not electronic, computer, or other technological aids are used in connection therewith), and if played in the same location as the bingo, pull tabs, punchboard, tip jars, instant bingo, and other games similar to bingo. Class II gaming also includes nonbanked card games, that is, games that are played exclusively against other players rather than against the house or a player acting as a bank. The act specifically excludes slot machines or electronic facsimiles of any game of chance from the definition of class II games. Tribes retain their authority to conduct, license, and regulate class II gaming so long as the state in which the tribe is located permits such gaming for any purpose and the tribal government adopts a gaming ordinance approved by the National Indian Gaming Commission. Tribal governments are responsible for regulating class II gaming with commission oversight.

The definition of class III gaming is extremely broad. It includes all forms of gaming that are neither class I nor class II. Games commonly played at casinos, such as slot machines, blackjack, craps, and roulette, would clearly fall in the class III category, as well as wagering games and electronic facsimiles of any game of chance. Generally, class III is often referred to as casino-style gaming. As a compromise, the act restricts tribal authority to conduct class III gaming.

Before a tribe may lawfully conduct class III gaming, the following conditions must be met: (1) the particular form of class III gaming that the tribe wants to conduct must be permitted in the state in which the tribe is located; (2) the tribe and the state must have negotiated a compact that has been approved by the Secretary of the Interior, or the Secretary must have approved regulatory procedures; and (3) the tribe must have adopted a tribal gaming ordinance that has been approved by the Commission chairperson.

Revenues from tribal governmental gaming must be used in one or more of five specific areas:

- funding tribal government operations or programs;
- providing for the general welfare of the Indian tribe and its members;
- promoting tribal economic development;
- donating to charitable organizations;
- helping fund operations of local government agencies.

Three-fourths of gaming tribes devote all of their revenue to tribal governmental services, economic and community development, neighboring communities, and charitable purposes, and do not give out per-capita payments. Tribal government services, economic and community development, general tribal welfare, charitable donations and any requirements for aid to local governments must be provided for before a tribe can file for a "Revenue Allocation

Plan"; per-capita payments must be approved by the Secretary of the Interior as part of the plan. Only about one-fourth of tribes that are engaged in gaming distribute per-capita payments to tribal members, who must pay federal income tax on these payments.

While the Indian Gaming Regulatory Act compromised tribal sovereignty by imposing the requirement that tribes enter into a compact with the governor of the state in order to engage in economic development by gaming, the statute soon opened a remarkable opportunity for a renaissance in tribal enterprise, well being, and affirmation of culture.

When the citizens of Oregon authorized a state lottery in 1984, they opened the door for gaming in the state. In time the State Gaming Commission expanded games of chance: Video Lottery, Keno, Powerball, Win for Life, Lucky Lines, Pick 4, and Sports Action. The state embrace of gaming predicated tribal gaming. In 1990 Dennis J. Whittlesey—a Washington, DC, attorney who had worked on restoration of tribes in Oregon and Washington as well as in cases involving events in the 1970s at Alcatraz Island, California, and Wounded Knee, South Dakota—drafted the first gaming compact in the state for the Cow Creek Band of Umpqua Tribe of Indians. It contained two remarkable features: a modest percentage of floor space for gaming operations (which was a test of whether there would be a challenge to the casino issue in the state), and a "most favored nations" clause that said the Cow Creeks had the right to negotiate with the governor for what any other tribe got through its compact.

The Cow Creek operation began modestly with a prefab metal building, gravel parking lot, and buried rubber reservoirs filled with sufficient water to meet fire insurance requirements. The Cow Creeks built a bingo hall on tribal land on Interstate 5 at Canyonville. In hopes of spurring economic development, the tribe had purchased a derelict motel and trailer park, cleaned up the property, and gotten it into trust status prior to IGRA. The land thus met the critical condition of the federal law: it was Indian land that was in trust status prior to the enactment of national standards for Indian gaming.

The Oregon Constitution prohibited casinos, but the matter was highly unclear. What was a casino? There was no definition. Further, the state had embarked on an ambitious gaming agenda to raise nontax revenues for education and delivery of social services. The Cow Creeks secured a Boston-based consulting firm, USA Research, Inc., to develop a business plan and find a potential joint-venture partner. In short order the plan and partner were in place, and in 1992 the Cow Creeks opened the bingo hall, which quickly evolved into Seven Feathers Casino. From modest beginnings, this facility soon grew to include a major convention facility, bingo hall, gaming area, restaurants, gift shop, four-story hotel, truck-travel center, three adjacent motels, and recreational vehicle park. The Cow Creeks also assumed the responsibility of accepting and purifying the wastewater from the City of Canyonville in a massive, tribally financed public works project.

No one challenged the implicit definition of "casino" in the Cow Creek compact template. In time, other tribes developed their own compacts with the state and, again, there was no challenge. Parallel to these events, the Oregon Gaming Commission continued to expand the state's involvement in gaming to the extent that its revenues exceeded $1 billion in 2006.

The route to casino projects proved challenging for several Oregon tribes. Both Siletz and Grand Ronde had to secure special legislation to permit construction on lands—parts of their former reservations—that were not in tribal trust ownership at the time of the passage of IGRA. The Confederated Tribes of Coos, Lower Umpqua, and Siuslaw sued twice in federal district court in Washington, DC, before they secured judicial affirmation that their casino site on the North Fork of the Siuslaw River qualified as "restored lands" to a "restored tribe" within the definitions laid out by IGRA. This prolonged process meant that they were the last of the Oregon tribes to engage in gaming.

The Burns Paiute, Klamath, and Warm Springs tribes faced other problems. Their lands were not located adjacent to major population areas. The "luck of the draw" under IGRA was that the opportunity to engage in gaming did not ensure market share or equity. Thus the Burns Paiute launched an initiative to try to secure lands near Ontario; the Warm Springs acquired a site at Cascade Locks and preliminary agreement by the Oregon governor of its eligibility for compact agreement; and the Klamath purchased lands in the Willamette Valley immediately south of Portland. These actions confirmed that Indian gaming as of 2006 remained filled with wild cards.

The impacts of IGRA on Oregon tribes were tremendous. Prior to gaming revenues, tribes struggled with bootstrap economic development programs. These were often labor-intensive and financially unrewarding. The returns proved modest for the immense investment of time, labor, and energy. Gaming was, from the outset, a different proposition. The nontaxed income had the potential to generate capital quickly, enabling tribes to diversify their investments in other enterprises. Gaming also generated a wide variety of jobs. These ranged from part-time to full-time employment and drew on an immense range of skills: bookkeeper, cook, waitress, dealer, hotel manager, entertainment coordinator, booking agent, advertising promoter, convention and event planner, security officer, maid, bus driver, and the like.

Gaming also provided the opportunity for employment to hundreds and hundreds of non-Indian workers in rural areas who were coping with significant layoffs in the 1990s from the timber industry, as well as other economic adjustments in Oregon. With gaming revenues, tribes rapidly expanded programs in education, housing, delivery of health care, and services for the aged and infants; they even developed tribal credit unions to assist steady workers with loans to purchase cars and trucks.

Under the Oregon compacting revisions, the tribes pledged to commit 7 percent of their annual receipts to philanthropy through separate, charitable foundations. By 2006 the Spirit Mountain Community Fund of the Confederated Tribes of Grand Ronde had funded more than $30 million in "good works" in northwestern Oregon. The commitments included exhibits at the Oregon Historical Society, assistance to the Hallie Ford Museum of Art in Salem, aid to Oregon State Parks, and grants to help fund the Indian Law Program at Lewis and Clark Law School.

Gaming revenues also fostered tribal abilities to enliven, renew, sustain, and protect their traditional culture. With resources in hand, the Confederated Tribes of the Umatilla Indian Reservation created the Tamástslikt Cultural Institute and the Confederated Tribes of Warm Springs constructed the Museum at Warm Springs. Tribal revenues were now available to pay for tribal elders and leaders to visit distant museum collections, for the tribes to encourage traditional arts, and for instruction programs in traditional languages.

Federal policy articulated in the Indian Gaming Regulatory Act and shaped by compacts with the state of Oregon generated remarkable new energies to drive Oregon tribes into the twenty-first century. The bleak years of enforced acculturation, capped by the disastrous policy of Termination, were turned in remarkable new directions in the 1990s. Oregon tribes embraced a restoration of hope and charted, for the first time in decades, their own destinies.

Chapter 12

Languages and Their Uses

BY DELL HYMES

Traveling down the Oregon Coast two hundred years ago, starting at the Columbia River, one would have found a different variety of language at almost every river mouth along the way: Clatsop at the Columbia, then Tillamook and Siletz, Yaquina and Alsea, Siuslaw and Umpqua, Hanis and Miluk, Coquille, Tututni, Shasta Costa, and Chetco. In all, there were six families of languages, none intelligible to the others.

Clatsop is one of three Chinookan languages found from the mouth of the Columbia to The Dalles. Tillamook and Siletz are Oregon outposts of the great Salish family of languages found throughout much of Washington, Idaho, Montana, and British Columbia. Yaquina and Alsea are a separate family, known today by the name Alsea. Siuslaw and Umpqua are a separate family, known today by the name Siuslaw. Hanis and Miluk are yet another family: Coos. Coquille, Tututni, and Chetco are varieties of the far-flung family known as Athabaskan, which is related to many of the languages of Alaska and northwestern Canada, on the one hand, and to Navajo and Apache, on the other.

Overleaf: A Paiute family was featured in the film The Earth is Our Home by the Oregon Council for the Humanities and Oregon Public Broadcasting.

Starting upriver from the mouth of the Columbia to The Dalles, one would have found mostly varieties of Chinookan, some three distinct languages in all: Clatsop and Shoalwater across from each other at the mouth, known today collectively as Chinook or Lower Chinook; Kathlamet, Wahkiacum, and Skilloot on both sides of the river between Astoria and the mouth of the Cowlitz, known collectively as Kathlamet; and groups known collectively today as Upper Chinook, including Multnomah at Sauvie Island and thereabouts, and similar varieties at the Cascades, Hood River, and The Dalles, with Sahaptin and its relative, Nez Perce, to the east.

Along the Willamette River, the Indians spoke another variety of Upper Chinook—Clackamas—near what is now Oregon City, and on the west bank and south, a series of three languages—Tualatin, Santiam, and Yoncalla, known collectively as Kalapuyan. If one pushed farther south, there would be Upper Umpqua, Galice, and Applegate—other varieties of Athabaskan, the first probably a separate language and the last two amongst the Takelma. Heading east, there would be the closely related Klamath and Modoc. Heading north from there along a trading trail and down the Deschutes, one might encounter four languages: Molale, Cayuse, Paiute, and Sahaptin.

All in all, Oregon has been home to a great many local dialects and varieties, some eighteen mutually unintelligible languages, and, so far as has been established, thirteen separate linguistic families.

How the Languages Developed

Each community was independent. Language change went on unforced, a result of the variation and local adaptation present in every community. Considering the changes that must have occurred to bring about so many different families, the languages surely have been in Oregon for a long time.

To be sure, a few of the languages may have arrived fairly recently. The Clatskanie in the northwest corner; the Coquille, Tututni, and Chetco of the southern coast; the Upper Umpqua, Galice, and Applegate inland all are branches of the Athabaskan family. The ancestors of the Athabaskan languages probably comprised the last migration into the New World across the Bering Strait, and those who moved south into the present United States probably did so within the last two thousand years. (Editor's note: This Bering Strait theory is now considered outdated by many scholars, some of whom have made plausible arguments for migrations from Asia along the coast rather than overland.) The Tillamook and Siletz belong to the great Salish family of languages, whose speakers lived adjacent to each other over large parts of Washington, British Columbia, and northern Idaho and Montana. It is hard to say whether the Clatsop and Shoalwater Chinook came between the Tillamook and the rest, taking over the mouth of the Columbia, or whether the Tillamook themselves moved. In eastern Oregon, the Paiute are connected to the Bannock, Shoshone, Ute, and other members of the Uto-Aztecan family, whose center of gravity is to the south (including Hopi and Aztec) and may have expanded into the area in recent times.

Certainly, the locations and boundaries of all the groups changed over time. Still, it is likely that most of the languages have been more or less in one place for many centuries and that most are related to one another as members of a single family that has been given the name Penutian. The most likely picture of the early history of language in Oregon is one of settlement by communities that spoke varieties of Penutian. Because their speakers settled in different places, the changes that took place in one community were independent of those that took place in another. As the differences accumulated—first in vocabulary and pronunciation, then in grammar—speakers of one community would no longer be able to understand those of another. As a rule of thumb, this usually takes about a thousand years. The differences between, say, Hanis and Miluk Coos or Kathlamet and Wasco Chinook must be at least this old. Still, the relationship between them remains evident in many details, even after six thousand years. For it to become difficult to recognize even a connection, as is the case with the separate families of Oregon, a long history is needed indeed.

One day it may be possible to demonstrate what is now merely a reasonable hypothesis: that besides Tillamook and Siletz (Salish), Paiute (Uto-Aztecan), and the Athabaskan languages, the languages of Oregon are related as members of a single family

A Takelma
Invocation
When a new moon rose, the Kalapuya, Takelma, and others would shout to it. Here is a Takelma invocation, as given by Frances Johnson:

I shall be blessed,
I shall go ahead.

Even if people say of me,
　"Would he were dead,"
I shall do just as you,
　I shall still rise.

Even if all kinds of things
devour you,
　Frogs eat you,
Everything,
　Lizards,

Even if they eat you,
　Yet you shall still rise,
I shall do just as you from
this time on—
　"Bo————!"

The Penutian families in Oregon are Chinookan, Sahaptian and Molallan, Cayusan, Lutuamian, Kalapuyan-Takelman, Alsean, Siuslawan, and Coosan. Other Penutian families are found in central California (Wintuan, Maiduan, Yokutsan, Constanoan) and in Alaska (Tsimshian). If these are indeed all related, Oregon is very likely the center from which they spread.

Before Chinook Jargon or Chinuk Wawa (see sidebar), many factors encouraged Indians to learn one another's languages. Their communities were small and often situated near villages where other languages were spoken. A spouse from another community would bring another language with her. Trade was important to obtain resources from other localities, and travel by canoe along waterways and the coast was easy and frequent. An individual might establish an enduring relationship with a partner in another place. Thus, people would learn at least some of another language and take up words with new sounds as names for new places, persons, and objects. These eventually would enter a community's speech. Also, the pronunciations of others sometimes would be imitated for amusement, and tellers of myths might have a character say something in another language.

Such multilingualism is probably the source of one striking similarity among the Indian languages of the North Pacific Coast, including Oregon. Their grammars and vocabularies are largely different, but they are largely alike in their sets of sounds. They have few vowels but many consonants, including some unfamiliar to European languages.

A Special Kind of Grammar

One of the most interesting things about languages is the way grammars develop to make it easy for speakers to express themselves in ways the culture considers important. Speakers of Klamath, for example, seem to have been interested in repetition and intensity and to have enjoyed repeating parts of words. One kind of "reduplication" conveys that the main action is by a single actor on several objects, by a single actor on a single object over a period of time, by several actors on a single object, and by several actors on several objects. Another kind of reduplication expresses persistent emotional and bodily conditions (such as feeling bad or having a burning sensation in the mouth), and repeated states of activity, such as twinkling stars, flickering lights, or wiggling the buttocks around. A third kind of reduplication expresses an especially intense, habitual,

Opposite: This chart, showing the classification of Oregon Indian languages, is from Oregon Indians: Culture, History & Current Affairs by Zucker, Hummel and Hogfoss (Western Imprints/Oregon Historical Society, 1983) and is used with permission. They note, "The phylum level of classification is questioned by many linguists and is particularly hypothetical for Penutian. Language families which contain only a single language are now called language isolates (e.g., Waiilatpuan and Lutuamian) and are included here for convenience. This chart omits sub-family divisions and lists only major dialects. Each village probably had its own dialect—a language area may be seen as a continuous chain of related dialects." Author Hymes made changes to the original chart where the asterisks appear. He also believes that work now being done will prove the phylum classification for Penutian to be correct.

Phylum	Family	Language	Dialect
Salishan	Salishan	Tillamook	Tilamook
			Siletz
Hokan (?)	Shastan	Shasta	Shasta
			Klamath River
Aztec-Tanoan	Uto-Aztecan	Northern Piaute	Northern Paiute
Na-Dene	Athabaskan	Claskanie	Clatskanie
		Umpqua	Upper Umpqua*
			Cow Creek
		Coquille-Tolowa	Galice-Applegate
			Coquille
			Tututni
			Tolowa-Chetco
			Kwatami
Penutian (?)	Chinookan	Coastal Chinook	Clastsop
		Middle Chinook*	Kathlamet*
		Upper Chinook (Kiksht)*	Clackamas
			Cascades
			Wasco
	Kalapuyan-Takelman(?)	Tualatin-Kalapuyan	Tualatin
			Yamhill
		Santiam Kalapuyan	Santiam
			Mary's River
			McKenzie
		Yoncalla Kalapuyan	Yoncalla
		Takelma	Takelma
			Latgawa
	Sahaptian	Sahaptin	Umatilla
			Warm Springs
		Nez Perce	Nez Perce
	Lutuamian	Klamath	Klamath
			Modoc
	Molallan	Molalla	Molalla
	Cayusan*	Cayuse	Cayuse
	Yakonan	Alsea	Yaquina
			Alsea
	Siuslawan	Siuslaw	Siuslaw
			Lower Umpqua*
	Coosan	Miluk	Miluk
		Hanis	Hanis

Indian Languages

This map, showing the Indian language groups in Oregon, is adapted from a map in Oregon Indians: Culture, History & Current Affairs *by Zucker, Hummel and Hogfoss (Western Imprints/Oregon Historical Society, 1983), with cartography by Jay Forest Penniman, and is used with permission. Each language group is further divided into a larger number of languages and dialects, depicted in the chart on page 249.*

Penutian Phylum   Salishan Family
Uto-Aztecan Family   Shastan Family
Athabaskan Family

or continuous condition or action (keeps swimming around and around underneath).

Speakers of Takelma seem to have taken great interest in specifying spatial relations and locations and, in the process, have made unusually elaborate use of names for body parts. The names can simply refer to body parts and their owner ("head-my," "mouth-my"). But these body parts can also suggest a location. "Head" can have the sense of "over" or "above"; "mouth, lips" can convey "in front"; "ear" can suggest "alongside"; "leg" can mean "under" or "away from view"; and "eye" has the sense of "to" or "at." When these new meanings are intended, "over the house" is literally "head" plus "house," and "underwater" is literally "leg" plus "water." Or the word for "leg" may be incorporated in a verb that means, "he washed his legs" and also in a verb that means "they put (food) away" (i.e., under platforms away from view).

Speakers of Sahaptin have evolved a language that gives great attention to the way in which an action is accomplished. Verb stems commonly have two parts. The second part names the act, while the first part identifies a means or manner. When asked how one says "cross the river," an elder at Warm Springs responded, "How do you want to go? Cross by swimming, cross by wading, cross by riding?" One would not just say "i-wáicha" ("he went across"); one would choose between "i-shúu-wáicha" ("he swam across"), "i-yáwash-wáicha" ("he waded across"), "i-xásu-wáicha" ("he rode horseback across"), "i-wishá-wáicha" ("he went across in a canoe"), or something else that expressed the means by which the crossing occurred. Other simple word elements can specify time, very general (rather than specific) modes of movement, and involved actions that in English would require several words: "with the hand," "push with the hand," "thrust, wield, push," "with the teeth or mouth," "pull, lift with the hand," "with an implement," "with the hands," "throw, place, lie down," and also "on the knees," "involving the head," "involving the ear," "with the eyes," "on hands and feet," "with the foot," "on the buttocks or bottom side," "creep on all fours," "hop or limp," "sit up," "jump," and a number of others. Thus, it is possible to say, in one word, "eating, he died," "seated, he sang," and so on.

In Chinookan, the gender of a word usually bears no relation to the object it names, except in the case of persons and large animals. The term for *horse* is the noun-stem *kiutan*. With the feminine prefix, it designates a mare (*a- kiutan*); with the masculine prefix, a stallion (*i-kiutan*). But the word for *mosquito* always has a feminine prefix: *a- p'únachikchik*. When asked if it was possible to use the masculine prefix instead, an elder speaker replied, "How could you tell the difference?"

These formal prefixes are far from irrelevant, however. There is an unusually large number of them that make several precise distinctions, as in the following Wasco forms:

n-	I
nd-	two of us (excluding you)
nsh-	we (more than two, excluding you)
m-	you (just one)
md-	you two
msh-	you (more than two)
tx-	we two (just you and I)
lx-	we (more than two, including you)
ch- or i(y)-	he, him
g- or a-	she, her
L-	it, someone
sht-	two of them
t-	they (more than two)

Moreover, such person-marking prefixes define the four parts of speech.

The verb is often the most complex kind of word in an American Indian language. In Chinookan an element that means "say" or "tell" or "give" cannot be said by itself. It has to be part of a word that begins with an element that indicates something about time (i.e., future, present, or a degree of distance in the past). And the word has to have at least one person-marker (the subject) to indicate who is doing or experiencing something. To say "she said," the one word has to have all three elements: *igágim*, or literally, "she said, a little while ago" (*ig-* immediate past, *a-* she, *-gim* "to say").

A verb can have two person-markers. The second marker indicates who or what is affected (the direct object). Some verbs, such as that for "to tell," have to have both. In Chinookan, "you told him (a little while ago)" is one word with four main elements: *igmiúlxam* (*ig-* immediate past, *m-* "you," *i-* "him," *-lxam* "to tell"; *u-* has to be there, but has no translatable meaning).

Some verbs can or must have three person-markers. The third indicates an indirect object. One way that two kinds of objects are used is to signal a difference between a means of doing something

Chinook Jargon

One Oregon language—Chinook Jargon or Chinuk Wawa—was created in relatively recent times and should not be confused with the Indian language from which it takes the name. Like other "jargons," or pidgin languages, Chinuk Wawa was a simplified form of speech that sprung up between people who did not speak one another's language. Much of its vocabulary was Chinookan in origin but stripped of that language's grammatical complexity. Other words were borrowed from Nootka of Vancouver Island, French (because of the French traders and missionaries), and English.

During the nineteenth century, Chinook Jargon spread rapidly and was used from Alaska to northern California and the Rockies during trade and also missionary instruction. Evidently it could be learned as a separate language with some rules of pronunciation and a word order of its own.

The Nootka words and records of early visits by trading ships have made it seem as though Chinook Jargon started on Vancouver Island after contact with non-Indians. However, long before whites came, Chinookan peoples had slaves—usually Indians who had been captured or traded and who spoke other languages. In such situations, the slaves would have had to learn just enough of their owners' language to carry out commands. Therefore, it seems almost certain that some simplified form of Chinook would have existed well before the first whites arrived at the Columbia River, as would simplified forms of the languages of other Northwest Coast peoples who held slaves, including the Nootka. Since Indians themselves traded over large distances, some words may have been shared. Early trading ships encountered these trade jargons, and the nineteenth-century influx of whites caused Chinook jargon to flourish. Toward the end of that century it declined, to be replaced by English as a lingua franca, yet many people retain some knowledge and use of Chinook Jargon today.

and who or what is affected by the doing. An English equivalent would be, "I will give it to her." In English this is said with six words; in Chinookan languages, this is said with one, but the one word, of course, has several parts.

In many languages it is reasonable to think of pronouns as substitutes for nouns, but in a language such as Wasco Chinook, the opposite is true: nouns are adjuncts to pronouns. In fact, a verb can be a complete sentence: one doesn't need a noun or separate pronoun. We must keep in mind that these languages historically were used face-to-face by people who knew a great deal about one another and the situation they were discussing.

Naming Things

Indian languages are also a copious source of names. Their speakers, who historically traveled by foot and canoe and depended on land and water for food, had an intimate knowledge of their environment and were attentive to each change in contour and vegetation, to each sign of animals or birds. To those who know only the names of highways and cities and who recognize only categories of things—trees, birds, flowers—a landscape may seem unvaried and almost empty. To an Indian community, however, a landscape is full of all the thousands of names by which the inhabitants know their world.

How Indian Communities Got Their Names

Different communities might have different styles of naming, to be sure. Along the Columbia River, speakers of Chinookan languages named communities after some special thing to be found among them. *Wasco* comes from the Wasco word for cup, and in their language their name would properly be Ga-thla-sqo, "the ones who have a cup" (literally, "the ones-their-cup"). The word refers to a natural stone bowl in which water once bubbled up for drinking (until it was destroyed in the building of the railroad). *Clackamas* comes from a word for vine maple. *Kathlamet* and *Clatsop* come from the same kind of name: "the ones-their-mat" and "their-tsap" (*-tsap* was a prized mixture of huckleberries and salmon; a definition of *-mat* is not known).

While every community has its name for itself, commonly used names can sometimes be traced to those outside of the community. For example, *Klamath* is a Chinookan name, referring of course to

Klamath Lake. Chinookan speakers who lived across from the Dalles came to be known as Wishram, a word in their neighbors' Sahaptin language. Chinook itself is a name applied to one group of Chinookan speakers near the mouth of the Columbia by their Salish-speaking neighbors. And along the Columbia, Lewis and Clark learned a name for the Paiutes of the Deschutes River that meant "enemies" to those who used it. Sometimes, a group was known by several names—some rather generic. Often it was enough to speak simply of "upriver people" and "downriver people."

Soldiers, governments, and scholars, however, wanted a single name for each group and a general name for as many as could be classed together. If they discovered that languages were related, they usually seized upon the fact. Thus, communities on the Columbia with related languages were christened with a Salish name for one of them: Chinookan. People who lived on the west side of the Willamette along the Tualatin, Santiam, Yoncalla, and other streams were all called Kalapuya. Klikitats, Yakimas, Teninos, and others were labeled Sahaptin.

History itself also has an effect. The Sahaptin-speaking peoples on the Warm Springs Reservation are known as "Warm Springs," for their long residence there. "Wasco" has become a common name for the Chinookan-speakers from various points along the upper Columbia. In general, the names one sees in maps and books today often were not known or used that way two hundred years ago.

Personal Story of Kalapuyan William Hartless

In the course of recounting the history of his people, William Hartless, a Mary's River (Pinefu) Kalapuya, said this about himself:

I am the only one now, I've been left alone, all my people have died. The only one now, I stay on. Once I am dead, my tribe will indeed be gone. My country—I am Kalapuya, at Corvallis my country, the Indian people name my country "Pínefu"—my tribe. So I am now indeed the last, I in my country.

How Individuals Were Named

Indian personal names had a different role than English personal names do. Often one's name was not for casual use, but functioned like a title. It had belonged to an ancestor and was given to honor the previous bearer and to promise that the new bearer deserved and perhaps would increase the honor.

Only family members could call a person by name, and everyone was expected to know it, for to ask would be improper. After the bearer died, the name could not be used again for a certain number of years, nor would one say the name of the dead person. Family members might change their own names rather than be pained by hearing the name their loved one had used for them.

In everyday life the title-like name was not much needed because people knew one another and often were related. Instead, people used terms of kinship, in part to be polite—even to people who were not relatives. Thus, one might say "Grandmother" to an old woman, "Nephew" or "Younger Brother" to a younger man, and so on. Myths and other stories are full of such usages.

In face-to-face conversation, pronouns also served very well. In speaking of oneself and others, one might distinguish economically between a "we" that included the person spoken to and a "we" that did not.

Speaking Properly

An important activity might give rise to a way of speaking not open to everyone. When men of the lower Rogue River went out to sea for fish or seals, they did not mention land animals or women. Anyone who broke the taboo had to be thrown overboard to save the rest from the anger of sea creatures. And the steersman, in giving directions, would speak as if a game were being played against the ocean. He would not say, "Paddle in that direction," but instead, "Hit the ball over that way" (if the game agreed upon was shinny). The uninitiated would be at a loss.

Some had an ability to understand that others did not. The Tillamook, Chinookans, and perhaps others considered infants to be born with a language of their own, which some had the power to interpret. Understanding was important, for each child was precious and might go back to the world from which it had come if its wants were not understood. Some could interpret what particular animals said as a warning, perhaps, or an omen. These gifts were usually acquired through success in a guardian-spirit quest.

In Indian communities there were also things one should and should not say. Everyone probably avoided the ordinary name for "grizzly bear" and "rattlesnake," using instead a respectful term such

Family Names

The modern pattern of a first name and a continuing family name is, of course, only a few centuries old, even in English and other European languages. *Miller* goes back to someone who was once "so-and-so the miller," *Johnson* to someone who was actually a "son of John," and *Newtons* to someone who was "so-and-so from Newton (new town)." For Indian people in Oregon, family names came about in the nineteenth century. Government officials and missionaries assumed everyone must have one. Sometimes a father's English first name was given to a family (Dick, Pat, Charley). Sometimes an Indian name was adapted (Simtustus, Suppah, Kuckup, Tufti, Wallulatum). And of course many English names were adopted, in some cases through marriage.

as "Grandfather" or "Ancestor." Nor did one speak the exact name of a person who had died.

Recounting Myths

Myths were part of the winter season and for practical and spiritual reasons were not to be repeated at any other time. One could quote them: seeing a coyote, one might say something the Coyote of the stories would characteristically say, such as "I'm hungry." But to tell myths outside of winter might bring rattlesnakes or other misfortune.

Myths themselves were not merely stories but dramatic performances, often told by an older person who might be specially invited to come to a house for several nights and be presented with gifts. Against the enclosed light of a smoldering fire, the narrator would develop a story using different voices for the various characters, highlighting their characteristic turns of expression, underlining foolishness and pathos with tone of voice, imparting emphasis with gestures. One or more members of the audience would be expected to respond at intervals, perhaps after every verse, with the equivalent of "yes" or "indeed." A child who fell asleep might be made to go bathe in a frozen river; but if all response ceased, clearly it would be time to tie off the story for the night.

Performance did not stop with the end of the story. There would be a formal phrase to signal "the end," then a phrase invoking good weather, and then perhaps instruction to the boys and the girls to find something associated with spring. These conventions suggest that the winter telling of myths was a world-renewal rite.

The language of myths would include some standard words, often related to a community's pattern for the repetition of important acts, such as rituals. Along the Columbia River and down the Willamette Valley, the pattern centered on the number five. Among many other groups it was four. In stories in which a scene was repeated, as when the last of several sisters succeeds, there would be five sisters and five scenes in the one case, and four in the other.

Traditional stories drew upon a set of underlying possibilities for giving shape, for arousing expectation and satisfying it, again and again, as the story progressed. Where the pattern number was five, sequences of three would also be used. Where the pattern was four, pairs were also used. That was the ordinary way. When intensity was desired, stories that usually used sequences of five and three might instead use pairs, and stories organized in sequences of two and four might instead use threes. These kinds of patterning were found at every level of a story, from the smallest units (sequences of lines and verses) to the largest (sequences of scenes and acts).

All of this patterning allowed a narrator to shape a story in the course of telling it. Though each story must have a certain series of incidents, there were options for organizing them. One part might be elaborated with what characters say, another not. One repetition of a scene with another brother might be spelled out in full, another repetition shortened. The whole would have satisfying form as long as what was said followed the patterns.

A Paiute Account of the Earth's Beginning

Traditions and traditional ways of speaking have continued to be used to address situations brought about by the coming of whites. A Paiute doctor, Sam Wata, connected the old and new laws in this way:

One time this was all water but just one little island. This is what we are living on now. Old Man Chocktoot was living on top of this mountain. He was living right on top of this mountain. In all directions the land was lower than this mountain. It was burning under the earth. Numuzoho was under there, and he kept on eating people.

The Star was coming. When that Star came, it went up into the sky, and stayed there.

When that Star went up, he said: "That is too bad. I pity my people. We left them without anything to eat. They are going to starve."

This Star gave us deer, an antelope, and elk, and all kinds of game.

They had Sun for a god. When the Sun came up, he told his people: "Don't worry, come to me. I'll help you. Don't worry, be happy all your life. You will come to me."

The Sun and the Stars came with the Water. They had the Water for a home. The Indian doctor saw them coming. He let his people know they were coming. There were many of them. The little springs of water are the places from which the silver money comes. It comes from the Sun shining on the water.

The first white man came to his land and saw that silver but he lost himself and didn't get to it.

Finally white people found this place and they came this way looking for the silver. Those white men brought cattle, sheep, pigs, and horses. Before they came, there were no horses in this land.

The Sun told his people, "Deer belong to you. They are for you to eat." These white men don't know who put the deer and other animals in this land.

I think it is all right for me to kill deer, but the white men say they will arrest me. Whenever I see cattle or sheep, I know they don't belong to me, I wouldn't kill them. I feel like going out and killing deer, but I am afraid. I am getting too old. Maybe the white people don't know about the beginning of this earth.

Though much of the art of telling myths has been lost today, much remains. The stories—some comic, some tragic, some stirring—still richly reflect human nature and its needs. And patterning is not limited to formal storytelling. Speeches and formal explanations display it. Everyday reports of experience and the giving of advice can use this rhetorical form—a touch of verbal art—as well.

A few examples illustrate different kinds of discourse and the main kinds of rhythm. Two—"A Takelma Invocation" (page 247) and "A Paiute Account of Earth's Beginning" (page 257)—proceed in rhythms of two and four. Another, a personal statement in Kalapuyan (page 254), proceeds in rhythms of three and five; and a fourth, a Klamath statement of advice (page 260), consists of a series of five pairs. Stories in Nez Perce often proceed in rhythms of three and five, but the morning speech given here uses two and four; it has four sections, each of which pairs an opening statement with three lines that amplify it, for four lines in all.

Many of the first languages of Oregon are no longer spoken, especially those of the western part of the state, where disease swept through early after settlers arrived. Some of the languages still are known by at least some speakers, and a number of communities have made efforts to preserve and teach them:

- The Confederated Tribes of the Coos, Lower Umpqua, and Siuslaw have had a language and heritage program for a number of years.

- The Confederated Tribes of the Warm Springs have long supported documentation and teaching of the languages of their reservation. Each issue of the bi-weekly newspaper, *Spilyay Tymoo* (Coyote News), devotes space to lessons in the three languages: Sahaptin, Wasco, and Paiute.

- The Klamath Tribes have had Klamath language taught in Head Start, kindergarten, and first grade classes in the local school for many years. Documentation work has also been done with Modoc and Northern Paiute (Uto-Aztecan languages).

- The Burns Paiute hold regular Elders Group Potlucks, which, in part, are opportunities for elders to socialize in the language. There is an effort to have language

classes in the public school, and one of the elders,
Ruth Lewis, works on documenting her own stories
and transcribing and translating texts of others.

- The Confederated Tribes of the Umatilla Indian
Reservation have an extensive program of documentation of Umatilla (Sahaptin), Walla Walla, and Nez
Perce. The program includes a linguist, Noel Rude,
who earlier helped develop materials for the Klamath.
There have been classes for each language one day
per week and, for the past several years, there have
been language classes at two local schools.

- The Confederated Tribes of Grand Ronde includes
descendants of several different western Oregon language communities. Few of each have survived, but
all shared Chinook Jargon as a lingua franca for trade
and other purposes. Recognizing this, Tony Johnson,
a Chinook descendent, has established a program for
it. (Contrary to what the word "jargon" might suggest, this language had considerable scope. Indeed,
narratives told in Chinook Jargon show the kind of
regular patterning found in narratives in other languages of the region.)

All these efforts come out of a widespread national and global
concern for the preservation and renewal of languages.

*A Nez Perce
Crier's Speech*
Many communities had
a crier, someone who
would go through a
camp at the beginning
of the day, hailing
the others and giving
advice. Here is one such
speech from the Nez
Perce (written down in
English, but reflecting
the Nez Perce pattern):

I wonder if everyone is up!
  It is morning.
  We are alive,
  So thanks be!
Rise up!
  Look about!
  Go see the horses,
  A wolf might have
killed one!
Thanks be that the
children are alive!
  And you, older men!
  And you, older women!
  Also that your friends
are perhaps alive in other
camps.
But elsewhere,
  there are probably those
who are ill this morning,
  and therefore the
children are sad,
  and therefore their
friends are sad.

Klamath Advice for Children

Among the Klamath, as among other groups, parents and elders instruct children and young people on many occasions. Such advice is essential to success in life. Klamath storytellers make use of three- and five-part patterning, and these two examples of advice, although in English, have five parts. The first is from a young mother to her four-year-old daughter:

> I am going to teach you.
> At home, you can wear any kind of clothes.
>
> Save your new clothes for when you go out.
> Patch your old clothes up.
>
> Everybody should learn to put his clothes away just right.
> If people see you doing that, they know you are doing all right.
>
> You have to learn how to cook.
> Everybody has to learn how to cook.
>
> You have to be busy and work.
> When you have nothing to do, that's when you get into trouble.

The second example is from an elderly father to a forty-year-old son.

> If you want people to think well of you, stay away from bad companions.
> People say bad things about anyone who gets into trouble.
>
> I say to you: Drinking is not good and costs lots of money.
> When a man saves his money, people say he is steady.
>
> When those men say, "Let's drink,"
> you say to them, "Give me the money instead of the drink."
>
> Then there's no trouble for anybody.
> Then everything is right.
>
> If there is no trouble, then everybody thinks good.
> This is good advice.

Chapter 13

From Petroglyphs to Powwows

BY BILL MERCER

Although much Native American art is based in tradition, it is not static. Historically, Native American art forms have undergone constant change as new ideas have been adopted and new materials incorporated. Tribes traded with one another not only for food, but also to acquire raw materials and other items that were not available in the local environment. Through this interaction, information and ideas were exchanged and broad cultural patterns developed. With the arrival of European, then American, explorers, traders, and settlers, Native Americans were able to acquire industrially manufactured goods, such as cloth and glass beads, that were immediately adapted to and employed in the creative process.

Today, there are many Native American artists working in Oregon, including artists whose family roots are here and artists whose cultural traditions are from outside the region. This has created a dynamic environment in which artists can interact and share ideas and personal experiences with one another. Some artists continue to work in traditional forms, such as basketry and beadwork, carrying on the traditions established for generations. Many of the traditional forms continue to play a vital role in ongoing ceremonies and also serve as expressions of cultural identity.

Overleaf: Artist Minerva Soucie holding her "Pauite Cradleboard with Hummingbirds." This cradleboard is made from a bent willow frame, woven with willow sticks, covered with tanned deer hide, and beaded designs. It is thirty-four inches and fits a newborn to a six-month-old baby. The cradleboard will be given to the artist's granddaughter, Kristeny, when she has children. Photo courtesy of Minerva Soucie.

Powwows, intertribal celebrations where Native Americans gather to dance and sing, are among the main venues for the expression of cultural identity. In some instances, the dances and songs are based on historical traditions, while in other instances they are innovative compositions that reflect contemporary life. During powwows, dancers often wear elaborately beaded clothing that reflects their cultural heritage and personal interests. A dancer's garb consists of numerous articles, each carefully created and instilled with personal meaning. In most circumstances, the garments are made not just by the dancer but also by relatives and friends, resulting in an ensemble that is a collaborative effort reflecting the ongoing vitality of the community and the traditional Native American arts.

Other contemporary Native American artists in Oregon work in media such as painting, printmaking, and sculpture; they participate in the international dialogue of contemporary art, while responding to the world around them both as individuals and as Native Americans. The following are only a few examples of Oregon-based Native American artists whose works are firmly based in a legacy of creativity and remain vibrant and dynamic.

Minerva Soucie (Burns Paiute)

Minerva Soucie is an artist and teacher who is intent on carrying on the basketry traditions of the Burns Paiute. As a girl, she learned about basketry by helping gather and prepare the materials, then carefully observing while her mother's aunt, Marion Louie, worked. Minerva completed her first cradleboard at about age twenty. Traditionally, Paiute cradleboards are made from wood and then covered with a piece of tanned deerskin decorated with beadwork. There is also a shade woven from willow that is located above the baby's head. Minerva is also skilled at weaving other traditional basketry forms, including the conical-shaped burden baskets that she often weaves in miniature.

After working for the United States Forest Service for twenty-four years, she now works for the Burns Paiute tribe and is more involved in basketry than ever before. She teaches younger tribal members the art of basketmaking and is an active member of both the Northwest and California Basketweavers Associations. Minerva has conducted research in several museums to increase her knowledge of basketry, prompting her to revive traditional forms and techniques, such as duck decoys made from cattail and bulrush. Her teaching, her research, and her own basketmaking are all done with the intention that the basketry of the Burns Paiute continues far into the future.

Current art form: Beadwork

Native American women have long been excellent artists adept at decorating their clothing and accessories with shells, pendants, porcupine quills, and other materials. Glass beads made in Europe were brought by traders to Oregon in the early nineteenth century, and they rapidly came into widespread use. The first available beads were limited to a palette of white, black, red, and blue, but by the middle of the nineteenth century, a wider range of colors became available, and these were used extensively to create works of intricate beauty.

Several basic beadwork techniques have been used traditionally throughout Oregon. The most common technique is an appliqué stitch using two needles and thread. The beads are strung on the first thread and tacked onto the surface to be beaded. Then, using a second needle, the second thread is run back through the beads, firmly sewing them onto the surface.

There were also two types of woven beadwork that were frequently used. One method uses a loom, with the beaded strip later being sewn onto the desired surface. The other is woven without the use of a loom and is a technique similar to twining basketry. This twined beadwork technique is extremely rare and found only among those tribes living along the Columbia River.

Beadwork is a major avenue of artistic expression in Indian culture, and is used to decorate a variety of objects, including clothing, bags, cradles, and horse gear. Flat bags, traditionally carried by women, are a prime candidate for beading, and it is on these bags that some of the finest beadwork occurs. Some bags are beaded with geometric designs and others with floral motifs. Some have complex figurative scenes that include realistically depicted humans, horses, elk, birds, and fish. Many of the scenes also include depictions of Mount Hood, as well as rivers and streams, as part of the narrative. Native people made these bags for their own use and to sell to collectors.

Lillian Pitt (Wishram/Wasco/ Cascade)

Lillian Pitt is one of the leading contemporary Native American artists in the Pacific Northwest. She was born on the Warm Springs Reservation and, although her other family members were artistic, she did not consider herself an artist as she was growing up. She eventually moved to Portland and became a hair stylist before retiring in the 1970s for health reasons. It was during this time that she took a ceramics class and immediately fell in love with working in clay. As Lillian says, "It was love at first touch." In the beginning, she was simply having fun and did not consider what she was doing to be art. However, she ultimately sold several of her raku-fired masks to the Navajo artist R. C. Gorman, who suggested that she have a show at a local gallery in Portland. This led to Lillian's inclusion in a major exhibition featuring contemporary Native American women artists, *Women of Sweetgrass and Sage*, that traveled to museums around the country.

Over the years, Lillian has continued to emphasize her personal heritage in her works, often incorporating rock art imagery, while expanding from ceramics to printmaking and metal sculpture. She often collaborates with other artists on large-scale public art works and enjoys the process of working with and learning from her colleagues. Lillian has been the recipient of the Governor's Arts Award from the State of Oregon, and a solo exhibition of her work, The Spirits Keep Whistling Me Home, has been installed at the Museum at Warm Springs and the Hallie Ford Museum in Salem, Oregon, as well as several other museums around the country, earning her both local and national acclaim.

Wasco Totem, 1994, wood, ceramic, copper, and beads (56" x 18" x 5") by Lillian Pitt. Courtesy of the Portland Art Museum.

Pat Courtney Gold (Wasco/Tlingit)

Pat Courtney Gold is an innovative artist who excels in working with basketry, textiles, and woven sculptures. Pat was born and raised on the Warm Springs Reservation and later attended Whitman College in Walla Walla, Washington, where she earned a degree in Mathematics-Physics. After graduating, she taught mathematics at Portland-area community colleges and spent eleven years as a mathematician and computer specialist.

Pat learned to weave traditional Wasco cylinder baskets by taking classes when she returned home on summer vacations from college. At that time, the Wasco tradition of full-turned twined baskets with geometric human and animal motifs was a dying art. Since then, however, Pat has helped to revive the tradition and now devotes her time to creating art and lecturing on Plateau tribal art and culture. She was a recipient of the State of Oregon Governor's Arts Award in 2000, and her baskets are in the permanent collections of many museums throughout Oregon, including the Portland Art Museum, the Museum at Warm Springs, Oregon History Center, Hallie Ford Museum, and the High Desert Museum. Many of Pat's baskets are immediately recognizable, as they combine traditional Wasco designs with contemporary themes that reflect her personal observations of Native American life in the twenty-first century.

Bud Lane (Chetco/Lower Rogue/Shasta)

Bud Lane is emblematic of a younger generation of Native Americans who, after spending a significant portion of their lives away from their tribal community, have begun to move back and assume major roles within the culture. Bud was raised in a large military family and, during his childhood, lived in various places both in the United States and abroad. However, he recalls regularly visiting family living on the Siletz Reservation and considering it to be home. After graduating from high school, he moved to Siletz and subsequently began to immerse himself in cultural activities, including the building of a longhouse and helping to revive interest in the Feather Dance. He also learned Coastal Athabaskan, one of ten or eleven native languages once spoken at Siletz, and learned to weave the traditional double-handled baskets from his colleague Robert Kentta.

Bud's interest in basketry grew in the late 1980s, and he started making basketry caps as well as other regalia for dancers to

Above: Sally bag, 1999, 10" x 6.5", by Pat Courtney Gold. Courtesy of the Portland Art Museum. Below: Cedar Hat by Bud Lane. Courtesy of Hallie Ford Museum, Willamette University.

wear during ceremonies. He began to weave baby baskets in 1993 and continues to create a variety of baskets and other traditional regalia, primarily for use within the Siletz community, and rarely sells his work to non-tribal members. In addition to working as an artist, Bud is employed by the Siletz Tribe to develop language programs and educational curricula based on traditional cultural values so that future generations of Siletz tribal members will be able to maintain the traditions of their ancestors.

Older art forms: Rock art

Rock art is the oldest surviving form of visual art created by Native Americans in Oregon. While there are no methods to establish the precise date when a particular image was made, it is generally believed that most of the rock art in Oregon was produced before the arrival of European Americans. Rock art can be found throughout the region, although it is more heavily concentrated in the eastern and southern portions of the state and along the Columbia River. There are two types of rock art. Petroglyphs are engravings, usually made by pecking the rock surface with another stone. Pictographs are paintings made with a variety of natural pigments, such as iron oxides, clay, and charcoal, that produced various shades of red, white, and black. The pigments were mixed with a binder of water, blood, urine, or eggs, and then applied to the surface by finger painting.

Although it is impossible to know the significance of rock art in the Indians' daily life, many rock art sites appear to have been carefully chosen. Some are situated on high points with commanding views. Some may have been places where hunters came to look for game and, while they were waiting, made images depicting the type of animals they were searching for. Hunters could also have come to these places to give thanks for successful hunts by recording images of the animals taken. Other sites, such as those located in rock shelters, were more private and may have been places where individuals went to fast and seek spiritual guidance. Still others functioned as calendrical devices and were situated to mark astronomical events such as the summer solstice.

Because rock art is not a language, there is no way to decipher the exact meaning of each image. An image might have meant a certain thing to the person who made it, but another individual might interpret the same image quite differently. Meanings can also change over time as the original intent is forgotten and new ideas emerge.

Most rock art imagery in Oregon falls into one of three categories: The first category consists of anthropomorphic images. These humanlike figures are usually drawn or engraved in a flat manner with arms and legs outstretched, while others are simply faces without bodies. Some have a series of lines radiating above their head as if to represent a headdress of some sort, but there is often little other detail. The second category is zoomorphic figures. Bighorn sheep are

Maynard White Owl Lavadour
(Cayuse/Nez Perce)

Maynard White Owl Lavadour is an extraordinary artist whose work is focused on traditional forms ranging from basketry and clothing to beadwork. He was raised on the Umatilla Reservation by his grandmother, Eva Lavadour, and his great-grandmother, Susie Williams, and says, "I feel very fortunate to have [had] the opportu-

depicted frequently, as are other quadrupeds such as lizards. Also fairly commonly represented are insects and birds, the latter recognizable by their outstretched wings. The vast majority of rock art motifs, however, fall into the third category: nonfigural and consisting of lines, circles, dots, and meanders that remain an enigmatic artistic legacy.

Closely related to rock art are carved stone items created in the precontact era, especially by those peoples living along the Columbia River. Most of these objects were made from the plentiful basalt, which could be shaped with tools made of harder stone. These objects included ring-shaped net weights, bowls, pestles, mauls, axes, and a variety of other useful implements. In addition to the utilitarian pieces, there are a few rare sculptural pieces that take anthropomorphic or zoomorphic form. These sculptural works range in size from just a few inches to nearly five feet and weigh as much as six hundred pounds. The smaller pieces may have been intended as personal charms or amulets, while the larger ones were probably meant to be public monuments, erected as boundary markers or village symbols. The anthropomorphic figures are often quite detailed and have distinguishing characteristics that include round, broad faces with an emphasis on the eyes and exposed skeletal features such as a rib cage or spinal column. Usually there is a navel and a waistline. Arms and legs are often represented only vaguely, if at all. Some of these figures are painted red and many appear to be wearing headdresses. Zoomorphic figures, which include owls, seals, and bighorn sheep, are frequently portrayed with exposed ribs and other characteristic features that make them immediately recognizable.

Other forms of sculpture include wooden spoons, as well as intricately carved horn bowls and ladles made from mountain sheep horns that were first softened, then steamed and worked into a distinctive shape. The horns were then carved with elaborate geometric designs that include concentric boxes, circles, and rectangles, as well as zigzag motifs usually placed around the rims. Anthropomorphic figures or faces that are carved in the same style as those found on stone sculptural works also show up on some bowls. A frequent representation on ladles as well as wooden spoons is a four-legged animal with pointed ears that may refer to Coyote, a major mythological character.

nity of being educated by many knowledgeable elders in all aspects of traditional life." Maynard also attended the Institute of American Indian Arts, where he earned a reputation as a master beadworker and won numerous awards at the Santa Fe Indian Market. His reputation grew after several of his works were selected to be included in the exhibition *Lost and Found Traditions: Native American Art 1965–1985*, which toured museums around the country. This exposure has provided him the opportunity to teach and give beadwork demonstrations both locally and nationally. In 1997 Maynard received the State of Oregon Governor's Arts Award. He is generally acknowledged to be one of the finest contemporary Native American beadworkers.

James Lavadour (Walla Walla)

James Lavadour is one of the leading Native American painters of his generation. He is a self-taught artist who has lived most of his life on the Umatilla Reservation, and his work is tremendously influenced by the topography of the region. His paintings are landscapes that reflect an intense personal connection to the local environment. James describes his painting technique as "gestures of memory" that have accumulated in his consciousness from countless hours hiking in the foothills and mountains near his home. An atmospheric, dreamlike quality often pervades his work. He sometimes combines individually painted panels into a single work of art.

James has completed several public art commissions throughout Oregon, and he has participated in many museum exhibitions, in-

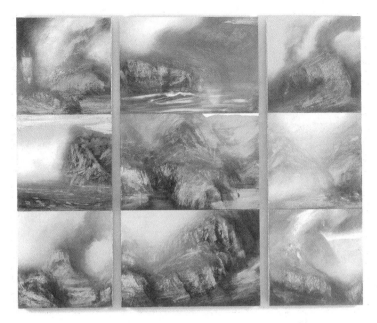

Bodies of My Body, 1992, oil on linen by James Lavadour. Courtesy of the Portland Art Museum.

cluding solo exhibitions at both the Portland Art Museum and the Pacific Northwest College of Art. In 1999 he received an honorary doctorate from Eastern Oregon University. In addition to his work as an artist, James devotes his time to the community. He was the founder of Crow's Shadow Art Institute, a nonprofit arts organization located on the Umatilla Reservation that provides art instruction and studio facilities for tribal members, as well as residencies for contemporary Native American artists from around the country.

Current art forms: Basketry

Basketry is an ancient art form developed by the native peoples of Oregon. However, because baskets are made from organic materials and oftentimes used extensively, very few examples predating the middle of the nineteenth century have survived. Among the oldest basketry items recovered by archaeologists are woven sandals that are ten to twelve thousand years old. Most of the basketry in museum collections today dates from the period of 1880 to 1940, when collectors and museums began to acquire Native American baskets in earnest.

In Oregon, Indians continue to produce a large variety of basketry using a wide range of materials and techniques. Weaving a basket requires great knowledge about the local environment and the characteristics of the plants that are used as weaving materials. Ideally, a weaver has to be familiar with the specific growing locations of particular plants, as well as the appropriate time to harvest them. Gathering the materials is a task that often involves the entire family, who offer songs and prayers of thanksgiving for the plants and for the opportunity to collect them. Once gathered, the materials have to be properly prepared. For instance, the outer bark of willow shoots has to be stripped away and the grasses cut into usable lengths. Some materials are also dyed in order to create colors used in designs. Once the materials are processed, the weaver might use any of a number of weaving techniques to create the desired form. A weaver might spend many hours over the course of weeks and even months working on a single basket.

Each tribal group in Oregon developed its own particular style of basketry. The style's characteristics are based on a combination of materials, weaving techniques, shapes, functions, and designs. In western Oregon and along the coast, basketmakers often work with juncus, grass, or hazel. Most of these baskets are made with various types of twined weaves. There is also very little decoration other than horizontal bands or simple geometric patterns. Siletz baskets typically are made from a combination of hazel and bear grass, and many of them have a distinctive double-braided handle. By contrast, around the turn of the century, Clatsop weavers produced basketry items that consisted mostly of flat mats and pouches made from cattails; they were left unadorned except for vertical strips of maidenhair fern sewn onto the surfaces.

Klamath-style baskets are typically made with tule and other materials collected from marshy areas around Klamath Lake. The Klamath basketmakers prepare and split their plant material into thin strips before using. The result is that the baskets are relatively soft and flexible. Most are twined, and a variety of unique forms can be created. The majority of Klamath baskets are relatively small bowls, although large, flat trays and truncated, cone-shaped hats worn by women were also common forms. The baskets have a warm brown tint with darker brown designs that are highlighted at times with red or bright yellow. Historically, the bright yellow material consists of porcupine quills dyed with wolf moss. The designs on Klamath baskets incorporate both geometric and figurative motifs, such as birds, which were used primarily on baskets made specifically for sale to collectors.

The people living at both Warm Springs and Umatilla make several distinctive types of baskets. One is called a cornhusk bag, which is usually identified with the Nez Perce, although many of the Plateau tribes, including weavers at Warm Springs and Umatilla, also create them. Cornhusk bags are flat, twined pouches. They are made from a variety of materials including cornhusk, Indian hemp, ryegrass, string, yarn, and raffia. Cornhusk bags were traditionally used to store food and, because they are woven without seams, were excellent at keeping whatever was inside free from dirt. Basketmakers wove the bags tightly, employing a continuous twining technique. Designs were either woven as part of the construction of the bag or embroidered onto the surface using brightly colored yarn. The majority of designs consist of bold geometric motifs featuring a combination of diamonds and triangles. By the end of the nineteenth century, as more and more bags were being sold to collectors, weavers began to incorporate figurative motifs, such as humans, horses, elk, birds, and trees, into visually complex scenes representing the local flora and fauna.

The cylinder basket is another distinctive type of twined basketry created by the tribes along the Columbia River. These baskets are sometimes referred to as "sally bags," a name given to them by traders who marketed these unique forms as having been made by an old lady named Sally. The makers twined these cylindrical bags in a manner similar to cornhusk bags, except that they are shaped into cylinders instead of flat pouches. The bags are usually made with materials that include Indian hemp, yarn, string, raffia, and grass. Traditionally, a woman attached the cylinder bag to a belt and wore it on her hip to hold the roots of wild plants that were collected for food, such as camas roots and wild onions. Many of the bags have geometric designs, but some have distinctive figurative designs that are characteristic of the Columbia River art style. The abstracted figurative designs include humans, fish, condors, elk, dogs, and horses. The human figures often have diamond-shaped heads and skeletal features that are stylistically similar to the motifs on sculptural works, such as the stone and horn bowls, made in the same locale.

In addition to the cornhusk and sally bags, the tribes along the Columbia River created a third distinctive type of basketry: the coiled basket. These coiled baskets are sometimes called berry baskets or Klickitat baskets, although they have been produced by all of the tribes along the Columbia River. They are made from cedar root and bear grass and have a consistent cylindrical shape that features a flat bottom and flaring sides. Most also have a series of loops around the rim. Traditionally, these baskets were used to gather huckleberries. Individuals would tie a small basket on their belt and drop the berries in as they were picked. When the smaller basket was filled, the berries would be transferred into a larger basket that remained on the ground. The larger basket was then covered with fresh leafy branches that were woven through the loops on the rim to keep the berries cool and moist. The baskets were decorated with a false embroidery technique known as imbrication, which required the weaver to take strips of bear grass and tuck them between the sewing element and the coils before being pulled tight. The result is a series of small loops of bear grass in contrasting colors on the surface of the basket. On some examples, the imbrication covers the entire basket and includes both geometric and figurative designs.

Chapter 14

The Great Basin

BY C. MELVIN AIKENS AND MARILYN COUTURE

Archaeological data show clearly that native people have lived around Malheur and Harney lakes in the northern Great Basin for well over ten thousand years. Geoarchaeological studies have found large spear points associated with ancient beach lines well above the level of the modern lakes. Flaked stone projectile points, scrapers, and other artifacts found on the Malheur National Wildlife Refuge also document extensive occupation of that locality, especially during and after middle Holocene times, or after about five thousand years ago. At Catlow and Roaring Springs caves, not far south of the lakes, evidence dates to eight thousand years ago, if not more. It includes sagebrush bark sandals, rabbit-skin robes, twined baskets, soft bags, nets, mountain mahogany digging sticks, grinding stones, flaked stone points, knives, and scrapers, as well as hunting weapons including both the atlatl and dart (early), and the bow and arrow (later). Other evidence from Blitzen Marsh, south of Malheur Lake, shows that people camped there often over the last twenty-five hundred years, and earlier evidence is hinted at. The bones of ducks, geese, suckers, chubs, and various large and small mammals are the remains of peoples' hunting activities. Traces of semi-subterranean house floors and light pole-framed structures known as wickiups have also been found there.

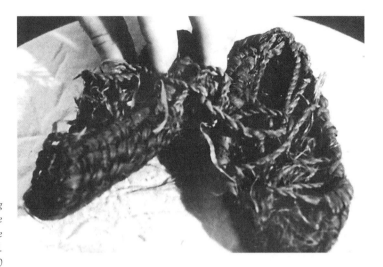

Among objects found at Roaring Springs and Catlow caves are well-preserved sandals. Those shown were for a small child. The sites were occupied 6,000 to 8,000 years ago.

All these finds, and the activities they represent, evoke in various ways the cultures of both the nineteenth-century Northern Paiutes, who were on the land when European Americans first arrived, and such peoples as the Klamath and Nez Perce, who at that time occupied adjacent regions. Thus, both ethnological and archaeological evidence fits well with the linguistic evidence, all of it suggesting that the ancestors of modern native peoples variably shared the northern Great Basin region over a very long period of time.

The Seasonal Round

The Burns Paiutes are descendants of the ancient people who lived in the Harney Valley of southeastern Oregon. Residents interviewed by Beatrice Blyth Whiting in the 1930s and by Marilyn Couture in recent times drew on their knowledge of local traditions to provide the following account of the annual seasonal round of the Wada Tika band of Northern Paiutes.

The Wada Tika ranged a broad territory around Malheur Lake, congregating for the winter along the shore in clusters of conical or domed, pole-framed lodges covered with tule mats that were made from a species of bulrush. They favored this area because even when cold weather limited travel, they could depend on being able to take some fish, waterfowl, small game, and marsh plants to supplement the foods prepared and stored during the warm months of the year.

Overleaf: Babies in cradleboards. In the Paiute languge, the cradleboard is called a hupe. Photo courtesy of Nevada Historical Society.

In April the first green shoots of spring appeared, and by May the thuga (*Lomatium cous*) and bitterroot (*Lewisia rediviva*) were ready to be dug from the hills forty miles north and east of the lake. Camas (*Camassia quamash*) was harvested in the lowland meadows as well. At the same season, salmon were starting to run in the head-waters of the Malheur River not far beyond the root grounds. While companies of women dug and dried roots for storage, men went on to set up salmon traps in certain streams or spear salmon. Women, along with their digging partners and accompanying children, might walk five to seven miles a day in search of roots. Families tended to return year after year to the same campsites near specific root grounds. With the root harvest completed, all joined in catching and drying the fish, an activity that continued through June.

During July and August, small household groups scattered widely. Their forays took them north beyond the high country near John Day and south beyond the Alvord Desert. In the north, they hunted the abundant deer, elk, bighorn sheep, and other animals. Groundhogs, another important food source, were hunted in differ-ent locations throughout the region and at different times, depend-ing on when the animals had accumulated enough fat, usually from May through July.

Salmon, steelhead, trout, and a wide variety of plant resources as well as familiar social networks drew the Wada Tika to the area now known as the Wallowa Whitman National Forest. Ponderosa pine nuts, cambium, seeds, roots, huckleberries, camas, tule roots, cattail pollen and roots, and juniper were among the resources that sustained them. The essential resources that drew them to this for-ested area, however, brought them closer to their northern neighbors, with whom relations were gener-ally strained, particularly after the Bannock

The Wada Tika spent the winter in conical or domed willow-framed lodges covered with tule mats made from a species of bulrush. These houses were clustered around Malheur Lake. Photo courtesy of Nevada Historical Society.

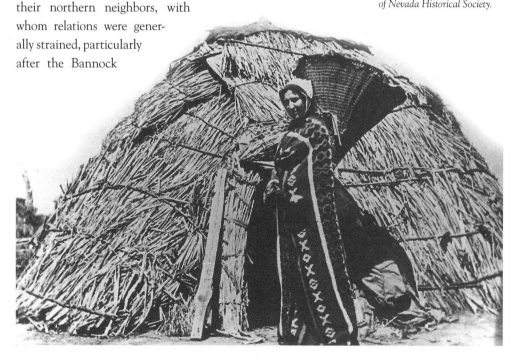

War. Sometimes the Wada Tika were the victims of wife raiding, slave trading, horse stealing, and other acts of aggression. At other times, they and their neighbors arranged a temporary peace for purposes of trade.

Groups that traveled south to the Alvord Desert area beyond Steens Mountain enjoyed varied plant resources including sunflower seeds and atsa (mustard seeds). They hunted deer and grouse, caught marmots, and collected crickets that could be pounded into cakes and dried for storage. In suitable places they fished or harvested chokecherries and buckberries.

In the fall, women would look along stream banks in search of chokecherries, which they picked, washed, and crushed between a hand stone (*mano*) and a flat grinding stone. The cakes were then formed by hand, dried in the sun and wind, and stored in buckskin bags. Before using the cakes, the women would soak them overnight in water, boil and strain the crushed seeds, and thicken the sauce to make a pudding.

In September, wada (*Sueda depressa*), with its abundant tiny black seeds, began to ripen along the alkaline shores of Malheur Lake. The Wada Tika, whose name means "wada eaters," reunited to gather and store large quantities of the seeds for the approaching winter. They also gathered the seeds of saltbush and other plants in the same Chenopod family as *Sueda depressa*.

In October and November the plant harvest was completed and the people turned to hunting bighorn sheep, deer, antelope, and jackrabbits. They stalked sheep and deer in the surrounding highlands. In open country, they trapped antelope—or surrounded and shot them—and drove jackrabbits into three-hundred-foot-long nets made of Indian hemp (*Apocynum*) cordage. Meat from the hunt was dried for winter stores, while hide, sinew, gut, and bone were used to make clothing, containers, and tools. No part of the animal was wasted. In December, the people, once again at the pivotal point of their annual cycle, settled into winter encampments around the lake.

Other Paiute bands—including the Elk Eaters, the Yapa Eaters, and the Salmon Eaters—ranged their own territories throughout Eastern Oregon. In fact, groups related by language and custom lived everywhere in the vast intermontane desert of Oregon, southern Idaho, Utah, Nevada, and eastern California. The "eater" names, by which many of these bands were called, drew attention to the special foods of their individual territories, and when circumstances dictated, communities shared in one another's abundant resources. Such exchanges were facilitated through a web of kinship maintained by intermarriage. Kinship ties could reach across hundreds of miles, giving members of any band access to the resources of a vast region—a great help when local foods were scarce.

In the spring, communities left the lakes for the annual root camp, where they and other people from a broader region congregated to catch up on the news and to trade, gamble, race horses, arrange marriages, and dig roots. The root camp represented a social and spiritual experience for all of the people.

Though the specifics varied according to local landscapes and resources, the wide-ranging, cyclical lifeway of the Wada Tika was characteristic of all Great Basin societies. Elevation, soil, and water dictated where particular plants and animals could be found, while the time of year determined the schedule of hunting and harvesting.

This pattern of life, which evolved to fit the Indians' landscape, emerged thousands of years ago. It continues today as Burns Indians hunt, fish, and gather traditional plant foods such as bitterroot, biscuit root, and camas lily bulbs. Now, however, the broad range of wild foods that once served as staples are eaten primarily as delicacies or used at special celebrations of traditional heritage.

Society

In Great Basin society, the roles of women and men were clearly defined. Women cared for the children and gathered plants for food, medicine, and the manufacture of useful items. They prepared the food, built shelters, tanned hides, made clothing, and wove baskets, cradleboards, and mats.

Feather headdress worn by Paiute men. Photo courtesy of Nevada Historical Society.

Men hunted deer, bighorn sheep, and antelope. They fished for salmon along the Drewsey River (the middle fork of the Malheur River) and for trout in various streams. They also manufactured tools of wood, stone, and bone; duck decoys of tule and cattails; and drums, rattles, game pieces, Indian-hemp rabbit nets, and ceremonial headdresses.

Men and women participated in some activities jointly. Both joined in salmon fishing and stalking groundhogs (marmots) in rocky areas with dogs and sticks. Men, women, and children also participated in the rabbit drives, with women and children usually tending the rabbit net or walking abreast while beating sticks together to chase the animals into the net.

In addition to being hunted for their meat, rabbits were also useful for their furs: they were captured during late fall or early winter, when their fur was rich and thick. After the rabbits were caught, they were immediately hit on the head, for if they were allowed to struggle, the meat would "taste tired." Usually, the rabbit meat was dried and stored for future use.

A rabbit-skin robe, requiring fifty rabbit pelts, was not only luxurious, but was also an essential item of clothing—as well as a

work of art. To fashion a rabbit robe, the maker would place an obsidian blade between his or her teeth, hold the pelt taut against it, and cut in a spiral pattern to produce a long strip of hide with fur attached. Each strip was stretched to dry, causing it to curl, which produced a hollow area inside the curl; this undoubtedly helped insulate the robe. The lengths of pelt were then sewn together with two-ply twined plant fiber to make a robe that would keep the maker warm, even in the cold and snow.

In the old days, a shaman or doctor—man or woman—was an important part of the community. Shamans would build a sweathouse in which to purify themselves. The small dome-shaped structures were framed with willows and well insulated with hides—or later with canvas tarps. Just outside the door, a fire was built to heat rocks. These were carried inside and placed in a central pit, where water was sprinkled on them. The shaman would steam and sweat before taking a dip in a nearby stream. Other community members would also take sweat baths for health and purification.

Agnes Hawley of the Burns Paiute Tribe is shown here in a rabbitskin robe, a luxuriant garment that kept its wearer warm and dry, even in cold, snowy weather. Photo courtesy of the Herbert W. Hawley Family.

Worldview

The Paiute people of the Great Basin held beliefs similar to those of the Indians of the Coast and Columbia Plateau—beliefs in animal and nature spirits, the spirit world, respect for the dead, spirit helper quests, and shamans. For them there was good and bad power: the power to make people love you, to cause misfortune, to bring sickness or death, and to heal. There were other specialized powers as well, for example, to lead antelope drives.

According to Beatrice Blyth Whiting, who interviewed Burns Paiute Indians in the mid-1930s, sorcery was a form of social control. The people maintained peaceful relations within the band by instilling a fear of sorcery or accusing individuals of sorcery. Because social cooperation was essential to the welfare of the group and sorcery could be used to encourage conformance to the rules of good behavior.

Language

The speech of Oregon's Northern Paiutes belongs to the Numic family of languages, which also includes Bannock, Shoshone, Comanche, Ute, Gosiute, and Southern Paiute. These sister languages seem about as closely related to each other as are the Romance languages of French, Italian, Romanian, Spanish, and Portuguese.

When first encountered by European American immigrants during the nineteenth century, Numic-speaking peoples occupied the entire Great Basin and extended various distances beyond it. Similarities in grammar and vocabulary suggest that all the Numic languages are descended from a single ancient speech community whose homeland was probably the main core of the Great Basin. In relatively recent times, Numic languages appear to have radiated from that core into, and in some cases beyond, the peripheries of the Great Basin to the edges of the Great Plains in the east, the Colorado Plateau in the south, the Sierra-Cascades foothills in the west, and the Columbia Plateau in the north. One prominent interpretation proposes that this apparent "Numic expansion" made Northern Paiutes the dominant people along the western and northern edges of the Great Basin about fifteen hundred years ago, while Southern Paiutes, Utes, and Shoshone became dominant from northeastern Arizona into northern Wyoming and Idaho after the collapse of northern Anasazi and Fremont corn-farming cultures between seven hundred and nine hundred years ago.

How and why might these shifts have occurred? The simplest and most likely answer is through relatively limited movements by Numic ancestors and their neighbors around the outer edges of the Great Basin, which were most likely triggered by long-term drying-out of the western climate and the changes this brought to human habitats. In the desert heartland of the Great Basin, where good hunting and gathering sites were widely scattered, the indigenous Numic peoples lived by ranging over large territories.

By comparison, groups who lived along the edges of the Great Basin, where streams and storms brought more water from major mountain zones, found more abundant resources and could establish larger and more permanent settlements. Along the western edge of the Great Basin, major hunting-gathering populations clustered around the lakes and marshes at the foot of the Sierra-Cascades. Along the eastern and southern edges of the Great Basin, major farming populations flourished for many generations.

When the western climate became significantly drier, however, as it did around the eras noted above, the farmers of the east and south had to choose whether to become hunters and gatherers or whether to remain farmers, which would require moving southward to regions with more available water. Different communities no doubt elected different options depending on individual circumstances. The hunter-gatherers of the western peripheries, some of whom were probably not Numic ancestors, could sustain their accustomed lifeways by moving only short distances into adjacent higher and wetter country. The places such people formerly occupied were left to their Numic neighbors, who knew from long experience how to make a living in an arid landscape. Much recent paleoclimatic research has shown that the Great Basin's climate has been highly variable over millennia; wet and dry cycles probably caused various communities to shift their ranges again and again in this manner. What we call the Numic expansion is by all odds only the most recent in a series of relatively small-scale population shifts that have occurred throughout the time of human occupation all over the desert west.

Chapter 15

The Oregon Coast

BY STEPHEN DOW BECKHAM

The coastal Indians' land was washed by the sea, bathed in fog and mist, covered with towering forests, and filled with dense underbrush. It was broken by mountains jutting into the ocean, cut by river valleys lying in isolated east-west directions, and fronted by the vast Pacific Ocean. In this rain-soaked region, the estuaries served as the food-rich places of livelihood, while the margins of bays provided secure village sites and access to the resources needed for daily life.

OUTSIDE OF AN INDIAN LODGE.

Coastal Indians lived in permanent villages during the winter—usually at the mouth of a river where fresh water and firewood were readily available. They covered their houses with large cedar planks. James Swan made this drawing of the gabled house and river canoes in the early 1850s and included it in his 1857 book The Northwest Coast: Or, Three Years' Residence in Washington Territory. *Illustration courtesy of Oregon Historical Society, #OrHi58495.*

In Oregon's coastal region life was rich in food and opportunity. Communication north and south was difficult. Prominent headlands jutting into the sea fractured the shoreline into a string of quiet, tidal estuaries and rivers running to the ocean. Visits and trade to the east necessitated journeys through dark forests and over the Coast Range. The diverse languages of the coastal zone testified both to the settlement of different people and the isolation of their homelands.

Subsistence

Coastal Indians had little need of an extensive seasonal round such as that found in other regions of Oregon. At low tide, their table was set. The food-rich intertidal zone abounded in mussels, chitons, snails, cockles, clams, and crabs. With prying and digging sticks, women and children eagerly worked the beaches to gather basic foods, while the men took salmon by spear, net, gaff, hook and line, and trap. They also constructed massive weirs of poles, literally damming the rivers and forcing the migrating schools of salmon, sturgeon, steelhead, and eels into their traps. Although the weirs were often difficult to maintain and repair after winter freshets, they proved their usefulness again and again. Weirs in tidewater were more permanent and used for harvesting diverse marine fish throughout the year on outgoing tides.

The men used bows and arrows or nets to hunt ducks and geese on the bays and coastal lakes. The Tillamook employed a unique basketry decoy covered with feathers to look like a duck. A man slowly stalked his prey by putting the decoy over his head, wading into the estuary, grabbing the duck's feet, and pulling it silently beneath the water until it drowned. Getting dinner was a wet and cold, but often productive, experience.

The men and boys also hunted a number of mammals using deadfall—log traps—carefully baited and mounted with rocks to ensnare and crush a bear, or pits dug on the far side of logs on game trails to trap unwary elk or deer. The animals would be impaled on sharpened stakes at the bottom of the pits.

During the course of the summer, the women and girls picked many baskets of berries—salmonberries in May, then thimbleberries and blackberries, and finally huckleberries and blueberries. To preserve the berries, the women dried some, such as salal, and packed them into cakes for later use. They also dug camas in the coastal meadows or in the uplands of the Coast Range.

Society

The Indians of coastal Oregon lived in permanent villages, usually located at the mouths of rivers. They favored sites with good drainage, visibility up and down the bay, a nearby source of fresh water, and abundant firewood. In time, the ground there accumulated a thick layer of broken shell, fire-cracked rock, charcoal, and other debris that has made it possible for archaeologists to trace back through thousands of years of history at some village sites.

In addition to the year-round, or permanent, villages, coastal Indians established berry-picking camps in the foothills of the Coast Range, as well as at blueberry bogs or huckleberry patches on the margins of lakes. In the fall, they often journeyed upriver to take

Lodges sheltered several families and provided room for sleeping, cooking, food drying, and storytelling. Tool and basketmaking often took place in lean-to-shelters, where better light was available. Illustration by A. T. Agate, 1841, engraved by R. W. Dodson, 1845. Courtesy of Stephen Dow Beckham and Oregon Historical Society, #OrHi4465.

freshwater mussels and the last lamprey eels from the spring run and to hunt for elk and deer. Because some of these more remote settings were gateways to inland valleys of complimentary abundance, they served as centers of trade and social interaction.

The people of this region erected a variety of structures, including semi-subterranean, plank-slab houses. Constructed over a shallow pit in the earth, framed with poles, and covered with large, finely hewn planks of cedar, these lodges might shelter a single family or several families. Design preferences varied. The Tillamook, for example, used a single-pitch shed roof, while other groups used a two-pitch gable roof. The Coos constructed some dwellings almost entirely underground, while the Tututni and Chetco built theirs nearly at ground level. Some of the peoples, especially those on the southwest coast, constructed sweat lodges where heated rocks sprinkled with water produced soothing sauna baths to cure illness, prepare a man for hunting, or bring good luck in gambling.

Other structures in the villages included windbreaks to quell the incessant north winds of summer and shelters for woodworking, basketmaking, or firewood. Dwelling units were often too dark or smoky for toolmaking and basketmaking, while lean-to shelters enabled craftsmen and -women to work in better light, protected from the elements.

Oregon's coastal Indians lived in a stratified social world in which there were three classes of people: free, rich, upper-class families; free, but poor and exploited, lower-class families; and, in some communities, a small number of slaves. The rich possessed power and ensured their wealth with strategic marriages and payment of a "bride price." They measured wealth in dentalium shells, dugout canoes, house planks, privileges to tell certain tales or hold political power, or—on the southern coast—in woodpecker scalps and obsidian display blades. The rich man who had ability served as the "headman." The village of a dozen to forty or more people constituted the tribe, though this body had no overarching political authority or tribal government. Among the Coast Indians, there was little evidence of social mobility except through gaming or marriage.

Languages

The linguistic complexity of the inhabitants of the Oregon seaboard mirrored the long residencies of many Indian groups. Major language stocks, from north to south, included the following:

Chinookan Family (Penutian)—Clatsop
Salishan Linguistic Isolate—Tillamook, Siletz
Yakonan Family (Penutian)—Yaquina, Alsea
Siuslawan Family (Penutian)—Siuslaw, Lower Umpqua
Coosan Family (Penutian)—Hanis, Miluk
Athabaskan-Eyak—Upper Coquille, Tututni, Shasta
    Costa, Chetco, Clatskanie

There were differences even within the various groupings of languages. Hanis and Miluk speakers, for example, both occupied Coos Bay, yet their languages were not mutually intelligible, though many Hanis and Miluk were bilingual to some degree. Similarly, the Athabaskan languages of southwestern Oregon were somewhat differentiated.

The Penutian language stock is perhaps the oldest in coastal Oregon. The Chinookan, Yakonan, Siuslawan, and Coosan speakers thus might lay legitimate claim to deep ancestry in the region. The Salishan-speaking Tillamook resided on the north-central coast. Either they were old-timers who had been shoved back from the mouth of the Columbia, or they were newer arrivals. Linguists are certain that the Athabaskan-speakers of southwestern Oregon's lower Rogue River and Curry County coast were, indeed, newcomers. Their language may be tied directly to that of the Apache and Navaho, or the Eyak on the Alaskan Coast.

Clothing, Technology, and Art

From northern California to the great fjords of southeast Alaska, the cedar was the tree of life to the Indians. As the sap rose in the spring, Oregon's coastal Indians stripped cedar bark, shredded it into strands, and wove capes and skirts. While women wore fringed, hula-like skirts for everyday labors, they wore tanned leather sheath dresses, capes, or wraparound skirts for special occasions. They decorated these garments with tassels of bear grass, shells, and even projectile points tied to buckskin thongs. They also used pounded cedar bark (the silky inner cambium layer) for baby diapers.

On special occasions, men wore a feather shirt and shell beads. Both men and women donned feather headdresses like the one worn by Coos Chief Doloose ("Jackson") in 1905. Photo courtesy Stephen Dow Beckham and the Bandon Historical Society.

For the men, clothing was simpler. Part of the year they went naked or wore leather breechclouts wrapped over a belt. In colder, wetter weather, they wore leather shirts, either open or laced across the chest, and leather leggings, which they tied to their belts.

For everyday labors, "Blind Kate," Coos, wore a fringed skirt and cape. Photo courtesy of Coos County Historical Society, North Bend, Oregon.

Men were usually bareheaded, while the women and girls often wore woven basketry caps. On special occasions, both men and women donned headdresses containing short, vertical feathers that extended across the forehead but did not have the dangling eagle-feather piece used by Plains Indians. Because leather shoes were impractical in the wet environment of coastal Oregon, they seldom wore moccasins.

Like Indians in other locales, the men bedecked themselves with body paints, favoring red ochre, which they obtained from quarries like that near Cape Perpetua and bonded with salmon eggs and saliva. Along the southern Oregon coast, pubescent women usually tattooed three vertical lines on their chins using indelible willow-bark charcoal that fixed the design for life. On the northern coast (and along the lower Columbia River), Indians of high status bound their infants in cradleboards, applying gentle but steady pressure to their skulls to shape them into distinctive, flat shapes from the tip of the nose to the crown of the head. Only slaves and some foreigners, they observed, had ugly round heads. Head-flattening extended into Alsea country but was rare south of the Siletz estuary.

The Indians of Oregon's coastal zone exhibited skills in woodworking, bone-carving, weaving, and stone-tool manufacturing. Unlike their distant cultural cousins who lived hundreds of miles to the north along the same Pacific shore, they did not carve totem poles, masks, elaborate houseposts, screens, or partitions in their dwellings. Their skills were able but simple.

Men manufactured dugout canoes, wooden scoops for use as bailers, spear handles, sinew-backed bows, and housing. Using their skills at lashing, they constructed pole frames for drying fish and meat, erected plank dwellings, hollowed out wooden bowls for cooking or holding foodstuffs, and wove eelpots for catching lampreys in late spring. The men also made arrow shafts by steaming slender poles of wood (to make them straight and true) and sanding them with sandstone, or by scouring rushes. To manufacture projectile points, knife blades, fleshers, and scrapers, they employed pressure flaking; to make hammers and other heavy tools, they pecked and abraded hard stones.

Coastal women were skilled at weaving. From the margins of lakes they gathered tules, which they sewed together to make rain capes and matting for partitions and floor coverings in their lodges. They also used spruce root and shredded hazel bark as basic materials for weaving a wide variety of baskets. Their nimble fingers produced basket hats, storage containers, baby cradles, drinking cups, cooking baskets, serving trays, and large clam baskets with heavy handles. The women often decorated these wares with overweave of bear grass (white), maidenhair fern stems (black), or materials dyed with alder bark (red). They preferred geometric designs, but the Chinookans sometimes wove animal or humanlike figures into the outsides of their baskets.

Oregon's coastal Indians have a rich oral literature. Melville Jacobs, who in the 1920s and 1930s made the most ambitious effort to record this literature, estimated that at the time of European American settlement in the 1850s, there were more than ten thousand tales known by the coastal Indians. Tragically, less than one-tenth of those accounts were recorded. Untold works—poems, epics, tragedies—vanished when the last speakers of the coastal languages died in the twentieth century.

Indians of high status bound their infants in cradleboards that shaped their heads into a distinctive flat shape, seen here in an early lithograph of Stum-Ma-Nu, a Chinook boy who died in 1839. Illustration courtesy of Oregon Historical Society, #OrHi77340.

The literature focused on how the land came to be and why things were the way they were. The tales mixed past and present. Some were set in a Myth Age, a time when only animals (who acted much like humans) occupied the earth. Others were set in a Transition Age, when animals and near-humans interacted. The near-humans, however, were sometimes incomplete, lacking fingers or even mouths. Then there was the Historic Past, the epoch when humans alone occupied the earth in an era that was bonded with things past. Time was a continuum along which things past seemed to flow into the present and in which modern realities were inextricably linked to the past.

Coyote, the "Trickster," appeared in a number of the oral traditions. He created things, caused trouble, got involved in many sexual escapades, and somehow always escaped the fate that would have overtaken a mere man. Coyote seemed human at times and was very clever. He and other supernatural heroes populated the literature and imaginations of Oregon's coastal peoples.

Worldview

Oregon's coastal Indians believed that many spirits inhabited the short days and dark nights of winter, the pall of fog and rain, and the vast virgin forests. These beings were both good and evil and might bring misfortune or even death to the unprepared person who encountered them. Signs of the spirit world were all around: terrible smells in the forest, ravaged rotten logs where wild creatures had fought or jostled for food, even sounds in the night. The trick was to stay clear of—or, if necessary, secure the proper skills for communicating with and managing—these supernatural companions.

This was best done through the right behaviors. At puberty, most boys and many girls went on spirit quests. Knowing that they faced this rite of passage between the ages of twelve and fourteen, young people went out alone at night to retrieve marked sticks from distant places—their first tests. Ultimately, each would go to a vigil site, often a lonely promontory overlooking the river or the sea, and prepare to gain a spirit helper.

These young people had to endure several days and nights of seclusion. They were prohibited from eating and were instructed to fast, pray, and dance. Above all, they were to wait. Even if they became scared, cold, and sick, they were to wait until the spirit world spoke. Ultimately, perhaps in the fourth or fifth day, each gained a spirit helper. These helpers might be animate or inanimate: otter, grizzly bear, blue jay, fir tree, or even flint, the stone from which some men made projectile points. Once a young person knew this helper, he or she was free to return to the village to perform a dance and a short song that revealed the guardian spirit's identity.

Those who had particularly strong helpers, or who aspired to become professional communicators with the spirit world, might go on successive quests or vigils. By gaining more helpers, they increased their abilities to cure the sick, bring good luck, or bring death or misfortune through their powers and incantations.

Such correct behaviors ordered Indian life. Many of the people of this region observed "first salmon" rites, believing that ritual observances ensured the bounty of the annual migrations of fish.

Some groups, such as the Athabaskan speakers at the entrance to the Rogue River, reportedly burned the hillsides near the river's mouth each year in the belief that this action would compel the fish to return. The worldview of the Indians along the shore included deference to the wealthy, respect for elders, and acceptance of the world where myth and reality blended to create a sense of place and belonging.

Chapter 16

The Plateau

BY EUGENE S. HUNN

The cultural area we call the Plateau is generally considered to be the vast region that straddles the Columbia River and follows its tributaries. Plateau culture spans portions of what is now British Columbia, Montana, Idaho, Washington, north-central and northeastern Oregon, and sometimes the Klamath Lake basin, which is adjacent to, but not part of, the Columbia River drainage. Seasonal temperatures vary greatly, as the Cascades cut off the Plateau from the moderating effect of marine air and leave a semidesert embraced by forested uplands.

Archaeologists have found abundant evidence of human occupation in the Plateau throughout the past ten thousand years. Well-documented early sites include Wakemap mound, at the site of the easternmost Chinookan village of Nixluidix, and Windust and Marmes rock shelters on the lower Snake and Palouse rivers. Evidence from these and other sites suggests that for the Plateau people, key resources—salmon, roots, fruits, and deer—were always important, though in varying proportions as climate and technologies changed. The stability of Plateau cultural ecological patterns was altered only—though radically—by the spread of Spanish horses from the Southwest (after about 1730), and later by guns imported from the expanding fur-trading frontier in the Plains and by the spread of smallpox and other Old World epidemic diseases (after about 1775). Remarkably, however, many of the Plateau lifeways are kept alive today.

Peoples and Languages

Celilo Falls, on the western edge of the Plateau, was the meeting place of two distinct Indian cultures: speakers of Sahaptian languages lived east of the falls and Chinookan speakers lived to the west, their lands stretching as far as the Pacific Ocean. Sahaptian speakers included those who spoke the related languages of Nez Perce and Sahaptin—a complex combination of the mutually intelligible dialects spoken in Oregon by the Cayuse, Umatilla, John Day, Celilo, Tenino, and Tygh Valley peoples. Judging by the internal diversity of this language family and its contiguous distribution, Sahaptian speakers must have occupied the Columbia River basin above the Dalles for many centuries.

In the Blue Mountains, after the winter snows melted, Umatilla and John Day people mingled with their Cayuse and Nez Perce relatives and friends, gathering, fishing, and hunting on the upper reaches of the Umatilla, Walla Walla, Grande Ronde, and Powder rivers. European Americans regarded the Cayuse as fierce warriors; however, the Cayuse were few in number and their terrain was located off the main rivers. The Nez Perce lived in the Wallowa River valley.

Parties of Northern Paiute or Shoshone lived on the southern marches of the Plateau. These groups raided northward on horseback or simply pursued their own seasonal rounds on the headwaters of the Columbia's southern tributaries. Their presence drove a wedge between two closer cultures whose languages were similar: Sahaptians on the Columbia River and the Klamath in what is now southern Oregon.

Overleaf: In this region, edible roots were the primary sources of food energy. The women gathered them using pointed digging sticks fashioned from strong woods and crafted with handles of stone, antler, or wood.

Facing page: The Plateau Indians took advantage of a complex environment that began at the Columbia River and stretched south to the Great Basin and Klamath area of the Western Interior and east to the Blue Mountains. The Indians' seasonal round began in the winter, when they remained in their winter villages making tools and weapons, holding dances, and subsisting on food gathered during the year. In spring few foodstuffs remained and small groups set out in search of Indian celery (Gray's lomatium) and spawning suckers and eels (Pacific lamprey). In April the women established camps in nearby canyons and harvested bitterroot and other lomatiums. May brought chinook salmon runs, and families moved to fishing sites along the Columbia. Then began a series of moves south and eastward to various types of fish from July through October; pick berries in the mountains; hunt; and gather Indian hemp, bulrushes, and tules with which to make tools, clothing, and shelters. Illustration is by Lynn Kitagawa and used with permission.

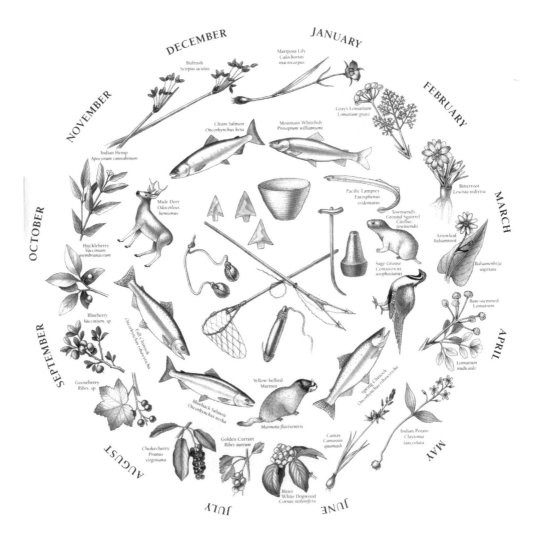

DECEMBER

Bulrush
Scirpus acutus

JANUARY

Mariposa Lily
*Calochortus
macrocarpus*

NOVEMBER

Gray's Lomatium
Lomatium grayi

FEBRUARY

Indian Hemp
Apocynum cannabinum

Chum Salmon
Oncorhynchus keta

Mountain Whitefish
Prosopium williamsoni

Bitterroot
Lewisia rediviva

OCTOBER

Mule Deer
*Odocoileus
hemionus*

Pacific Lamprey
*Entosphenus
tridentatus*

Townsend's
Ground Squirrel
*Citellus
townsendii*

MARCH

Huckleberry
*Vaccinium
membranaceum*

Arrowleaf
Balsamroot

Sage Grouse
*Centrocercus
urophasianus*

*Balsamorhiza
sagittata*

SEPTEMBER

Blueberry
Vaccinium, sp.

Fall Chinook
Oncorhynchus tshawytscha

Bare-stemmed
Lomatium

APRIL

*Lomatium
nudicaule*

Gooseberry
Ribes, sp.

Yellow-bellied
Marmot

Spring Chinook
Oncorhynchus tshawytscha

Blueback Salmon
Oncorhynchus nerka

Marmota flaviventris

Indian Potato
*Claytonia
lanceolata*

MAY

Chokecherry
*Prunus
virginiana*

Golden Currant
Ribes aureum

Camas
*Camassia
quamash*

AUGUST

Bitter
White Dogwood
Cornus stolonifera

JUNE

JULY

The Seasonal Round

The Plateau encompasses a variety of habitats, beginning near sea level along the Columbia River and rising to the Cascades' volcanic summits. The region has six major life zones, each characterized by dominant plants that grow and mature in stages each year, beginning in the low elevations and moving gradually into the higher ones. The Plateau Indians took advantage of this complex habitat and its long harvest season by following a highly mobile "seasonal round" as they gathered their food.

The seasonal round of a family from the John Day River, for example, would begin during the winter, when home was a tule-mat longhouse in a village containing several such houses. Each house contained several families, two of whom shared each hearth or fireplace. Explorers Lewis and Clark described a cluster of these villages opposite the mouth of the Umatilla River containing five, fifteen, and twenty-four houses respectively, with thirty-two persons counted in one house. They estimated the collective population of that village to be fifteen hundred.

Typically, winter villages were established near the Columbia or on the lower reaches of its major tributaries, sheltered from the wind and located near a source of driftwood, which was used for fuel. In this season, opportunities for hunting, fishing, and gathering were severely limited and people sustained themselves on dried stores of roots, fish, and berries. During the long winter months, they manufactured and maintained their tools, recounted myths, held spirit power dances (which were sponsored by Indian doctors), and paid social visits.

The winter's fast was broken in late February as the tribes harvested Indian celeries and again in March as they caught spawning suckers, both of which could be found near the winter villages. In April, the women might establish camps a few miles from the river in tributary canyons and, from these, climb adjacent ridges seeking bitterroot and various tuberous *Lomatiums*—key starchy staples. Back at the village, they would dry these roots for storage and prepare *sapolil* (flour), salmon meal, and other foods for trade.

In early May, when spring chinook salmon runs peaked, fishing intensified at strategic locations throughout the Columbia Basin, including at the Long Narrows, downstream of Celilo Falls on the mainstem of the Columbia River. Later, as summer and fall chinook and other salmon runs arrived, the preferred harvest location moved up the Columbia to Celilo Falls, where families with traditional fishing sites often moved for the duration of the runs. John Day families then dismantled their winter lodges and began a series of moves southward, camping successively at Rock Creek, Olex, Condon, Fossil, and Spray—then moving east to Monument and south again, climbing to the camas meadows in the Fox Valley, and then (after white settlers arrived) going on to John Day for the Fourth of July celebrations. When they returned to the river, these families would be laden with food that they stored in special pits at the winter village sites.

When fishing efforts shifted to Celilo Falls, families without claims could fish there, but only with permission from the families who owned the sites. At Celilo and elsewhere, people focused on salmon and steelhead, intercepting successive runs that began with blueback (sockeye) salmon in July, peaked with fall chinooks in early September, and ended with silver (coho) and dog (chum) salmon in October. Many families left the river during the heat of late summer to go on berry-picking expeditions in the mountains, which were kept open and productive by intentional burning. While the women gathered and dried quantities of huckleberries, the men hunted.

By harvesting local wild plants and animals, the Columbia River Indians provided virtually all of their own food, shelter, tools, and medicine at this time. For Sahaptin-speaking Indians (those who lived east of the Dalles), these included thirty-five species of edible roots, thirty kinds of fruits and nuts, eight kinds of edible greens, twenty-one kinds of fish, thirty-seven kinds of birds, and thirty-one kinds of mammals. In addition, Plateau Indians recognized well over a hundred species of medicinal plants. Other plants—principally Indian hemp and tules (a species of bulrush)—were used in making tools, clothing, and shelters. Each species was named, and its harvest seasons and preferred habitats were well known, as were techniques of harvest, preparation, and storage.

For the Indians of the Plateau, edible roots were the primary sources of food energy, in contrast with neighboring regions, which emphasized seed, acorn, bison, game, or fish. The Plateau was also characterized by strong seasonal contrasts that required substantial food supplies to be dried for winter use. Within the region, however, subsistence strategies varied. West of the Dalles, the Chinookan peoples lived; they controlled trade and exchanged their surpluses of dried salmon for upland products, allowing them to remain on the river throughout the year. These Indians ranged as far west as the Pacific Ocean and were, in some ways, similar to coastal Indians. On the eastern edge of the Plateau, Nez Perce and Cayuse peoples placed greater emphasis on hunting deer, elk, and bison.

Plateau Indians lived in longhouses covered with tule mats. Each house was home to several families and a village contained many houses. Tule-mat walls could keep out the blazing heat of summer as well as the sub-zero cold of a Plateau winter. Red Elk and his sister are shown in front of their tule-mat longhouse. Photo by Major Lee Moorhouse, courtesy of Knight Library, University of Oregon Negative #4786.

Society

Plateau society did not countenance kings and distrusted the exercise of power, instead highly prizing the right to lead one's own life. It may be hard for us today to imagine how a society can function without judges, courts, police, or executive officers, yet Plateau society succeeded for millennia without such institutions of social control.

Throughout the region, people were linked by reciprocal moral obligations among kin, trading partners, and friends. These obligations were established and maintained by gift exchanges of food, valuable manufactured items, or services. For example, marriages were cemented by a series of formal gift exchanges among corresponding kin of the bride and groom and by the groom's bride-service, akin to a dowry, for his parents-in-law. Such exchanges continued periodically throughout the marriage, and if one partner died, they were carried on by means of the levirate and sororate (preferred marriages of a widow or widower to a sibling or cousin of the deceased spouse).

Among the people of the Plateau, social control and leadership were in the hands of several respected individuals. Children had their first taste of discipline from "whippers," and each village was home to one or more chiefs, a status often—though not invariably—passed from father to son. Chiefs did not command, but led by example and rhetorical inspiration; their speeches were amplified and broadcast by a herald, who helped sustain the dignified reserve expected of chiefs. These chiefs were rarely if ever shamans—Indian doctors whose extraordinary spiritual powers were harnessed to the work of curing. Rather, they might be individuals distinguished as warriors, salmon

Raised caches were used for storing food or building material. Photo by Edward S. Curtis, courtesy of Oregon Historical Society, #OrHi67539.

chiefs, or leaders of root-digging or hunting parties, depending on their personal character and ability. The shamans themselves were revered but might also have been feared because of the deadly potential of their powers.

The people of the Plateau also held war captives from northeastern California, who were captured and sold by Klamath intermediaries or taken on raids by war parties along the Columbia. Among the Chinookan peoples on the Columbia, slaves were apparently quite numerous and were roughly treated, but among Sahaptian peoples they were rare and most often were treated as if they were family.

Extended family ties remain at the core of Plateau Indian social life today. Traditional kinship usage, in which cousins and siblings are equated, is still evident in the common use of the terms "aunt" and "uncle" to include the first and second cousins of one's parents. Also, funerals and memorials continue to be important occasions for reaffirming the overriding importance of traditional kinship ties.

Clothing, Technology, and the Arts

Plateau peoples of earlier generations survived in the face of a harsh climate through their detailed knowledge of ecology, but also by virtue of their technology. They had implements—digging sticks, bows and arrows, nets and fishing spears, and dugout canoes—made of various local woods, hemp, obsidian, and other natural materials. They also had carrying bags and baskets, tule mats and mat-covered lodges, and clothing of softened hides. The knowledge of how to manufacture, employ, and repair each item has been passed from generation to generation by precept and example.

A detailed knowledge of ecology and technology helped the Plateau peoples survive. For fishing, they crafted long dugout canoes. The Plateau Indians also traded for other canoes, such as the Chinookan canoe that had a lighter head and tail and a wider area inside for trade goods and family storage. This 1897 photograph was taken near Celilo Falls on the Columbia River. Faintly visible in background, on the other side of the river, are utility poles and some temporary structures used for fishing. Photo courtesy of Oregon Historical Society, #OrHi018927.

The largest portion of the Plateau Indian tool kit was made of plant materials. Indian hemp, for example, was essential for making string for bindings, for knotting fish and rabbit nets, for twining carrying bags and a special Plateau hat, and for making a woman's "time ball," her personal record of the important events of her life. Tules were cut, dried, and sewn into mats to sit and sleep on or to eat from. Because their cylindrical stems are filled with a cellulose matrix that traps air, tules make wonderful insulation. For this reason, lodges with tule-mat walls could keep out the subzero cold of a Plateau winter. The elegant Klickitat baskets, for which Plateau Indians are famed, were woven of cedar root and decorated with bitter cherry bark and the leaves of bear grass.

Although deer and elk were prized for their meat, they were perhaps even more important for their skins. These were softened by being soaked in a fatty solution of deer brains and sturgeon heads, then carefully scraped and stretched, and finally cut and sewn for clothing. Moccasins, leggings, shirts, and full-length ceremonial dresses—plain or highly decorated—were the products of this craft. The decorative designs were traced in porcupine quill, shell, and natural dyes.

The creative talents of the Plateau Indians were most fully expressed in the verbal art of storytelling. In 1976, during the winter—the customary season for myth telling—Elsie Pistolhead, a sixty-seven-year-old Columbia River Indian, told from memory, in Sahaptin, nearly seventy Coyote stories—a full sixteen hours on tape. Elsie's remarkable recitation of her people's oral literature is testimony to the importance of that literature in the culture of the Plateau.

The stories, all of which feature Coyote as the central figure, are myths that tell of a primordial time, an age during which animals were fully human and from which the present humanized world was ordained. Here, Coyote is frequently described as a trickster and a fool, but he is much more than that: he is everyman, acting out human fantasies and fears and inspiring moral behavior, while making the world safe for "the [Indian] people who are coming soon," to use the characteristic Plateau myth refrain.

The mythology of the Plateau Indians is an oral tradition, properly appreciated at once as dramatic performance (ranging from burlesque to tragedy), as poetry, and as sacred text—the "Indian bible." Some of the stories have been preserved in written form, but much is lost in this translation. Also lost is the wealth of common experience and cultural values that informed the traditional audience's appreciation of the tales' humor and dramatic power.

Religion

In everyday Plateau life, religion did not exist as a separate sphere of belief and practice set apart from the secular. Rather, spirit power was thought to be manifest in all things—a form of belief called "animism," in which plants, animals, and other natural forces possess will and intelligence. This belief establishes a moral community, which transcends human society and strongly sanctions respect for nature. This attitude of respect was reinforced in Coyote stories and periodic thanksgiving feasts.

In one aspect of the Plateau Indians' animistic lives, children were sent questing until a spirit revealed itself to them, taught them a song, and promised a lifelong alliance. Once such revelations occurred, individuals revealed their spirit powers only in an indirect way—in their character and achievements and at winter spirit dances—for to speak of those powers was to lose them. Thus, the relationship between individual and spirit was intensely personal and private. In the case of shamans, their extraordinary healing power came from several especially powerful spirit allies.

In historical times, the focus of Plateau Indian religious expression shifted from the relationship between individuals and their spirit powers to communal worship, whether Christian or distinctively Indian. The Sacred Dance religion (also known as the Longhouse religion, Seven Drums religion, or Dreamer religion and closely allied with the Feather Dance religion still practiced today on the Warm Springs Reservation) is the dominant Indian church in the Plateau today. This religion may have roots in precontact communal dance ceremonies, such as were witnessed by David Thompson at the John Day River in 1811.

The specific, modern forms of these religions owe much to a series of revelations by Plateau prophets prominent in the nineteenth century. Of these, Smohalla of Priest Rapids, Washington, is best known, but others also experienced miraculous resurrection, returning from death's door with instructions for the proper conduct of communal worship as a means of personal expiation and communal salvation. Sacred Dance worship now focuses on respecting indigenous sacred foods, public testimonials, and the reinforcement of social ties at funerals, memorials, and name-giving rites—which in many respects are similar to coastal potlatches.

Native and nonnative scholars have suggested that nineteenth-century Plateau prophecy led to cultural revitalization after the many deaths from epidemic diseases, such as smallpox and measles, that had been introduced by white settlers. The traditional curing of Indian doctors was ineffective in the face of these new diseases, which tore at the Plateau tribes' social fabric. In traditional Plateau religion the dead were a danger to the living, and showing appropriate respect to the dead was essential to the health of those still living. This remains true today, when the ghosts of deceased relatives are still thought to cause serious illness. During those trying times, Sacred Dance worship gave the people of the Plateau the will to survive.

Chapter 17

The Western Interior

BY KATHRYN ANNE TOEPEL

Archaeological research has established that the lifeways practiced by the
hunters and gatherers of the Western Interior were in existence for a very long
time. A number of archaeological sites—including Cascadia Cave in the
western Cascades, the Marial Site in the Rogue River Valley, and several
localities along the Long Tom River west of Eugene—have been identified
through radiocarbon dating as being between six thousand and ten thousand
years old. Stone tools and charred plant remains found at these sites indicate
the existence of a long-standing way of life focused on hunting and root
gathering. Both linguistic evidence and the emphasis on root crops suggest that
the early peoples of the Western Interior may have migrated into the area from
the Plateau many thousands of years ago.

The Kalapuya Indians occupied most of the interior valleys of western Oregon for thousands of years, inhabiting the expansive Willamette Valley and spilling south into the Upper Umpqua Basin. A number of distinct bands unrelated to the Kalapuya lived in smaller valleys in southwestern Oregon, including the Upper Umpqua, the Rogue River, and the Klamath Lakes basins in the Cascade Mountains. Sandwiched between coastal peoples to the west of the Coast Range and Plateau groups east of the Cascades, the Indians of western Oregon shared some similarities with the people of these neighboring areas, while adapting to the rain-drenched drainages of the Interior.

Overleaf: For the Klamath Indians, situated at the conjunction of the Western Interior and Great Basin regions, wokas (water lily seeds) were an important food. This Klamath woman is grinding the seeds. Photo by Edward S. Curtis, courtesy of the Smithsonian Institution #76-91.

Subsistence Round

A diverse environment composed of prairie and oak savannas, oak and fir groves, forests, marshes, and lakes produced an abundance of foods for the Indians of the Western Interior valleys. Their annual subsistence round was divided into two general seasons: summer and winter. They spent the summer months, from about March to

The Kalapuya Year

The Kalapuya year was divided into twelve lunar months, beginning with the first new moon in late August or early September. Month names reflect the annual growing cycle and the importance of particular foods.

September *First month*	After the harvest the Indians are still out. Small groups are still living in their summer camps scattered across the valley, collecting acorns, berries, and camas roots. Prairie burning begins for tarweed seed harvesting.
October *Hair [leaves] falls off*	Wapato harvest time begins in the northern Willamette Valley, and the northern Kalapuya groups move to camps close to the lakes where the wapato grows. Groups in the southern Valley complete their camas harvesting.
November *Approaching winter*	The Kalapuya prepare their winter houses for the coming cold weather.
December *Good month*	The weather becomes colder but is still mild. The Kalapuya settle into their villages for the winter.
January *Burned breast*	The winter becomes cold and the old people sit so close to the house fires that their chests get singed. The Kalapuya spend much time in their winter houses, feeding the fires. Winter dances begin.

October, in temporary open camps, moving about the valley floors and foothills to harvest roots, nuts, seeds, and berries as they ripened. Before the winter rains began in earnest, though, the people returned to their permanent villages.

Among the plants they collected were acorns, wapato (wild potato), hazelnuts, ipos (an edible root), arrowroot, sego lily, tule, cattail, and a variety of berries. One of the most important harvests involved camas, the bulbs of which are similar in appearance, but not in taste, to onion. The small camas bulbs, which have a flavor some say is like sweet potatoes, were first harvested in March or April when they were most tender. Then, in June, they were harvested in great quantities, roasted in below-ground rock ovens, and prepared for winter storage.

Another staple food, the tarweed seed (similar to a sunflower seed), was ready for harvesting by late summer. After collection, the tarweed plants were set afire, and the seeds were beaten from the stalks into basketry or buckskin platters. Then the seeds were parched, ground into flour, and sometimes mixed with mashed cooked camas and hazelnuts.

February *Out of provisions*	The end of winter finds the Kalapuya short on stored provisions, and it is a lean time. Hunters spend more time in the woods trying to find game.
March *First spring*	People begin to leave the winter village, making short camping trips to gather food, including the first shoots of camas, which are only finger high at this time.
April *Budding time*	The Kalapuya make more trips onto the valley floor as the camas grows higher.
May *Flower time*	The camas begins blossoming as the Kalapuya leave their winter houses to camp out for the summer. The spring runs of salmon head up the Willamette River and its tributaries.
June *Camas harvesting*	The camas becomes fully ripe. The women begin to gather and dry camas bulbs for the following winter, an activity pursued until September or October. The people also catch all sorts of fish. Berry picking begins.
July *Half-summer-time*	Weather is hot and dry. The Kalapuya begin to collect hazelnuts and caterpillars.
August *End of summer*	The weather remains hot as the people continue to gather a variety of berries, nuts, and roots in preparation for the winter.

Game, waterfowl, and fish supplemented this plant diet. Deer were numerous, and elk were available both on the valley floor and in the upland forests. In addition, birds (wild goose, grouse, duck, quail, pigeon) and small mammals (squirrel, rabbit, raccoon, beaver) were trapped and cooked by roasting or boiling. To boil food, hot stones from the fire were placed with wooden tongs into a watertight basket containing a stew or soup.

Eels, crawfish, freshwater shellfish, trout, suckers, and salmon were also caught from rivers and lakes, and the fish were roasted, boiled, or dried for winter storage. In addition, large quantities of dried salmon were obtained through trade along the Columbia River.

The early inhabitants of the Western Interior were able to increase the abundance of the prairie plants upon which they depended. In the fall they frequently set fires on the valley floor to maintain vast areas of open prairie, which served not only to make seed harvesting much easier, but also to roast grasshoppers (a delicacy) and clear out undergrowth between trees, thus making berry picking and acorn harvesting easier.

Society

The winter village was the basic social group for the Indians of the Western Interior. Each village consisted of related families. Suitable marriage partners were found outside the village group during foraging trips, trading forays, or social visits with relatives. Once married, a woman usually joined her husband's village.

Clusters of closely related villages, recognized as bands, shared a common territory, usually a particular river basin. Each village had its own rights of access to some resources, such as a particular tarweed patch, but other resources such as camas or game animals, were considered to be available to all villages within the band.

In each village, leadership roles were filled by the most qualified people. Some social distinctions were made on the basis of wealth, with the wealthiest member of a village often known as the head chief. Although wealth was gained or lost with relative ease, the distinction between freemen and slaves was never confused. While the origin and extent of slavery in western Oregon is unclear, it may have been a relatively recent practice, playing a particularly important role among those groups living near the trading centers of Oregon City and the Columbia River, and among the Klamath, who were frequent visitors to these centers.

People built villages and camps to fit the needs of the seasons and occupied the dwellings in accordance with their place in the subsistence round. They built winter lodges—rectangular semi-subterranean or earth-banked structures with bark roofs and central fireplaces that extended up to sixty feet on a side—at permanent village sites, often to house more than one family.

During the warmer months, the winter village residents splintered into smaller groups for increased mobility. While these groups were hunting or on the move from one food-gathering place to another, they set up temporary camps under oak or pine trees or sometimes in the open, often not building shelters, but, if necessary, constructing windbreaks of boughs, brush, or grass as the weather required.

Sweathouses, used for purification purposes, were often erected next to rivers or streams near camps or villages. These small round structures, large enough for a few individuals, consisted of bent hazel sticks with a covering of fir boughs and dirt. Inside, fired stones provided the heat for steam baths.

With the exception of enclaves of Athabaskan speakers in southwestern Oregon and near the lower Columbia River, speakers of the Penutian stock of languages occupied the Western Interior. This language stock was composed of the Kalapuyan Family (including three Kalapuyan languages), the Siuslawan Family (Siuslaw and Lower Umpqua languages), and the Molala, Klamath-Modoc, and Takelman languages (which are believed to have no close relationships to any other surviving languages).

The presence of these diverse but distantly related language families in western Oregon strongly suggests that Penutian speakers were in the region for thousands of years. In western Oregon, the language distribution appears to have centered on river basins, following the natural boundaries of mountains and drainage breaks.

A Klamath woman carries a load of wood, circa 1920. Photo courtesy of Oregon Historical Society, #OrHi65927.

Sweat lodges were an integral part of village life. They were often made of layers of earth covered with planks. Photo courtesy of Cow Creek Band of Umpqua Indians.

This seems the case for the Kalapuya in particular, who spoke a number of dialects within their three language groups along the entire length of the Willamette Valley. These three groups were Tualatin-Yamhill, spoken in a small portion of the lower Willamette Valley upstream from the falls at Oregon City; Santiam, which included dialects in the middle and upper Willamette Valley; and Yoncalla, whose speakers occupied the upper Umpqua drainage basin south of present-day Cottage Grove.

Clothing, Technology, and the Arts

Relatively few descriptions of Western Interior dress and adornment exist, but it is apparent that the amount and type of clothing varied with the seasons. The basic dress throughout the year included leather moccasins and leggings for the men and a leather or grass apron or skirt, sometimes with leggings and moccasins, for the women. Botanist David Douglas, who visited the Umpqua Valley in June 1826, observed the dress of the Yoncalla Indians he had met:

> The dress of the men is skins of the small deer undressed, formed into shirts and trousers, and those of the richer sort striped and ornamented with shells. … The women, a petticoat like that worn by Chenook [Chinook] females, and a sort of gown of dressed leather, in form differing from the men's only by the sleeves being more open.

When the weather turned colder, both men and women wore caps of fur or basketwork, along with heavier shirts, trousers, or gowns. Fur cloaks or robes were sometimes made of gopher, squirrel, or deer hides sewn together with deer sinew.

Social status was often reflected in an individual's personal adornment. For example, designs tattooed on arms, legs, and faces with a sharp piece of bone and blackened with cinder from the fire were not just marks of beauty but also indications of social status. Natural pigments of red, white, or green were often used as ornamental face paint. Both men and women were also fond of necklaces, armbands, and nose- and earplugs fashioned from beads made of salmon backbones, marine shells, bone, trade beads, feathers, porcupine quills, and strips of otter skin.

Like the Chinook and northern coastal groups, the Western Interior Klamath-Modoc and the northern Kalapuya groups practiced the head-flattening of infants, accomplished in the cradleboard. The Klamath regarded an unflattened head with derision, saying it was "slavelike," while they admired flattened or "good" heads. However, many groups in the interior of western Oregon did not practice head-flattening.

In much of western Oregon, little remains of the native inhabitants' technology. Although archaeological excavations have unearthed an ever-growing collection of native artifacts, these consist mostly of stone tools, as organic materials are poorly preserved in the acidic valley soil. However, we do have a few sporadic descriptions of material culture in the literature of early European American arrivals.

Marshes and lakes produced an abundance of food. This Klamath man in a dugout boat hunts for ducks among the cattails and tules, 1923. Photo by Edward S. Curtis, courtesy of Oregon Historical Society Negative #OrHi 78079.

Before the introduction of historic trade goods, tools and utilitarian items were fashioned from locally available materials such as wood, grasses, stone, bone, shell, and skins. After about 1750, however, European American trade items, including glass and metal beads, and other metal items, became increasingly important.

Although all groups in western Oregon built canoes for water transport, woodworking was a largely undeveloped art. Because horses were not available until sometime after 1800, land travel was undertaken on foot.

Spears, clubs, and bows and arrows were basic hunting equipment, as was an array of snares, traps, and decoys. Fishing was accomplished by many means, including spears, detachable harpoon heads, line and hook, clubs, lures and bait, basket traps, and rock dams. Items frequently used in daily activities included cordage, basketry, stone mortars and pestles, digging sticks for root gathering, knives, and scrapers.

Grasses and bark were used as basketry materials and twined into both soft and rigid items. In western Oregon, the basketry of the Klamath-Modoc Indians is the best known. They used tule, cattails, and swamp grasses to twine bowls, hats, gambling or sifting trays, and circular baskets. Burden baskets and storage baskets were made of a more open twine weave. Rigid loop containers included seed beaters, ladles, and winnowing baskets. Other basketry items included trays, two-handled baskets, fish traps, cradles, and twined flat bags. Water baskets were made by coiling rather than twining. Less durable weavings of tule and grasses were made into bedding and house coverings. Cordage was often fashioned from nettle bark and flax fibers and made into

During the Wilkes Expedition of 1841, Joseph Drayton drew this sketch of Indians fishing with dipnets from plank platforms at Willamette Falls. Illustration courtesy of Oregon Historical Society, #OrHi46193.

nets. Rope was made of willow bark or twisted hazel sticks, or braided from grasses, tule, hide, and nettle fibers.

Unlike the well-known and gifted woodcarvers in the heart of the Northwest Coast culture area who carved large totem poles and the like, the people of the Western Interior expressed their artistic bent in everyday items that were often decorated, such as grinding tools and basketry. Small anthropomorphic sculptures called *henwas* were used by Klamath-Modoc shamans and were often artfully decorated. Rock art, though not often found in western Oregon, served as an aesthetic, and presumably religious, outlet. To a great extent, the people expressed their artistic sense through the manner in which they tattooed and arrayed themselves.

Worldview

Among the Indian people of western Oregon, the world was reflected in a rich mythological heritage. Various animals and supernatural beings inhabited the myths that recounted, in part, how the trickster Coyote created the world, Willamette Falls, sickness, and the technique of net fishing for salmon, and how he engaged in a number of amusing adventures and misadventures along the way. Winter was the traditional time for telling stories, which served to convey morals and practical information to the youngsters.

The animals and beings represented in mythology also had a real existence in everyday life for the peoples of the Interior. Many of these mythical beings were guardian spirits or spirit powers who guided individuals through their lives and provided them with luck, strength, and protection. To acquire one or more powers, children approaching puberty were sent alone to a mountain place to seek a vision. After several days of fasting and little sleep, questers were often rewarded with a visit from a spirit power or dream power. Sometimes during vision quests, a spirit seeker would mound or stack stones as part of the path to a prophetic dream. The remains of these vision quests are still found in the upland regions of western Oregon today.

Men and women who acquired strong spirit powers were known as shamans and served as highly respected healers and ceremonial leaders. Shamans were primarily responsible for curing diseases and wounds, but occasionally they also acted to recall lost souls, control the weather, foretell the future, and locate lost or stolen objects.

Acknowledgments

The Oregon Council for the Humanities and the editor wish to extend their heartfelt thanks to the following people.

The authors were, of course, indispensable. So many of them went beyond the call of duty to answer questions, help with myriad details, and provide suggestions, contacts, sources, and photos. We are so grateful for their hard work, patience, diligence, and good humor. Before the authors began their work, we relied on an advisory committee to establish the publication's broad outlines and objectives. We turned often to individual committee members throughout this process, seeking and receiving advice, support, and assistance. Members of that group, some of them also authors, include representatives of the nine federally recognized tribes: Ron Brainard, chair, and Bob Garcia, former vice chair of the Confederated Tribes of Coos, Lower Umpqua and Siuslaw Indians; Roberta Conner, director of Tamástslikt Cultural Institute, and her mother, Leah Conner, Confederated Tribes of the Umatilla Indian Reservation; Robert Kentta, cultural specialist of the Confederated Tribes of Siletz Indians; Bernice Mitchell, tribal council member of the Confederated Tribes of the Warm Springs; Michael Rondeau, government operations officer for the Cow Creek Band of Umpqua Tribe of Indians; Minerva Soucie, elder of the Burns Paiute Tribe; June Shell-Sherer, former secretary of the Confederated Tribes of the Grand Ronde; Gerald Skelton, culture and heritage director of the Klamath Tribes; and Ken Tanner, chief of the Coquille Indian Nation. Other members of the advisory committee are Stephen Dow Beckham, professor of history at Lewis & Clark College; Bob Conklin, owner of Timber Press; Bill Lang, professor of history at Portland State University; David Liberty (Umatilla), assistant librarian of StreamNet Library; Lillian Pitt (Warm Springs), artist; Olney Patt, Jr., executive director of the Columbia River Inter-Tribal Fish Commission; Karen Quigley, executive director of the Oregon Commission on Indian Services; and Mary Wood, professor of law at the University of Oregon School of Law.

The authors and the editor express their gratitude to the many other individuals who answered many questions and provided information, clarification, inspiration, and perceptive and helpful review: Affiliated Tribes of Northwest Indians; Howard Arnet; Chief David Brainard and other tribal council members, Confederated Tribes of Coos, Lower Umpqua and Siuslaw Indians; Garland Brunoe, former chair, Confederated Tribes of Warm Springs; R. Scott Byram; Torina Case, secretary, Klamath Tribes; Phil Cash Cash, anthropology linguist,

University of Arizona, Confederated Tribes of the Umatilla Indian Reservation; Rochelle Cashdan; Marilyn Couture; Marshall Cronyn; Debra Croswell, public affairs manager of the Confederated Tribes of the Umatilla Indian Reservation; Bobby David; Taylor David, media relations for the Klamath Tribes; Anita Dragan; Scott Delancey, Department of Linguistics at the University of Oregon; Arthur Dye, formerly of Ecotrust; Neva Eggsman; David Ellis; Susan Fillin-Yeh; Andrew Fisher, professor of history at the College of William & Mary; Allen Foreman, chair of the Klamath Tribes; the Honorable Elizabeth Furse of the Institute for Tribal Government at Portland State University; Pat Courtney Gold (who also let us photograph her lovely hands for the cover); Roberta Hall, professor emeritus of anthropology at Oregon Sate University; Charles Haller, tribal council coordinator of the Confederated Tribes of Grand Ronde; Suzanne Hanchett; Katherine Harrison, former chair of the Confederated Tribes of Grand Ronde; David Hatch, former council member of the Confederated Tribes of Siletz Indians; Dino Herrera; Ken Hymes; Don Ivy, director of cultural resources for the Coquille Indian Tribe; James Jackson; Jerald Jackson; Philip Jackson, elder of the Klamath Tribes; Craig Jacobson, vice president of Ecotrust; Wendell Jim; Deanie Johnson, language specialist for the Confederated Tribes of Warm Springs; Jean Johnson; Orin Kirk; Klamath Tribes Culture and Heritage Department staff; Marianne Keddington-Lang, Oregon Historical Society Press; Tori Lahr; Bud Lane, tribal council member and native language teacher for the Confederated Tribes of Siletz Indians; Bill Layman, author, *River of Memory*, and the University of Washington Press; Carole Leon, director of the Museum at Warm Springs; Diane LeResche; Perri McDaniel; Shelley Matthews; Elwood Miller; Robert Miller, professor of law at Lewis & Clark Law School; Antone Minthorn, chair of the board of trustees for the Confederated Tribes of Umatilla Indian Reservation; tribal representatives from Nine Tribes Education Cluster; Stephanie Ohles; June Olson, former cultural resources director of the Confederated Tribes of Grand Ronde; Jeff Ostler, professor of history at the University of Oregon; Evaline Patt, archivist for the Museum at Warm Springs; Floy Pepper; Patricia Whereat Phillips, Confederated Tribes of Coos, Lower Umpqua and Siuslaw Indians; Beth Piatote, professor of ethnic studies at the University of California at Berkeley; Louie Pitt, Jr., director of governmental affairs for the Confederated Tribes of Warm Springs; Karen Quigley, director of the Oregon Commission on Indian Services; Arlita Rhoan, language specialist for the Confederated Tribes of Warm Springs; Diane Rodriquez, public information officer for the

Confederated Tribes of Siletz Indians; Christopher Roth; Howard Roy, cultural development coordinator, Confederated Tribes of Coos, Lower Umpqua, and Siuslaw Indians; Sue Schaffer, chair of the Cow Creek Band of Umpqua Tribe of Indians; Sherri Shaffer, chief executive officer of the Cow Creek Band of Umpqua Tribe of Indians; Myra Shawaway, director of the Confederated Tribes of Warm Springs; Kathleen Shaye-Hill; Gerald Skelton, director of culture and heritage for the Klamath Tribes; Valerie Switzler, language specialist for the Confederated Tribes of Warm Springs; Chris Tanner, tribal librarian and newspaper editor for the Coquille Indian Tribe; Siobhan Taylor, public affairs director for the Confederated Tribes of Grand Ronde; Brad Victor, Oregon Department of Education; Dallas Winishut, language specialist for Confederated Tribes of Warm Springs; and Adrian Witcraft.

For assistance in securing photographs and illustrations for the book, we wish to thank the following museums, archivists, curators, and photographers: Bandon Historical Society; Stephen Dow Beckham; Lucy Berkley, Oregon Historical Society; Nan Cohen of the University of Washington Archives; JoAnne Cordis of Central Oregon Community College Library; Debra Croswell of the *Confederated Umatilla Journal*; Jeremy Five-Crows of the Columbia River Inter-Tribal Fish Commission; Kathrine French; Andrew Fuller of Ecotrust; Kent Goodyear of Ecotrust; Craig Jacobsen of Ecotrust; Jeana Harrington of Oregon Commission on Indian Services; Debbie Johnson of Oregon State University; Lawrence Johnson; Norman Johnson of Oregon State University; Lynn Kitigawa; Amanda Kohn of the Portland Art Museum; Lesli Larson of the Knight Library at the University of Oregon; Roberta Lavadour; Jack T. Lee; Carole Leon, director of the Museum at Warm Springs; Toby McClary and others at *Smoke Signals*, Confederated Tribes of the Grand Ronde; Randall Melton and Dallas Dick, Tamástslikt Cultural Institute, Confederated Tribes of the Umatilla Indian Reservation; Ralf Meyer of Green Fire Productions; Museum of Natural History at University of Oregon; Daisy Njoku of the National Anthropological Archives at the Smithsonian Institution; John Olbrantz of Hallie Ford Museum; Evaline Patt, archivist of the Museum at Warm springs; Wil Phinney of the *Confederated Umatilla Journal*; Karen Quigley of Oregon Commission on Indian Services; Ray Ramirez of the Native American Rights Fund; Kay Reid of the Institute for Tribal Government; Joanna Cohan Scherer, visual anthropologist of the Smithsonian Institution; Alison T. Stenger; Deward Walker, Jr.; Chuck Williams; Edward C. Wolf of Ecotrust; Elizabeth Woody; Jennifer Viviano of Viviano Design; Shirod

Younker; and Jeff Zucker and the Oregon Historical Society's Western Imprints.

We owe a huge debt of gratitude to these individuals and the many others who were responsible for originally conceiving this volume and bringing to life the first edition: Richard Lewis, former OCH executive director; Carolyn Buan, first edition editor; and Jeanne Galick, graphic designer. We also very much appreciate former OCH executive director Christopher Zinn, who realized the importance of republishing *The First Oregonians* and started us on the path to a second edition. Thanks also to Allison Dubinsky, Sherry Smith, and Leigh van der Werff for their editing, proofreading, and indexing help during the production phase of this book.

Major funding for this second, revised edition came from the Spirit Mountain Community Fund of the Confederated Tribes of Grand Ronde and also from the Cow Creek Band of Umpqua Tribe of Indians, Coquille Indian Tribe, Confederated Tribes of Siltez Indians, Confederated Tribes of the Umatilla Indians, and Confederated Tribes of Warm Springs. We give them our special thanks for making this project possible.

We would also like to gratefully acknowledge the staff at Oregon State University Press, particularly Jo Alexander, Tom Booth, and Mary Braun, for sustaining their belief and interest in this project even when there was so much uncertainty.

For a project as collaborative and complicated as this, it is difficult to offer adequate thanks to all the individuals who have contributed. For those whose help we may have failed to acknowledge here, we thank you, and ask your forgiveness.

Selected Bibliography

Aberle, David F. "The Prophet Dance and Reactions to White Contact." *Southwestern Journal of Anthropolgy* 15 (1959): 74–83.

Ackerman, Lillian A. "Sexual Equality in the Plateau Culture Area." Ph.D. diss., Washington State University, 1982.

———, ed. *A Song to the Creator: Traditional Art of Native American Women of the Plateau*. Norman: University of Oklahoma Press, 1996.

Affiliated Tribes of Northwest Indians, Economic Development Corporation. *A Travel Guide to Indian Country: Oregon Edition 2005–2006*. Portland, Oregon: Affiliated Tribes of Northwest Indians, Economic Development Corporation, 2005.

Aikens, C. Melvin. "Adaptive Strategies and Environmental Change in the Great Basin and its Peripheries as Determinants in the Migrations of Numic-Speaking Peoples." In *Across the West: Human Population Movement and the Expansion of the Numa*, edited by David B. Madsen and David Rhode, 35–43. Salt Lake City: University of Utah Press, 1994.

———. "Archaeology of the Northern Great Basin: An Overview." In *Man and Environment in the Great Basin*, edited by David B. Madsen and James F. O'Connell. Special Memoirs of the Society for American Archaeology, 2. 1982.

Alexie, Sherman. *Old Shirts, New Skins*. Illustrated by Elizabeth Woody. Los Angeles, California: UCLA American Indian Studies Center, 1993.

Ames, Kenneth M., and Herbert G. D. Maschner. *Peoples of the Northwest Coast: Their Archeology and Pre-History*. Portland, Oregon: Thames Hudson. 1999.

Barber, Katrine. *Death of Celilo Falls*. University of Washington Press: Emil and Kathleen Sick Lecture-Book Series in Western History, 2005.

Baughman, Mike, and Charlotte Cook Hadella. *Warm Springs Millennium: Voices from the Reservation*. Austin: University of Texas Press, 2000.

Beckham, Stephen Dow. "History of Western Oregon Since 1846," in *Northwest Coast*, vol. 7, ed. by Wayne Suttles. *Handbook of North American Indians*. Edited by William C. Sturtevant. (Washington DC: Smithsonian Institution, 1990), 180–196.

———. *The Indians of Western Oregon: This Land Was Theirs*. Coos Bay, Oregon: Arago Books, 1977.

———. *Land of the Umpqua: A History of Douglas County, Oregon*. Roseberg, Oregon: Douglas County Commissioners, 1988.

———, ed. *Oregon Indians: Voices from Two Centuries*. Corvallis: Oregon State University Press, 2006.

———. *Requiem for a People: The Rogue Indians and the Frontiersmen*. Corvallis: Oregon State University Press, 1996.

Beckham, Stephen Dow and Robert M. Reynolds. *Lewis and Clark: From the Rockies to the Pacific*. Portland, Oregon: Graphic Arts Center Publishing Co., 2002.

Beckham, Stephen Dow, Rick Minor and Kathryn Ann Toepel. *Native American Religious Practices and Uses in Western Oregon*. Eugene: University of Oregon Anthropological Papers, 31, 1984.

Beeson, John. *John Beeson's Plea for the Indians: His Lone Cry in the Wilderness for Indian Rights: Oregon's First Civil-Rights Advocate*. Medford, Oregon: Webb Research Group, 1994.

Blyth, Beatrice. "Northern Paiute Bands in Oregon." In *Tribal Distribution in Eastern Oregon and Adjacent Areas*, edited by Verne F. Ray, *American Anthropologist*, 40 (1938): 402–05.

Boit, John. "Remarks on the Ship 'Columbia's' Voyage from Boston. In *Voyages of the Columbia to the Northwest Coast*, 1787–1790 and 1790–1793. Boston: Massachusetts Historical Society, 1941.

Boyd, Robert T., ed. *Indians, Fire and the Land in the Pacific Northwest.* Corvallis: Oregon State University Press, 1999.

———. *People of The Dalles: The Indians of Wascopam Mission.* Lincoln: University of Nebraska Press, 1996.

Byram, R. Scott. "Scoquel, Coquelle, and Coquille," *Changing Landscapes: Stustaining Traditions, Proceedings of the 5th and 6th Annual Coquille Cultural Preservation Conferences*, Ivy, Donald B., and R. Scott Byram, eds. pp. 121–138. North Bend, Oregon: The Coquille Indian Tribe, 2002.

Cashdan, Rochelle. *Indians of the Northwest.* Perspectives on History Series. Carlisle, Massachusetts: Discovery Enterprises, Ltd., 1998.

Cebula, Larry. *Plateau Indians and the Quest for Spiritual Power, 1700–1850.* Lincoln: University of Nebraska Press, 2003.

Clements, William M. *Oratory in Native North America.* Tucson: University of Arizona Press, 2002.

Cohen, Fay G. *Treaties on Trial: The Continuing Controversy Over Northwest Indian Fishing Rights.* Seattle: University of Washington Press, 1986.

Columbia River Inter-Tribal Fish Commission. *Chinook Trilogy: My Strength Is From the Fish* (30 min), *Empty Promises, Empty Nets* (30 min.), *Matter of Trust* (30 min.) Portland, Oregon: Columbia River Inter-Tribal Fish Commission, 1995. VHS.

Cone, Joseph. *Celilo Falls and the Remaking of the Columbia River.* Corvallis: Oregon Sea Grant, Oregon State University, 2005. DVD, 31 min.

———. *A Common Fate: Endangered Salmon and the People of the Pacific Northwest.* Corvallis: Oregon State University Press, 1995.

Cone, Joseph and Sandy Ridlington. *The Northwest Salmon Crisis: A Documentary History.* Corvallis: Oregon State University Press, 1996.

Confederated Tribes of Coos, Lower Umpqua and Siuslaw Indians. *Arrow Chain: Reclaiming our Heritage.* Coos Bay, Oregon: Confederated Tribes of Coos, Lower Umpqua and Siuslaw Indians, 1995. VHS, 28 min.

———. *Coos, Lower Umpqua and Siuslaw Indian Tribes: A Historical Perspective.* Coos Bay, Oregon: Confederated Tribes of Coos, Lower Umpqua and Siuslaw Indians, 1977.

Confederated Tribes of Siletz Indians. *The People Are Dancing Again.* Siletz, Oregon: Confederated Tribes of Siletz Indians, 1996, VHS remastered 2002, 28 min.

Confederated Tribes of Siletz Indians. Skookum Tillicum: The Strong People of Siletz. Siletz, Oregon: Confederated Tribes of Siletz Indians, 2002. VHS, 34 min.

Confederated Tribes of the Warm Springs Reservation of Oregon. *The People of Warm Springs.* Warm Springs: Confederated Tribes of the Warm Springs Reservation of Oregon, 1984.

Connolly, Thomas J. *Newberry Crater: A Ten-Thousand-Year Record of Human Occupation and Environmental Change in the Basin-Plateau Borderlands.* Salt Lake City: University of Utah Press, 1999.

Coos, Lower Umpqua, and Siuslaw Confederated Tribes. *Providing for Restoration of Federal Recognition to the Confederated Tribes of Coos, Lower Umpqua, and Siuslaw Indians: Report to Accompany HR 5540.* Washington DC: Government Printing Office, 1984, 9p.

Couture, Marilyn D., Mary F. Ricks and Lucile Housley. "Foraging Behavior of a Contemporary Northern Great Basin Population." *Journal of California and Great Basin Anthropology* 8, no. 2 (1986): 150–60.

Craig, Carol, "Reawakening the Spirit: Yakama Tribe Leads Rededication of Willamette Falls Fishery." In *Wana Chinook Tymoo,* issues 2 & 3. Portland, Oregon: Columbia River Inter-Tribal Fish Commision, 1994.

Cressman, Luther Sheeleigh. "Klamath Prehistory: The Prehistory of the Culture of the Klamath Lake Area, Oregon." *Proceedings of the American Philosophical Society* 46, no. 4 (1956): 375–513.

———. *The Sandal and the Cave: The Indians of Oregon.* Reprint, Corvallis: Oregon State University Press, 1981.

Curtin, Jeremiah. *Myths of the Modocs.* Boston: Little, Brown & Co., 1912.

Curtis, Edward S. *The North American Indians,* vol. 7, *The Yakima, the Klickitat, the Salishan Tribes of the Interior, and the Kutenai; vol. 8, The Nez Perce, Walla Walla, Umatilla, Cayuse, and the Chinookan Tribes;* vol. 13, *The Hupa, the Yurok, the Karok, the Wiyot, Tolowa and Tututni, the Shasta, the Achomawi, and the Klamath.* Northwestern University Library, http://curtis.library.northwestern.edu/.

d'Azevedo, Warren L., ed. *Great Basin.* Vol. 11, *Handbook of North American Indians.* Edited by William C. Sturtevant. Washington DC: Smithsonian Institution Press, 1986.

De Smet, Pierre-Jean. *Oregon Missions and Travels over the Rocky Mountains in 1845–1846.* New York: Edward Dunigan, 1847.

Deloria, Vine, Jr., ed. *American Indian Policy in the Twentieth Century.* Norman: University of Oklahoma Press, 1993.

———, *Spirit and Reason: The Vine Deloria, Jr. Reader.* Golden, Colorado: Fulcrum Publishing, 1999.

Deloria, Vine, Jr. and Raymond J. DeMaille. *Documents of American Diplomacy: Treaties, Agreements, and Conventions, 1775–1979,* vols.1 & 2. Norman: University of Oklahoma Press, 1999.

Deloria, Vine, Jr. and Clifford M. Lytle. *The Nations Within: The Past and Future of American Indian Sovereignty.* Austin: University of Texas Press, 1998.

Deloria, Vine, Jr. and David E. Wilkins. *Tribes, Treaties, and Constitutional Tribulations,* Austin: University of Texas Press, 2000.

Deur, Douglas E. "A Most Sacred Place: The Significance of Crater Lake among the Indians of Southern Oregon." *Oregon Historical Quarterly* 103, no. 1 (2002): 18–49.

Devon A. Mihcsuah, ed. *Repatriation Reader: Who Owns American Indian Remains?* Lincoln: University of Nebraska Press, 2000.

Dietrich, William. *Northwest Passage: The Great Columbia River.* Seattle: University of Washington Press, 1995.

Dompier, Douglas. *The Fight of the Salmon People: Blending Tribal Tradition with Modern Science to Save Sacred Fish.* Philadelphia, Pennsylvania: Xlibris Corporation, 2005.

Douthit, Nathan. *A Guide to Oregon South Coast History: Including an Account of the Jedediah Smith Exploring Expedition of 1828 and its Relations With the Indians.* Coos Bay, Oregon: River West Books, 1986.

———. *A Guide to Oregon South Coast History: Traveling the Jedediah Smith Trail.* Corvallis: Oregon State University Press, 1999.

———. *Uncertain Encounters: Indians and Whites at Peace and War in Southern Oregon 1820s–1860s.* Corvallis: Oregon State University Press, 2002.

Drew, Charles S. Lt. Col. *Account of the Origin and Early Prosecution of the Indian War in Oregon.* Fairfield, Washington: Ye Galleon Press, 1973.

Dupris, Joseph C., Kathleen Shaye Hill and William H. Rodgers, Jr. *The Si'lailo Way: Indians, Salmon, and Law on the Columbia River.* Durham, North Carolina: Carolina Academic Press, 2006.

Dwyer, Mindy. *Coyote in Love.* Seattle: Alaska Northwest Books, 1997.

ECONorthwest. *The Contributions of Indian Gaming to Oregon's Economy in 2005: A Market and Economic Impact Analysis for the Oregon Tribal Gaming Alliance.* Portland, Oregon: ECONorthwest, 2007. www.econw.com/reports/2005_OTGA.pdf

Epps, Garrett. *To an Unknown God: Religious Freedom on Trial.* New York: St. Martin's Press, 2001.

Farris, Glenn J. "Women's Money: Types and Distributions of Pine Nut Beads in Northern California, Southern Oregon, and Northwestern Nevada." *Journal of California and Great Basin Anthropology* 14, no. 1 (1992): 55–71.

Fisher, Andrew H. "Tangled Nets: Treaty Rights and Tribal Identities at Celilo Falls." *Oregon Historical Quarterly* vol. 105, no. 2 (Summer 2004).

Fowler, Catherine S. "Subsistence," in *Great Basin*, vol. 11, edited by Warren L. d'Azevedo. *Handbook of North American Indians.* Edited by William C. Sturtevant. (Washington DC: Smithsonian Institution, 1986), 64–97.

Fowler, Catherine S. and Sven Liljeblad. "Northern Paiute," in *Great Basin,* vol. 11, edited by Warren L. d'Azevedo. *Handbook of North American Indians.* Edited by William C. Sturtevant. (Washington DC: Smithsonian Institution, 1986), 435–65.

French, David. "Wasco-Wishram." *In Perspectives in American Indian Culture Change,* edited by Edward H. Spicer, 337–430, Chicago: University of Chicago Press, 1961.

Gidley, Mick, ed. *Edward S. Curtis and the North American Indian Project in the Field.* Lincoln: University of Nebraska Press, 2003.

Glover, Richard, ed. *David Thompson's Narrative, 1784–1812.* Toronto: Chaplain Society, 1962.

Goddard, Ives, ed. *Languages.* Vol. 17, *Handbook of North American Indians.* Edited by William C. Sturtevant. Washington DC: Smithsonian Institution Press, 1996.

Gogol, John M., ed. "Benjamin Gifford, Photographer Among the Columbia River Indians." American Indian Basketry. Volume II, No. I. Whole Issue No. 5. Portland, Oregon: American Indian Basketry, 1982.

———. "The Columbia Plateau Indians and Twined Basketry of Indians of Western Washington and Vancouver Island (Part 1)." American Indian Basketry. Vol. I, Nos. 1, 2, and 3. Portland, Oregon: American Indian Basketry, 1979.

———. "Cornhusk Basketry of the Columbia Plateau Indians." American Indian Basketry, vol 1. No. 2. Portland, Oregon: American Indian Basketry, 1980.

———. "Klamath, Modoc, and Shasta Basketry." American Indian Basketry: Vol. III, No. 2, Whole Issue No. 10, Portland, Oregon: American Indian Basketry, 1983.

———. "Traditional Arts of the Indians of Western Oregon." American Indian Basketry and Other Native Arts. American Indian Basketry. Vol IV. No. 2, Whole Issue 14. Portland, Oregon: American Indian Basketry, 1984.

Gold, Ruben, ed. *Original Journals of the Lewis and Clark Expedition, 1804–1806.* New York: Antiquarian Press, 1959.

Glover, Richard, ed. *David Thompson's Narrative, 1784–1812.* Toronto: Chaplain Society, 1962.

Grafe, Steven. *Peoples Of The Plateau: The Indian Photographs of Lee Moorhouse, 1898–1915.* Norman, Oklahoma: University of Oklahoma Press, 2006.

Gunther, Erna. 1926. "An Analysis of the First Salmon Ceremony." *American Anthropologist* 28 (1926): 605–17.

———. "An Further Analysis of the First Salmon Ceremony." University of Washington Publications in Anthropology 2 (1928): 129–73.

Haines, Francis. "The Northward Spread of Horses Among the Plains Indians." *American Anthropologist* 40, no. 3 (1938): 429–37.

Hall, Roberta L. *The Coquille Indians: Yesterday, Today and Tomorrow.* Lake Oswego, Oregon: Smith, Smith, and Smith, 1984.

Hall, Roberta L., and Don A. Hall. "The Village at the Mouth of the Coquille River: Historical Questions of Who, When and Where." *Pacific Northwest Quarterly* 82, no. 3 (1991): 101–08.

Harless, Susan E., ed. *Native Arts of the Columbia Plateau: The Doris Swayze Bounds Collection.* Seattle: University of Washington Press, 1998.

Hines, Donald M. *Celilo Tales: Wasco Myths, Legends, Tales of Magic and the Marvelous.* Issaquah, Washington: Great Eagle Publishing Inc., 1996.

———.*The Forgotten Tribes: Oral Tales of the Teninos and Adjacent Mid-Columbia River Indian Nations.* Issaquah, Washington: Great Eagle Publishing, 1991.

Hines, Gustavus. *Oregon: Its History, Condition, and Prospects.* Buffalo, New York: George H. Derby & Company, 1851.

Hirschfelder, A., P. F. Molin and Y. Wakim. *American Indian Stereotypes in the World of Children: A Reader and Bibliography.* Lanham, Maryland: Scarecrow Press, 1999.

Hodge, Frederich Webb. "Cayuse." In *Handbook of American Indians North of Mexico,* vol 4/4 (1912). Reprint: Scituate, Massachusetts: Digital Scanning, 2003.

Hood, Susan. "Termination of the Klamath Indian Tribe of Oregon." *Ethnohistory* 19, no. 4 (1972): 379–92.

Hunn, Eugene S. with James Selam and Family. *Nch'I-Wana, The Big River: Mid-Columbia Indian People and Their Land.* Seattle: University of Washington Press, 1990.

Hymes, Dell. *In Vain I Tried To Tell You: Essays in Native American Ethno-poetics.* Philadelphia: University of Pennsylvania Press, 1981.

———. *Language in Culture and Society.* New York: Harper and Row, 1964.

————.*Now I Know Only So Far: Essays in Ethnopoetics*. Lincoln: University of Nebraska Press, 2003.

————, ed. *Reinventing Anthropology*. 2d ed. New York: Barnes and Noble, 2001.

Ivy, Donald B. and R. Scott Byram. Changing Landscapes: "Sustaining Traditions," Proceeding of the Fifth and Sixth Annual Coquille Cultural Preservation Conferences. North Bend, Oregon: Coquille Indian Tribe, 2002.

Jessett, Thomas E. *Indian Side of the Whitman Massacre*. Pamphlet. Fairfield, Washington: Ye Galleon Press, 1972.

Jones, Suzi, and Jarold Ramsey, eds. *The Stories We Tell: An Anthology of Oregon Folk Literature*. Oregon Literature Series, vol. 5. Corvallis: Oregon State University Press, 1994.

Josephy, Alvin M., Jr. *The Nez Perce Indians and the Opening of the Northwest*. New Haven: Yale University Press, 1965.

Kappler, Charles J., ed. *Indian Affairs: Laws and Treaties, vols.1 & 2*. Washington DC: Government Printing Office, 1904.

Karson, Jennifer, ed. *As Days Go By: Our History, Our Land, and Our People—the Cayuse, Umatilla, and Walla Wall*. Seattle: University of Washington Press, 2006.

Kasner, Leona Letson. *Survival for an Artifact—Siletz Indian Basketry*. Newport, Oregon: Lincoln County Historical Society, n.d.

Keyser, James D. *Indian Rock Art of the Columbia Plateau*. Seattle: University of Washington Press, 1992.

Kinkade, Dale M. "History of Research in Linguistics," *in Northwest Coast*, vol. 7, edited by Wayne Suttles. *Handbook of North American Indians*. Edited by William C. Sturtevant. (Washington DC: Smithsonian Institution Press, 1990), 98–106.

Kinkade, Dale M., William W. Emendorf, Bruce Rigsby, and Haruo Aoki. "Languages," in *Plateau*, vol. 12, edited by Deward E. Walker, Jr. *Handbook of North American Indians*. Edited by William C. Sturtevant. (Washington DC: Smithsonian Institution Press, 1998), 49–72.

Knudson, Ruthann, and Bennie C. Keel, eds. *Public Trust and the First Americans*. Corvallis: Oregon State University Press 1995.

LaLande, Jeffrey M. *The Indians of Southwest Oregon: An Ethnohistorical Review*. Corvallis, Oregon: Oregon State University Press, 1991. 66p.

Lampman, Evelyn Sibley. *Treasure Mountain (Eager Beaver Book)*. Illustrated by Richard Bennett. Reprint, Portland: Oregon Historical Society Press, 1990.

Lesley, Craig. *River Song*. New York: Picador USA, 1999.

Lesley, Craig. *Winterkill*. New York: Dell, 1984.

Liberty, David M. "It's Never Too Late to Give Away a Horse." *Oregon Historical Quarterly*, vol. 105, no. 1 (Spring) 2004.

Linn, Natalie. *The Plateau Bag: A Tradition in Native American Weaving*. Johnson County Community College, n.d.

Lomahaftewa, Gloria, ed. *Glass Tapestry: Plateau Beaded Bags from the Elaine Horwitch Collection*. Phoenix, Arizona: The Heard Museum, 1993.

Loring, J. Malcom and Louise Loring. *Pictographs and Petroglyphs of the Oregon Country*. Los Angeles: Institute of Archaeology, University of California, Los Angeles, Monographs 21/23, 1996.

Leuthold, Steven. *Indigenous Aesthetics: Native Art Media and Identity.* Austin: University of Texas Press, 1998.

McKeown, Martha (Ferguson) and Archie W. McKeown. *Come to Our Salmon Feast.* Portland, Oregon: Binford & Mort, 1959.

McKeown, Martha (Ferguson). *Linda's Indian Home.* Portland, Oregon: Binfords and Mort, 1959.

Mercer, Bill: People of the River: Native Arts of the Oregon Territory. Seattle, University of Washington Press, 2005.

Miller, Jay, and William R. Seaburg. "Athapaskans of Southwestern Oregon," *Northwest Coast*, vol. 7, edited by Wayne Suttles. *Handbook of North American Indians.* Edited by William C. Sturtevant. (Washington DC: Smithsonian Institution Press, 1990), 580–88.

Miller, Robert J. *Native Americans, Discovered and Conquered, Thomas Jefferson, Lewis and Clark and Manifest Destiny.* Westport, Connecticut: Praeger Publishers, 2006.

Miller, Wick R. "Numic Languages," in *Great Basin*, vol. 11, edited by Warren L. d'Azevedo. *Handbook of North American Indians.* Edited by William C. Sturtevant. (Washington DC: Smithsonian Institution Press, 1986), 98–106.

Moss, Madonna L., and George B. Wasson. "Intimate Relations with the Past: The Story of an Athapaskan Village on the Southern Northwest Coast of North America." *World Archaeology* 29 (1998): 317–32.

Mudge, Zachariah Atwell. *Sketches of Mission Life Among the Indians of Oregon.* Fairfield, Washington: Ye Galleon Press, 1983.

Murray, Keith A. *The Modocs and Their War.* Norman: University of Oklahoma Press, 1959.

Nabokov, Peter, ed. *Native American Testimony: A Chronicle of Indian-White Relations from Prophecy to Present, 1492–2000.* New York: Penguin Books, 1999.

O'Donnell, Terence. *An Arrow in the Earth: General Joel Palmer and the Indians of Oregon.* Illustrated by Karen Beyers. Portland: Oregon Historical Society Press, 1991.

Olson, Kristine. *Standing Tall: The Lifeway Of Kathryn Jones Harrison, Chair of The Confederated Tribes Of The Grand Ronde Community.* Portland and Seattle: Oregon Historical Society Press in association with University of Washington Press, 2005.

Peterson, Emil R. and Alfred Powers *A Century Of Coos and Curry.* Portland: Binsford and Mort, 1952.

Pevar, Stephen L. *The Rights of Indians and Tribes.* 3d ed. An ACLU Handbook. Carbondale: Southern Illinois University Press, 2002.

Phinney, Archie. "Coyote and the Swallowing Monster." In *Coyote Was Going There: Indian Literature of the Oregon Country*, edited by Jarold Ramsey, 9–12. Seattle: University of Washington Press, 1977.

Poupart, John, C. Martinez, J. Red Horse and D. Scharnberg. *To Build a Bridge: Working with American Indian Communities.* 4th Printing. St. Paul, Minnessota: American Indian Policy Center, 2001.

Prucha, Francis Paul. *The Churches and the Indian Schools 1888–1912.* Lincoln: University of Nebraska Press, 1979.

Ramsey, Jarold W., ed. *Coyote Was Going There: Indian Literature of the Oregon Country.* Seattle: University of Washington Press, 1977.

Rau, Violet. *Authentic North American Oregon Indian Clothing for Special Times.* Little Bears Go Visiting Series. *Toppenish, Washington:* Celia Totus Enterprises, 1988.

Ray, Verne F. *Primitive Pragmatists: The Modoc Indians of Northern California.* Seattle: University of Washington Press, 1963.

Relander, Click. *Drummers and Dreamers.* Caldwell, Idaho: Caxton Printers, 1956.

Reddick, SuAnn M. "The Evolution of Chemawa Indian School: From Red River to Salem, 1825–1885," *Oregon Historical Quarterly* 101 (Winter 2000): 444–65.

Richards, Kent D. *Isaac I. Stevens: Young Man in a Hurry.* Pullman: Washington State University Press 1993.

———, ed. "*Isaac I. Stevens and Joel Palmer Treaties, 1855–2005.*" *Oregon Historical Quarterly* 106 (Fall 2005) Special Issue.

Riddle, George. *History of Early Days in Oregon.* Riddle, Oregon: The Riddle Enterprise, 1920.

Ridlington, Sandy and Joseph Cone, eds. *The Northwest Salmon Crisis: A Documentary History, 1854–1994.* Corvallis: Oregon State University Press, 1996.

Robbins, William G. *The Great Northwest: The Search for Regional Identity.* Corvallis, OR: Oregon State University Press, 2001.

———. *The Native Context and the Arrival of Other Peoples,* in Section 1, *This Land-Oregon* of The Oregon History Project. Portland: Oregon Historical Society, 2002. www.ohs.org/education/oregonhistory/narratives/chapter.cfm?chapter_ID=0005F5DE-71D5-1DDA-B57D80B05272FE9F

Roberts, Wilma, and Carolyn Z. Shelton, ed. *Celilo Falls: Remembering Thunder, Photographs from the Collection of Wilma Roberts.* The Dalles, Oregon: Wasco County Historical Museum Press, 1997.

Ronda, James P. *Lewis and Clark Among the Indians.* Lincoln: University of Nebraska Press, 1984.

Ross, Richard E. "Prehistory of the Oregon Coast," in *Northwest Coast,* vol. 7, edited by Wayne Suttles. *Handbook of North American Indians.* Edited by William C. Sturtevant. (Washington DC: Smithsonian Institution Press, 1990), 554–59.

Rubin, Rick. *Naked Against the Rain: The People of the Lower Columbia River, 1770–1830.* Portland, Oregon: Far Shore Press, 1999.

Ruby, Robert H. and John A. Brown. *A Guide to the Indian Tribes of the Pacific Northwest,* vol. 173 of *Civilization of the American Indian.* Rev. ed. Norman: University of Oklahoma Press, 1992.

———. *Indians of the Pacific Northwest.* Norman, Oklahoma: University of Oklahoma Press, 1981.

Schlick, Mary. *Columbia River Basketry: Gift of the Ancestors, Gift of the Earth.* Seattle: University of Washington Press, 1994.

Schwartz, E. A. *Rogue Indian River Indian War and Its Aftermath 1850–1980.* Norman: University of Oklahoma Press, 1997.

———. "Sick Hearts: Indian Removal on the Oregon Coast, 1875–1881." *Oregon Historical Quarterly* 92 (1991): 229–64.

Scott, Leslie M. "Indian Diseases as Aids to Pacific Northwest Settlement." *Oregon Historical Quarterly* 29 (1928): 144–61.

Seaburg, William R. and Pamela Amoss, eds. *Badger and Coyote Were Neighbors: Melville Jacobs on Northwest Indian Myths and Tales* (Northwest Readers). Corvallis: Oregon State University Press, 2000.

Siuslaw Indians. Florence, Oregon: Siuslaw Pioneer Museum, n.d.

Smith, Courtland. *Salmon Fishers of the Columbia.* Corvallis: Oregon State University Press, 1979.

Smohalla. "Smohalla's Ghost-dance Cosmogony." In *Coyote Was Going There: Indian Literature of the Oregon Country,* edited by Jarold Ramsey. Seattle: University of Washington Press, 1977.

Sobel, Elizabeth, and Gordon Bettles. "Winter Hunger, Winter Myths: Subsistence Risk and Mythology Among the Klamath and Modoc." *Journal of Anthropological Archaeology* 19, no. 3 (2000): 276–316.

Spier, Leslie "Klamath Ethnography." In *University of California Publications in American Archaeology and Ethnology,* vol. 30. Berkeley: University of California Press, 1930.

———. "Tribal Distribution in Southwestern Oregon." *Oregon Historical Quarterly* 28, no. 4 (1927): 358–76.

Stern, Theodore. *Chiefs and Change in the Oregon Country: Indian Relations at Fort Nez Perces, 1818–1855, vol. 2.* Corvallis: Oregon State University Press, 1996.

———. "Ideal and Expected Behavior as Seen in Klamath Mythology." *Journal of American Folklore* 76, no. 299 (1963): 21–30.

———. "The Klamath Indians and the Treaty of 1864." *Oregon Historical Quarterly* 57, no. 3 (1956): 229–73.

———. "Klamath and Modoc," in *Plateau,* vol. 12, edited by Deward E. Walker, Jr. *Handbook of North American Indians.* Edited by William C. Sturtevant. (Washington DC: Smithsonian Institution Press, 1998), 446–466.

———. *The Klamath Tribe: A People and their Reservation.* American Ethnological Society, Monograph 41. Seattle: University of Washington Press, 1965.

Stern, Theodore, Martin F. Schmitt, and Alphonse Halfmoon. "A Cayuse-Nez Perce Sketchbook." *Oregon Historical Quarterly* 81 (Winter) 1980: 341–76.

Stewart, Hilary. *Artifacts of the Northwest Coast Indians.* Blaine, Washington: Big Country Books, 1981.

———. *Cedar: Tree of Life to the Northwest Coast Indians.* Seattle: University of Washington Press, 1995.

———. *Indian Fishing: Early Methods on the Northwest Coast.* Seattle: University of Washington Press, 1994.

———. *Looking at Indian Art of the Northwest Coast.* Seattle University of Washington Press, 1979

———. *Stone, Bone, Antler and Shell: Artifacts of the Northwest Coast.* Vancouver BC: Douglas & McIntyre Publishing Group, 1996.

Stowell, Cynthia D. *Faces of a Reservation: A Portrait of the Warm Springs Indian Reservation.* Portland: Oregon Historical Society Press, 1989.

Strickland, Ron. *River Pigs and Cayuses: Oral Histories from the Pacific Northwest.* Corvallis, Oregon, 2001.

Strong, Emory. *Stone Age on the Columbia.* Portland, Oregon: Binford and Mort, 1960.

Sullivan, Maurice, ed. *The Travels of Jedediah Smith.* Santa Ana, California: The Fine Arts Press, 1934.

Suttles, Wayne, ed. *Northwest Coast.* Vol. 7, *Handbook of North American Indians.* Edited by William C. Sturtevant. Washington DC: Smithsonian Institution Press, 1990.

Swan, James G. *The Northwest Coast or, Three Years' Residence in Washington Territory.* 5th edition. Seattle and London: University of Washington Press, 1857.

Thompson, Courtenay. *Tribal Status Still Elusive Concept for Americans* Washington DC: Newhouse News Service, 2000. www.newhouse.com/archive/story1a080700.html

Thompson, Laurence C. and Dale M. Kinkade. "Languages," in *Northwest Coast,* vol. 7, edited by Wayne Suttles. *Handbook of North American Indians.* Edited by William C. Sturtevant. (Washington DC: Smithsonian Institution Press, 1990), 30–51.

Townsend, Richard. *Indian Sovereignty in Oregon.* Salem: Association of Oregon Counties, August 2003. www.klamathbasincrisis.org/tribes/IndianSovereigntyOregon.pdf

Tamastslikt Cultural Institute. "The Story of the Confederated Tribes of the Umatilla Indian Reservation." Confederated Tribes of the Umatilla Indian Reservation: Mission, Oregon, n.d.

Ulrich, Roberta. *Empty Nets: Indians, Dams and the Columbia River.* Corvallis: Oregon State University Press, 1999.

Walker, Deward E., Jr. *Mutual Cross-utilization of Economic Resources in the Plateau: An Example from Aboriginal Nez Perce Fishing Practices.* Washington State University, Laboratory of Anthropology, Report of Investigations 41. Pullman: Washington State University Press, 1967.

———. "New Light on the Prophet Dance Controversy." *Ethnohistory* 16, no. 3 (1969): 245–55.

———, ed. *Plateau.* Vol. 12, *Handbook of North American Indians.* Edited by William C. Sturtevant. Washington DC: Smithsonian Institution Press, 1998.

Washburn, Wilcomb E., ed. *History of Indian-White Relations.* Vol. 4, *Handbook of North American Indians.* Edited by William C. Sturtevant. Washington DC: Smithsonian Institution Press, 1988.

Whereat, Donald. "Authentic American Indian Speeches from the Heart." *Oregonian* 7 March 1992, sec. DO6.

Williams, Chuck. *Bridge of The Gods, Mountains of Fire: A Return to the Columbia Gorge.* New York: Friends of the Earth; White Salmon, Washington: Elephant Mountain Arts, 1980.

Wolf, Edward C., *Klamath Heartlands: A Guide to the Klamath Reservation Forest Plan.* Portland, Oregon: Ecotrust, 2004.

Woody, Elizabeth. *Hand into Stone: Poems.* Contact II Publications

———. *Luminaries of the Humble.* University of Arizona Press, 1994

———. *Seven Hands Seven Hearts: Prose and Poetry.* Illustrated by Jaune Quick-to-See Smith. Portland, Oregon: Eighth Mountain Press, 1994.

Woody, Elizabeth, Edward C. Wolf and Seth Zuckerman. *Salmon Nation: People, Fish, and Our Common Home.* Portland, Oregon: Ecotrust, 2003.

Youst, Lionel and William R. Seaburg. *Coquelle Thompson, Athabaskan Witness: A Cultural Biography.* Vol. 243 of *The civilization of the American Indian.* Norman: University of Oklahoma Press, 2002.

Youst, Lionel. "*She's Tricky Like Coyote: Annie Miner Peterson, an Oregon Coast Indian Woman*," vol. 224 of *The Civilization of the American Indian*. Norman: University of Oklahoma Press, 1997.

Zenk, Henry B. "Siuslawans and Coosans, " in *Northwest Coast*, vol. 7, edited by Wayne Suttles. *Handbook of North American Indians*. Edited by William C. Sturtevant. (Washington DC: Smithsonian Institution Press, 1990), 572–579.

Zenk, Henry. "Kalapuyan," *Northwest Coast*, vol. 7, edited by Wayne Suttles. *Handbook of North American Indians*. Edited by William C. Sturtevant. (Washington DC: Smithsonian Institution Press, 1990), 547–546.

Zucker, Jeff, Kay Hummel and Bob Hogfoss. Oregon Indians: *Culture, History and Current Affairs: An Atlas and Introduction*. Portland: Oregon Historical Society Press, 1983. 229p.

Authors

C. MELVIN AIKENS is professor emeritus of anthropology, director of the Museum of Natural History, and former director of the Archaeological Field School at the University of Oregon. He has written extensively about the Great Basin.

STEPHEN DOW BECKHAM is the Pamplin Professor of History at Lewis & Clark College and author of numerous works on Oregon Indians. His most recent books include *Lewis and Clark: From the Rockies to the Pacific* and *Oregon Indians: Voices from Two Centuries.*

LAURA BERG is a Portland-based writer, editor, and communication specialist whose work primarily involves Indian tribes and natural resource protection, particularly salmon restoration.

MARILYN COUTURE is an anthropologist who has divided her time teaching at Linfield College in Portland, Oregon, and Maui Community College in Hawaii. She has collected oral stories from numerous elders of the Burns Paiute Tribe.

DOUGLAS DEUR is a geographer with expertise in American Indian views, uses, and management of the landscape and in the environmental history of Northwestern North America generally. He has worked closely with the Klamath Tribes in their efforts to document places of enduring cultural significance. Born and raised in Oregon, Doug is affiliated with the University of Washington's Pacific Northwest Cooperative Ecosystem Studies Unit and is an adjunct professor with the University of Nevada, Reno, Department of Geography.

YVONNE HAJDA is a Ph.D. researcher and consultant in social and cultural anthropology, specializing in the ethnohistory of Northwest Indians. She is based in Portland.

EUGENE HUNN is professor of anthropology at the University of Washington. From 1976 to the early 1990s, he focused his studies on the Sahaptin language and Plateau ethnography and ecology, working with James Selam, an elder from John Day River.

DELL HYMES grew up in Portland, where he graduated from Reed College. He is professor emeritus of anthropology, at the University of Virginia, where he taught linguistic anthropology, Native American mythology, ethno-poetics, and Native American poetry. He is the author of numerous books.

JENNIFER KARSON is the publications coordinator for the Tamástslikt Cultural Institute—the museum of the Confederated Tribes of the Umatilla Indian Reservation—and a doctoral candidate in socio-cultural anthropology. She recently edited *As Days Go By: Our History, Our Land, and Our People—the Cayuse, Umatilla, and Walla Walla.*

ROBERT KENTTA is a Siletz tribal member of Shasta and Applegate River Athabaskan descent. He has served as the cultural resources director for the Confederated Tribes of Siletz since 1993. He is an historian, traditional weaver, regalia maker, and singer in traditional ceremonies.

BILL MERCER is the former curator of Native American art at the Portland Art Museum and the author of *People of the River: Native Arts of the Oregon Territory.*

BRENT MERRILL is the former editor of the Grand Ronde tribal newspaper *Smoke Signals*. A member of the tribe, he is a journalist, photographer, and information specialist who has worked for the Northwest Indian Fisheries Commission, the Northwest Indian College, and several newspapers and other publications. Merrill lives with his family on Grand Ronde reservation.

WIL PHINNEY is a journalist and the editor of the acclaimed tribal newspaper, the *Confederated Umatilla Journal*.

MICHAEL RONDEAU is the Cow Creek tribe's government operations officer and a member of Roseburg Area Chamber of Commerce. A Cow Creek tribal member, he is descended from the Rondeau and Dumont families, who have long been active in the tribe's governmental affairs.

HOWARD P. ROY is the cultural education manager for and a member of the Confederated Tribes of the Coos, Lower Umpqua, and Siuslaw Indians. He has more than twenty years experience working for tribal governments and private business.

MINERVA T. SOUCIE has held many positions with her tribe, the Burns Paiute, including tribal chairperson. In 2006 she retired as the tribe's education specialist. For many years, Minerva also worked as a forestry technician for the Snowy Mountain Ranger District, Ochoco National Forest. She is a basketweaver, teacher, artist, storyteller, and speaker and writer on Paiute history and cultural resources. She recently contributed to an anthology about women artists and a collection of video-recorded interviews with tribal leaders from across the country.

KATHRYN ANNE TOEPEL received her Ph.D. in anthropology from the University of Oregon and is now co-director of Heritage Research Associates, a private consulting firm in Eugene that specializes in Pacific Northwest archaeology and history.

GEORGE B. WASSON JR. is the great grandson of Kitzenjinjum and Gishgia, grandson of Susan Adulsah and George R. Wasson, and one of five children of George B. Wasson and Bess Finley. He has retired after more than twenty years at the University of Oregon in academic counseling and administration and is now a council member of the Coquille Indian Tribe.

ELIZABETH WOODY is the author of three books of poetry and a recipient of the American Book Award, the Hedgebrook's J. T. Stewart Award, and the William Stafford Memorial Award for Poetry from the Pacific Northwest Booksellers Association. While a member of the Confederated Tribes of the Warm Springs, she also has Navajo and Yakama ancestry. She is currently the director of indigenous leadership for Ecotrust in Portland, Oregon.

Index

Photographs, special caption information, and figures are indicated with *italic* type, e.g., *12f, 32c.*

Established in 1971, Oregon Council for the Humanities is an independent, nonprofit affiliate of the National Endowment for the Humanities that offers Oregonians the opportunity to reflect upon and discuss the critical issues and ideas of our time. OCH programs and publications include Oregon Chautauqua, Humanity in Perspective, Young Scholars, Commonplace Lectures, and *Oregon Humanities* magazine.

www.oregonhum.org